What's Wrong with NATO and How to Fix It

What's wrong? Series

Paul Harris, *What's Wrong with Climate Politics and How to Fix It*

Simon Hix, *What's Wrong with the European Union and How to Fix It*

Bill Jordan, *What's Wrong with Social Policy and How to Fix It*

Bessma Momani and Mark R. Hibben, *What's Wrong with the IMF and How to Fix It*

Thomas G. Weiss, *What's Wrong with the United Nations and How to Fix It*, 3rd edition

Rorden Wilkinson, *What's Wrong with the WTO and How to Fix It*

What's Wrong with NATO and How to Fix It

Mark Webber, James Sperling
and Martin A. Smith

polity

First published in 2021 by Polity Press

Polity Press
65 Bridge Street
Cambridge CB2 1UR, UK

Polity Press
101 Station Landing
Suite 300
Medford, MA 02155, USA

ISBN-13: 978-0-7456-8261-7
ISBN-13: 978-0-7456-8262-4 (pb)

A catalogue record for this book is available from the British Library.

Library of Congress Cataloging-in-Publication Data
Names: Webber, Mark, author. | Sperling, James, author. | Smith, Martin A., author.
Title: What's wrong with NATO and how to fix it / Mark Webber, James Sperling and Martin A. Smith h.
Other titles: What is wrong with North Atlantic Treaty Organization and how to fix it
Description: Medford : Polity Press, 2021. | Series: What's wrong? | Includes bibliographical references and index. | Summary: "A penetrating diagnostic of the world's most powerful military alliance"-- Provided by publisher.
Identifiers: LCCN 2020038353 (print) | LCCN 2020038354 (ebook) | ISBN 9780745682617 (Hardback) | ISBN 9780745682624 (Paperback) | ISBN 9780745682655 (ePub)
Subjects: LCSH: North Atlantic Treaty Organization. | European Union. | National security--European Union countries. | European Union countries--Foreign relations.
Classification: LCC UA646.3 .W433 2021 (print) | LCC UA646.3 (ebook) | DDC 355/.031091821--dc23
LC record available at https://lccn.loc.gov/2020038353
LC ebook record available at https://lccn.loc.gov/2020038354

Typeset in 10.25 on 13 pt Scala by Servis Filmsetting Ltd, Stockport, Cheshire
Printed and bound in Great Britain by TJ Books Limited

Contents

Tables and Boxes

Tables

Boxes

Preface and Acknowledgements

Writing on matters of contemporary importance always faces the challenge of relevance. How will a book's analysis and proposals stand up as events carry on regardless of the authors' prognostications? This is a question we asked ourselves many times as this volume progressed. A book originally conceived in 2013 has had to take on board the Ukraine crisis of 2014; the election of Donald Trump in 2016; Brexit; a major reconfiguration of NATO's mission in Afghanistan; and the worsening of political order to NATO's south in the Middle East and North Africa. The manuscript had been drafted by early 2020 with all these events accommodated. Then came the COVID-19 pandemic. For some, this is an event of such magnitude that it amounts to a 'year zero' in international politics. If that judgement were true, much of our analysis would have become instantly redundant. It would be like finishing a book on terrorism the week before 9/11. But such a view may well prove false. This is not to minimize the ghastly and extensive effects of COVID-19. Pandemics, by definition are grave, but history suggests that they are also often temporary. Public health interventions, vaccines and acquired immunity could well mean that within a few years the disease is but 'a disturbing memory'.[1] Equally, as Joseph Nye has suggested, the pandemic 'might not change the world'.[2] This may seem a hopelessly optimistic view from the vantage point of November 2020, as COVID-19 marches across the globe. But Nye's point is a sensible one. The big issue of global politics –

the rise of China and America's adjustment to it – will play out regardless. Equally, NATO's perennial issues – the ones that have structured this book – will remain. To ignore COVID-19 would, however, have been perverse. In finishing the book, we have thus taken into consideration the evolving landscape of international response, but we have not been deflected from retaining a structure for the book that talks to NATO's longer-standing issues – those that pre-date the COVID-19 crisis and those that will outlast it. In short, we have dealt with the pandemic as an important, but second-order, issue (the book's concluding chapter explains how and why). Our thanks are owed here to one external reader who suggested that the pandemic could best be conceived as 'magnifying' but not replacing 'existing trends and fault lines' facing the Alliance.

Getting the book over the finishing line in such turbulent times owes much to the forbearance of Louise Knight and Inès Boxman at Polity. Their patience in the face of more than one delay in the book's delivery is much appreciated. The final push was also made possible by the generosity of the University of Birmingham, which afforded Mark Webber an extended sabbatical to complete the writing and editing. In addition, we would like to acknowledge a range of friends, colleagues and interlocutors, all of whom have fed ideas into the analyses (perhaps sometimes unwittingly). Thanks are owed to Derek Averre, Wyn Bowen, Lawrence Chalmer, Malcolm Chalmers, Lorenzo Cladi, Fabrizio Coticchia, Albert Covelli, Adam Crawford, John Deni, David Dunn, Spyros Economides, Nico Faso, Trine Flockhart, Rita Floyd, Alex Garrido, Tim Haughton, Ben Kienzle, David Logan, Sonia Lucarelli, Jennifer Medcalf, Hugo Meijer, Philip Mizen, Alex Moens, Jaimie Orr, Jack Porter, Patrick Porter, Adam Quinn, Jens Ringsmose, Sten Rynning, Jamie Shea, Thierry Tardy, Keery Walker, Nick Wheeler, Richard Whitman, Ben Wilkinson, Michael J. Williams and Katharine Wright. This book sits alongside others published by Polity addressing the question of *What's Wrong* with international organizations. Two of these were of some influence in shaping our thinking. We would thus like to thank Simon Hix and Thomas Weiss for their insights on, respectively, the European Union and the United Nations. If these have been transposed wrongly to NATO in any way, the responsibility is ours not theirs.

Finally, a personal note. The book was finalized during what historians might one day refer to as the age of social distancing and lockdown. This meant a lot of time spent with friends and family as homes became offices, and deadlines merged with domestic schedules. The deferred gratification that attends any writing project was intensified in these circumstances. Our thanks are, therefore, owed to Eddie, Della, Joy, Theo, Sheila and Victoria.

Mark Webber, James Sperling and Martin A. Smith
November 2020

Abbreviations

ACO	Allied Command Operations
ACT	Allied Command Transformation
AGS	Alliance Ground Surveillance
AMF	Allied Command Europe Mobile Force
ASEAN	Association of Southeast Asian Nations
AWACS	airborne warning and control system
BMD	ballistic missile defence
CARD	Coordinated Annual Review on Defence
CDPSP	*The Current Digest of the Post-Soviet Press*
CFE	Conventional Forces in Europe
CFI	Connected Forces Initiative
CPG	Comprehensive Political Guidance
CSBMs	Confidence and Security Building Measures
CSCE	Conference on Security and Cooperation in Europe
CSDP	Common Security and Defence Policy
CT	counter-terrorism
DCI	Defence Capabilities Initiative
EDF	European Defence Fund
EDSTAR	European Defence Standards Reference System
eFP	enhanced Forward Presence
ESDI	European Security and Defence Identity
EU	European Union
EUCOM	[US] European Command
EUGS	EU Global Strategy

FNC	Framework Nations Concept
GPS	Global Positioning System
IISS	International Institute for Strategic Studies
INF	Intermediate-Range Nuclear Forces
ISAF	International Security Assistance Force
ISR	intelligence, surveillance and reconnaissance
ISTAR	intelligence, surveillance, target acquisition and reconnaissance
JEF	Joint Expeditionary Force
JISR	joint intelligence, surveillance and reconnaissance
KFOR	Kosovo Force
MAP	Membership Action Plan
MARCOM	Maritime Command
MENA	Middle East and North Africa
METO	Middle East Treaty Organization
MPCC	Military Planning and Conduct Capability
NATO	North Atlantic Treaty Organization
NDPP	NATO Defence Planning Process
NNEC	NATO Network-Enabled Capabilities
NORDEFCO	Nordic Defence Cooperation
NRC	NATO–Russia Council
OAF	Operation Allied Force
ORS	Operation Resolute Support
OSCE	Organization for Security and Cooperation in Europe
OUP	Operation Unified Protector
PESCO	Permanent Structured Cooperation
PfP	Partnership for Peace
PJC	[NATO–Russia] Permanent Joint Council
SAC	Strategic Airlift Capability
SACEUR	Supreme Allied Commander Europe
SALIS	Strategic Airlift International Solution
SATCOM	satellite communications

SEATO	South East Asia Treaty Organization
SHAPE	Supreme Headquarters Allied Powers Europe
SIPRI	Stockholm International Peace Research Institute
STANAGs	standardization agreements
tFP	Tailored Forward Presence
UN	United Nations
UNCLOS	United Nations Convention for the Law of the Sea
VJTF	Very High Readiness Joint Task Force
WHO	World Health Organization

Introduction: What *Is* Wrong with NATO?

There would appear to be much wrong with the North Atlantic Treaty Organization. To its detractors, NATO (or 'the Alliance') has been written off as 'irrelevant'.[1] During the 2016 presidential campaign, Donald Trump called it 'obsolete'.[2] French President Emanuel Macron has suggested NATO is 'experiencing [. . .] brain death'.[3] Hence, so the argument runs, if NATO did not exist, no one in Europe or North America would any longer want to create it.[4] In this book, we outline the problems that beset the Alliance, but also put forward ways of addressing them. To declare our position up front: NATO, we argue, is salvageable and worth keeping. This book is structured around identifying what its problems are and then showing how they can be treated. Before doing so, however, it is worth outlining some of the broader issues which condition NATO's state of affairs.

NATO's Predicament

Does NATO still have a credible sense of purpose rooted in the realities of contemporary international politics? During the Cold War, when NATO faced off against the Soviet Union and its Warsaw Pact allies, this was a question hardly worth asking. The enemy was obvious, as was the means of countering it – through the combined military efforts of the US and its European allies. The end of the Cold War and the dissolution of the Soviet Union in 1991 thus raised the question of what, if anything, NATO had left to do. It was a view common in the early 1990s that NATO was ill suited to a world without a powerful adversary.[5] And despite an intervening quarter-century of adaptation and deployment – in the Balkans, Libya, Afghanistan and NATO's eastern flank facing Russia – that argument persists. NATO plays only a marginal role in countering three of the major threats affecting European security: the war in Syria, jihadist-inspired terrorism and migration flows from the Sahel and the wider Middle East. That NATO is positioned against these threats in such an unimpressive fashion owes much to its own crisis of conviction. Over the last three decades, NATO has compensated for the absence of a common agreed enemy of the Cold War type by acting reactively, dealing with crises as they arise according to the dictates of geography (as in the Balkans), American leadership (as in Afghanistan) or geopolitical 'muscle memory' (as in its response to Russia).[6] Behaving in this way demonstrates a certain strategic and institutional flexibility but belies an underlying divergence of priorities among allies as well as the absence of any overarching sense of commitment to a common cause.[7]

NATO's sense of drift is also evident in its own internal political dynamics. Strains between the US and its Canadian and European allies have been part and parcel of NATO's history. During the Cold War, the US took a dim view of Europeans' reluctance to spend sufficiently on defence. For their part, some European governments (most notably in France and West Germany) suspected that the American commitment to the defence of Europe was lukewarm. Division, however, has worsened since the Cold War's end. This is a theme we take up in later chapters. In brief, each US president has witnessed a different but escalating set of problems in the transatlantic relationship. For President Bill Clinton it was centred on the Balkans. For his successor, George W. Bush, it was over the

Iraq war of 2003. The administration of Barack Obama, meanwhile, complained openly about the unwillingness of certain allies to spend adequately on defence. Unease in Washington was mirrored by disquiet in Europe – at US unilateralism and the shift of America's strategic priorities away from Europe. NATO was caught up in these currents. Its internal divisions over Iraq were described as the Alliance's 'near-death experience'.[8] Secretary of Defence Robert Gates warned in 2011 that NATO had 'a dim, if not dismal future'.[9]

Mutual suspicion reached its zenith with the election of Donald Trump in 2016. Trump went on to criticize NATO in a manner unparalleled among previous American presidents. Paradoxically, the level of material support for European defence actually increased in the Trump years. But words matter, and Trump's broadsides against NATO as well as individual allies (he openly criticized France and Canada and reserved a particular animus for Germany) generated deep anxieties that the US could one day abandon its NATO commitments.[10] NATO scepticism has not been limited to the US. We have already noted the comments of the French President. In 2016, Turkish Foreign Minister Mevlüt Çavuşoğlu suggested his country would 'think of exit' from NATO owing to a perceived lack of solidarity for coup-threatened President Erdoğan.[11] The Prime Minister of Iceland, Katrín Jakobsdóttir, has said her country 'shouldn't be [a] member of NATO'.[12]

Beneath these voices of transatlantic dissent lurks a deeper problem: the withering away of political community. NATO throughout the Cold War claimed to be the upholder of liberal democratic values. Such a position was, admittedly, compromised by the Alliance's undemocratic minority: the Salazar dictatorship in Portugal and the occasional military rulers of Greece and Turkey. But in juxtaposition to Soviet communism, the claim had some mileage. Despite the end of the

Cold War, such arguments continued to be made, providing (as we will see in Chapter 1) justification for NATO's military interventions as well as the policy of membership enlargement. But NATO's value-based orientation now seems less and less convincing. NATO's newest members, Montenegro and North Macedonia, were admitted despite distinctly patchy records of democratic compliance. NATO's military mission in Afghanistan has long been detached from an initial hope that it would incubate political and social reform in the country. And a number of NATO allies – Turkey, Hungary, Poland, Italy and the US under Trump – have succumbed to strains of national chauvinism in their foreign policies that are profoundly damaging to the Alliance's bonds of solidarity. Brexit, although a withdrawal from the European Union (EU), has been seen, similarly, as undermining trust and goodwill among the UK and its NATO allies. Such political currents are, according to *New York Times* columnist Roger Cohen, 'the greatest [ever] challenge to the Atlantic alliance and the civilization it has sustained'.[13]

No, NATO Is Not Finished

In view of these deep-seated problems, one might simply conclude that NATO is beyond repair. Why bother attempting to fix it if by doing so an 'institutional dinosaur' is kept on life support? Far better to give NATO a 'dignified retirement', dividing its functions between Europe and America, with states in the former seeking alternative Europe-wide solutions to their common defence thereby leaving the US and Canada to pursue their security interests unencumbered by European responsibilities.[14] This is a view we reject. NATO certainly has its problems, but to do away with the organization would worsen and not improve the security position of its members. Reforming NATO, rather, is the more realistic and preferred course of action. Occasionally, political leaders have intimated at withdrawal from the Alliance, but none of NATO's members has advocated its dissolution. Any argument for doing so is unpersuasive. The alternative case presented in this book, for a reformed NATO, is framed by five starting assumptions.

NATO is not in terminal decline

Declinist views have characterized much commentary and scholarship on NATO. But time after time, such views have proven wrong. During the Cold War, the Suez Crisis of 1956, French withdrawal from NATO's integrated military commands in the 1960s and differences in the early 1980s between the Reagan administration and some European governments over how to deal with the Soviets were all seen as evidence of internal corrosion. However, as Wallace Thies has convincingly argued, the Alliance's 'self-healing tendencies' of democratic membership, internal democratic decision-making and institutional complexity ensured the accommodation of its members' interests, and with it ongoing resolve in facing down the Soviet bloc.[15]

Declinist positions resurfaced at the Cold War's end only to be confounded by NATO's repurposing in the 1990s. By 1995, one analyst was able to write that 'European security was once again dominated by the NATO alliance and US leadership, perhaps to a greater extent than even in the last years of the Cold War.'[16] The prompt for that verdict was the Alliance's decisive aerial intervention in Bosnia. Operation Deliberate Force, launched in August 1995, served as the catalyst for the Dayton Peace Accords, which finally brought a semblance of political stability to the troubled Balkan region. It also marked NATO's entry into peacekeeping (60,000 NATO personnel would go on to be deployed to Bosnia, the largest military deployment in Europe since World War II). NATO undertook a further air operation four years later. Operation

Allied Force pushed the Serb leader Slobodan Milošević to a peace deal over Kosovo and paved the way for the entry of the KFOR (Kosovo Force) peacekeeping mission to the troubled province. A smaller-scale NATO intervention in neighbouring Macedonia in 2001 also had a decisive effect in restoring political order. NATO's attentions then moved to the far-off theatre of Afghanistan. In 2003, it assumed formal responsibility for the International Security Assistance Force (ISAF). ISAF would prove NATO's most complex and demanding mission of the post-Cold War period, entailing both nation-building and gruelling counter-insurgency warfare. In 2015, a new non-combat mission, Operation Resolute Support, was initiated. These missions (along with a further aerial campaign, Operation Unified Protector, in Libya in 2011, and the return to collective defence in the face of Russia's actions against Ukraine after 2014) have not been without their problems, as was noted above. But even if one accepts the criticism that NATO operations have lacked an overarching sense of strategic purpose, taken together they are nonetheless a measure of allied staying power.[17]

An organization whose purpose is to protect the security of its members will necessarily have to confront its enemies and face down threats. Dealing with crisis – whether in the Balkans, Afghanistan, Libya or on NATO's eastern flank facing Russia – is simply part and parcel of what NATO does. To infer from such a state of affairs that NATO itself is 'in crisis' is a mistaken leap of logic.[18] Time and again, the Alliance has proven its naysayers wrong as it has responded, rather than surrendered, to some of the tough security challenges of the late twentieth and early twenty-first centuries.

NATO is unique

If we accept that NATO is here to stay, an argument still needs to be made as to why this is a good thing. The merits of that argument rest, in large part, on NATO's own claims to performance: how effectively the Alliance has executed its various missions and, related to this, how convincing have been the reasons for pursuing them. We shall return to these themes throughout the book. Here it is worth putting them in context. Our second assumption is that NATO can undertake operations and, indeed, engage in its full range of activities (military exercises, ballistic missile defence [BMD], nuclear deterrence, partnerships, joint intelligence, surveillance and reconnaissance [JISR], cyber defence, air and maritime patrols, and so on) owing to the development of some unique characteristics.

Ostensibly, NATO is simply a treaty-based alliance of states, a fairly conventional category in international politics. It is, however, much more besides. Since the signing of the North Atlantic Treaty in 1949, the number of NATO allies has grown (from the original twelve to thirty today) and, in parallel, NATO has developed a sophisticated institutional set-up. NATO, consequently, is as much an international organization as it is a military alliance. We will have more to say on this in Chapter 1. The point here is that these 'institutional assets', although initially developed during the Cold War, have proven flexible enough to ensure significant NATO adaptation in the three decades since.[19] Adaptation has, operationally speaking, not always generated the right results; it has also been painful as NATO has had to learn by doing in the field of operations. Yet adaptation has certainly been dramatic. In the Balkans, Afghanistan and Libya, NATO laid down a series of firsts – in terms of its willingness to work with non-NATO partners, its ability to provide massive and sustained concentrations of force on land, sea and air, and the expansion of its geographical area of operations.[20]

Alongside these formal structures, NATO has also developed all manner of informal practices of social and political interaction. Allies working in an organization premised on transparency and consensus have thus developed feelings of familiarity and trust in their mutual relations.[21] It was noted above that political community, one outgrowth of this dynamic, has been eroded. But an equally important aspect of community remains. NATO is the exemplary case of a 'pluralistic security community'. Its members hold 'dependable expectations of peaceful change' in their relations with one another such that war between them is rendered unthinkable.[22] A willingness to desist from violence among one's peers may be a minimum condition of community, but, given Europe's history, it is an undeniably important one. The anchoring of Germany within NATO has put paid to any fear among its neighbours of German military revanchism. NATO has also played a role in mitigating the antagonism between Greece and Turkey. The embrace of new members among some former Yugoslav republics is premised on doing something similar in the Balkans.

Both its informal and formal characteristics place NATO at some remove from more transient coalitions of the willing. Modern warfare is rarely conducted by states acting alone. Even powerful states such as the US have come to rely on allies to give added legitimacy to their cause or to widen the pool of assets upon which they can call. Here, a temporary coalition has certain advantages: flexibility of purpose, fluidity of decision-making and ease of dissolution when its purpose has been served. Coalitions, not alliances as such, fought wars against Iraq in 1990/1 and 2003, and since September 2014 a global coalition has battled ISIS in Iraq and Syria. Yet coalitions by their very nature lack the embedded structures and assets of a permanent alliance such as NATO. NATO's internal politics may mean sluggish decision-making, and capability asymmetries among its members often give rise to burden-sharing disputes. But when NATO acts, it enjoys the benefits of interoperability, unity of command and pooled resources – all of which are an aid to 'effectiveness [...] robustness and adaptability'.[23]

There is no substitute for NATO

The particular institutional form the Alliance has taken marks it out from other organizational alternatives. The EU, the United Nations (UN) and the Organization for Security and Cooperation in Europe (OSCE) can all lay claim to promoting security. None, however, is possessed of the institutional and military assets described above. None would have been capable of mounting combat operations in the Balkans, Libya and Afghanistan, or of replicating NATO's Readiness Action Plan to provide reassurance to the Baltic States and Poland in the face of Russian military might.

Three other points are also worth making by way of comparison. First, the US and the UK have consistently given priority to NATO. That choice determined NATO's European ascendancy at the end of the Cold War. London and Washington have ever since been lukewarm about the idea of an EU role in military security for fear that it will encroach upon alliance prerogatives. As the UK exits from the EU, such scepticism is only likely to increase. Non-EU Turkey has adopted a similar stance. France and Germany, by contrast, have tended to talk up the security and nascent military functions of the EU, but neither has ever contemplated abandoning NATO in order to support a distinct European alternative.

Related to this, NATO enjoys a privileged position in the 'organizational ecology' of international security provision.[24] Once the Alliance's primacy had been asserted at the end of the Cold War, possible alternatives became complementary to its efforts not substitutes for them. Thus, in Bosnia, NATO worked alongside the UN to enforce a series of Security Council Resolutions. NATO's peacekeeping force in the country eventually gave way to an EU operation (EUFOR Althea), a mission reliant on close cooperation between the EU Military Staff and NATO's Supreme Headquarters Allied Powers Europe (SHAPE). In Kosovo, similarly, KFOR has worked alongside OSCE and UN missions. And in Afghanistan, both ISAF and Resolute Support have been mandated by the UN. Here, EU and UN agencies have carried out significant roles alongside NATO.

Third, NATO has a distinct transatlantic dimension. Membership of Canada and the US means it can legitimately claim to be the institutional expression of the Western group of states. Commentators have warned of 'Westlessness' – a sense of drift, division and disorientation among the countries of North America and Europe[25] – but NATO remains the principal connection binding Europe to what is still the world's pre-eminent military power. A similar security blanket is also enjoyed by America's East Asian allies, Japan and South Korea, but NATO is unique in anchoring that guarantee within a multilateral setting. The Alliance cannot claim a membership as large as either the UN or the OSCE, but it has been able to avoid the gridlock that has characterized both those two bodies. Generally speaking, NATO fosters a pragmatic spirit of cooperation among its members generated by their engagement in multiple operations and decision-making formats. Here, consensus is an asset not an obstacle, requiring prolonged and patient interactions, which over decades has sustained a strong sense of shared purpose. We acknowledge that NATO's sense of political community is under strain, but the *practices* of the Alliance remain robust.[26]

NATO is strategically aware

Since the end of the Cold War, NATO has been engaged in an ongoing search for a compelling strategic vision. As we will see in Chapter 5, it has not found that task easy. But here two points can be made by way of mitigation. The first relates to the complexity of the security environment that NATO has had to deal with. Comparison with Cold War NATO may be unflattering but it is also unfair. Faced with the singular, overarching threat of Soviet power, strategy came relatively easy. Since the Soviet Union's demise, the security challenges facing the Alliance have been multiple in number, form and direction. NATO, consequently, cannot mobilize toward a single set of objectives (deterrence, defence and dialogue, as in the Cold War) focused on a clearly identified foe. Rather, it has had to shift focus according to the most pressing threat or issue at any given time.

Responsiveness of this type is no bad thing if it is consciously considered. Indeed, a second point of mitigation is that NATO has purposively shifted its operational focus on several occasions. On this basis, it has been able to claim that it is multi-purpose. In the words of the 2010 Strategic Concept, the Alliance seeks to fulfil the three 'essential core tasks' of collective defence, crisis management and cooperative security. As one seasoned NATO official has acknowledged, pursuing all three tasks simultaneously is extraordinarily testing.[27] The Alliance, in this sense, is a victim not of inaction but of ambition.

No organization is perfect

Political organizations are rarely without fault, and few, if any, are perfect – able to act in complete accordance with the organization's environment, to exercise flawless leadership and to mobilize resources efficiently and effectively to achieve its goals. While virtually all serious analysis would accept this as a starting point, opinion then differs on exactly how far organizations are constrained in action and effect.

An influential strand of realist opinion regards international organizations as mattering 'only on the margins'. Such bodies operate primarily because states (and great powers in particular) harness organizations for their own ends. This may mean a temporary meeting of minds, but the cooperation that results is always fragile, temporary and likely to relapse toward more competitive ways of doing things.[28] A somewhat different take (but an equally pessimistic one) argues that organizations develop entrenched ways of doing things and so become inherently inefficient. Rigid thinking and inflexible behaviour are especially evident in an organization's bureaucracy, but such patterns can also influence state members who become socialized into bad habits. The outcome is a dysfunctional organization, unresponsive to its environment, preoccupied with process and wedded to policies that end up being ineffective and self-defeating.[29]

If we accept such views, then NATO would have to be judged against a very low bar, it being just one more flawed and ineffectual international body. Such a starting point would colour both our diagnosis of the problems besetting the Alliance and prescriptions for how to attend to them. We would, in short, steer to a rather limited range of options aware that NATO's influence in the world was constrained and its future uncertain. Such a view is not without its merits. Indeed, even NATO's defenders hold to some of its assumptions, not least the view that the Alliance is an arena in which the interests of its members are presented and sometimes collide, and that, ultimately, the US runs the show.

The following chapters demonstrate, however, that such a view is overstated and, in certain regards, inaccurate. The premise we follow in this book is aligned more with the institutionalist view that organizations can have significant effects.[30] This does not mean that organizations are detached from their members – far from it. NATO, we suggest, has endured precisely because it serves its members' interests. It offers 'value-added' to the allies in the shape of permanent, tried and trusted military and political cooperation. It goes beyond an alliance of convenience, coordinating defence and security in ways the allies could achieve neither alone nor in temporary coalition.

NATO's distinct qualities do not, however, make it immune from the external challenges that have bedevilled other bodies. There is a view that the international system has entered a particularly unsettled time, one for which the current crop of international organizations (which largely originated after World War II) are ill suited. All organizations have to deal with uncertainty, but the chain of events beginning with the financial crash of 2008, and continuing with the Eurozone crisis, Russia's annexation of Crimea, the 2015 migration crisis, Brexit, the election of Trump, the rise of populist politics in Europe and the COVID-19 pandemic, has been seen as ushering in a new dark age of problems.[31] Such problems are, of course, real but perhaps no more troubling than those of previous decades. Robert Keohane argued in 1975 that 'the world is in a profound political and economic crisis' which has imposed severe 'constraints on effective cooperative action'.[32] The end of the Cold War gave rise to similar soul-searching as international organizations were immediately found wanting in the face of multiple crises, not least the wars in the former Yugoslavia.[33] In 2007, Edward Newman wrote that a 'crisis of multilateralism' had typified much commentary on international organisations throughout the decade of the 2000s.[34]

The lesson one might draw here is twofold: that crises tend to typify international politics over time and that international organizations are central to how these crises play out. This is not to say that international organizations are always equal to the task, but as NATO's case demonstrates, an organization can persist and adapt in the face of cumulative crises. What interests us, and what this book seeks to explore, is whether NATO's adaptation to date is sufficient and how much further it should go.

In Summary

The approach we take in the remainder of this book, then, is informed by a generally sympathetic view of NATO. We regard the Alliance as indispensable to European and transatlantic security. The international security order would be much worse off if NATO were to systematically fail or to exit global affairs. But while NATO has its virtues, it is also in need of reform. The Alliance has not been resistant to change, and there is a cottage industry of academic and think-tank opinion dedicated to changing it for the better.[35] This does not make our study unnecessary. NATO's importance requires that it be a subject of ongoing scrutiny, and that studies such as ours take on board contemporary challenges and political circumstances. We write this book as major changes impact the international system: the legacy of a Trump presidency that renounced many of the principles of multilateralism; a China and Russia that are pushing back against American claims to global leadership; and a worldwide pandemic that undermines the benefits of global interconnectedness. NATO is, in some ways, touched by all of these global shifts. But to appraise the Alliance, we have focused on a set of problems for which its members are directly responsible and over which, therefore, they can exert some influence. Some of these problems we have already encountered in this chapter. The four we have chosen to structure the book around are significant because they go to the heart of how NATO conducts its affairs and how the Alliance relates to its security and political environment. Tackling them will make a profound difference to NATO's fortunes. They can be summarized as follows:

- task proliferation (the pitfalls of doing too much);
- over-reliance on American leadership and a failure of European responsibility;

- limits on resources and an inability to obtain an effective allocation of defence capabilities;
- a divisive and dangerous relationship with Russia.

We cannot 'cure' NATO – like every organization, it will always be found wanting in some way. But we can recommend treatment. The fixes to its problems we see as follows:

- doing less but better (task discretion);
- rebalancing the responsibilities of leadership toward Europe;
- aligning missions with effective and efficiently allocated capabilities;
- constructing a realistic partnership with Russia.

Our purpose, then, is clear: to lead NATO toward a healthy recuperation. In this spirit, the book concludes with a summary of how the Alliance ought to prioritize its efforts and so ensure that it remains fit for purpose in the years to come.

Part I

Problems

CHAPTER ONE

Doing Too Much: The Problem of Task Proliferation

NATO's first major 'ill' – doing too much – is arguably a problem of success. Three of NATO's seven decades have fallen within the post-Cold War period, and it has accumulated a wide range of functions in consequence. Such adaptation and repurposing is clearly preferable to stasis and irrelevance. But accumulating more and more functions, with multiple institutions, policies and new members and partners to match, has also stored up problems. Taking on an extra commitment may seem logical in isolation, but when these multiply it can result in a dissipation of energy and a lowering of effectiveness. The magnitude of NATO's problem is, therefore, not to be underestimated. Here we outline its various aspects. In Chapter 5, we offer some routes by which the problem can be addressed.

Task Proliferation

NATO, so the well-worn saying goes, was created to keep 'the Russians out, the Americans in and the Germans down'. Attributed to NATO's first Secretary General, Lord Ismay, this summary indicates that even during the Cold War, the Alliance had a broad remit. NATO also developed features unusual in a traditional alliance, establishing procedures for political consultation, scientific cooperation and disaster management. Yet for all this, the Alliance's defining objective was to balance and deter Soviet power. Here, as the 1974 Declaration on Atlantic Relations put it, 'the common defence' of NATO equated to 'the defence of Europe' alongside the air- and sea-space on the continent's flanks – in the north Atlantic and the Mediterranean.[1]

This continental focus did not go unquestioned. During the 1950s, a debate unfolded on the possibilities of a global NATO. Secretary General Paul-Henri Spaak, French President Charles de Gaulle and deputy Supreme Allied Commander Europe Field Marshal Bernard Montgomery all argued that the Alliance should assume responsibilities beyond the defence of Europe. Fading colonial powers Portugal, Belgium and the Netherlands, meanwhile, felt the NATO allies should coordinate their activities at the United Nations.[2] In the face of American indifference, however, such ideas came to nothing. The US was at times frustrated at the reluctance of its allies to lend their support to its military campaign in Vietnam or to the defence of Israel, but it did not envisage NATO as a vehicle to pursue the global competition with the Soviet Union (or, for that matter, the People's Republic of China). Consequently, there was no agreement on a role for the Alliance 'out-of-area'. When the allies went to war – the Belgians in the Congo, the Americans in Vietnam, the French in Algeria or the British over the Falkland Islands – NATO was not involved. And while the Alliance was busy organizing the collective defence – through force planning, standardization, exercises, air and naval patrols, territorial defence, communications, command structures and so on – not once did it conduct a mission involving force. 'Throughout the entire period of the Cold War,' the Alliance website notes, 'NATO forces were not involved in a single military engagement.'[3]

The narrow predictability of NATO's position was turned upside down by the end of the Cold War. We shall say more on this historic moment below, but in short, the Alliance proved able to move with the times. The Soviet Union – or what would soon become Russia – was downgraded as a threat and NATO amazon.com

SMhhNRyxkT

Purchase Order #: US Lib - books
Your order of December 1, 2021 (Order ID 112-5640417-1421848)

Qty.	Item	Item Price	Total
1	**What's Wrong with NATO and How to Fix it** Webber, Mark --- Paperback **0745682626** 0745682626 9780745682624	$26.95	$26.95

This shipment completes your order.

Subtotal	$26.95
Order Total	$26.95
Paid via credit/debit	$117.00

Return or replace your item
Visit Amazon.com/returns

0/MhhNRyxkT/-1 of 1-//DCN2-CART-A/next-1dc/0/1202-00:30/1201-21:12 SmartPacSr

foresaw greater opportunities for dialogue and cooperation with its erstwhile adversary. In parallel, NATO's strategic mission was modified. The Alliance, the new Strategic Concept of 1991 declaimed, would proceed from a 'broad approach to security', embracing for the first time crisis management alongside collective defence.[4] Having made this leap forward, NATO has in the intervening years been involved in a constant process of change. Since the Cold War's end, the Alliance has nearly doubled its membership; has developed partnerships with over forty countries around the world as well as with the EU (in 1990, the partnership concept didn't even exist); has added cyber and space to its domains of operations alongside land, sea and air; has run major operations in Afghanistan, the Balkans, Libya, the Mediterranean Sea and elsewhere; has developed a counter-terrorism remit; and following the 2014 Ukraine crisis has repositioned itself to counter the rising threat from Russia. In a significant step, NATO's 2019 London Declaration pointed to a potential new role in addressing 'China's growing influence'.[5] The Alliance has thus taken on many new – and simultaneously held – tasks. Such 'pragmatic functionalism' means NATO has been able to stake a claim to international relevance in a fluid security environment, while at the same time meeting the needs of a diverse membership, and steering toward the priorities of its leading state, the US. The Alliance, in other words, has survived because it has found 'new things to do'.[6] Indeed, it keeps on finding new things to do. To adapt, innovate and prepare for the future is why, to its defenders, NATO is 'not only the longest lasting alliance in history. It is the most successful alliance in history.'[7]

Strategic Overload

But the accumulation of tasks also has its downsides. NATO has taken on more than it can cope with and it makes claims to competence it cannot possibly fulfil. This problem of 'overload' was identified by the political scientist Anthony King back in the mid-1970s when analysing the growing demands placed upon domestic governments.[8] It is a problem that also applies to international organizations. Overload has informed much of the debate on NATO's post-Cold War evolution. As the Alliance has moved forward, scholars, think-tank analysts and politicians have lined up either to praise its adaptive creativity or to warn against over-stretch and a dilution of purpose. The latter position focuses on the downsides of NATO's acquisition of new tasks, and its absorption of new members through enlargement.

During the 1990s, NATO took decisive steps on both counts. It adopted the Partnership for Peace (PfP) programme in January 1994, launched an air campaign and peacekeeping mission in Bosnia, signed the Founding Act with Russia in May 1997, and in 1999 welcomed the Czech Republic, Hungary and Poland as new members. In March 1999, meanwhile, NATO launched Operation Allied Force (OAF) – a seventy-eight-day aerial bombing campaign that dislodged Serbian forces from Kosovo. The Alliance was thus in the thick of the action, but as the decade ended, some observers argued that it was now doing too much. NATO, Michael E. Brown argued, had become 'preoccupied with activities unrelated to vital interests'. The high costs of military operations and the likelihood of serial failures, he suggested, threatened to inflict 'irreparable damage' upon it.[9]

As NATO moved into the 2000s, it acquired more new members (seven states joined in 2004) and more tasks. The operation in Afghanistan was the Alliance's most significant undertaking after 9/11, but NATO also staked out a broader counter-terrorism role and extended its partnership programmes beyond the former communist states and the Mediterranean to embrace the Gulf region as well as a diverse group of 'partners across the globe' that included Japan, Australia and New Zealand. A lack of strategic and operational focus now emerged as a real problem. The Alliance, Beatrice Heuser suggested in 2002, was in danger of 'becom[ing] so amorphous and so ill-defined that it will be useless for anybody'.[10] Six years later, the UK House of Commons Defence Committee noted similarly that NATO's diversification had made its 'role and purpose' unclear both to its members and to its citizens.[11]

The Alliance at that point was certainly very busy. But as its own Secretary General, Jaap de Hoop Scheffer, noted, the sheer range and difficulty of missions meant its resources were stretched as never before.[12] As defence budgets plunged in the aftermath of the 2008 global financial crisis, this would become a recurrent theme. According to the 2010 NATO Parliamentary Assembly, several allies were of the view that 'NATO is already stretched beyond its capabilities' and should be wary of taking on new commitments.[13] The termination of the Alliance's combat role in Afghanistan in 2014 offered little respite. That development coincided with the Ukraine crisis and NATO's refocusing on Russia. To this revived front to the east, the Alliance also staked out a role to its south in the Middle East and North Africa (MENA) as well as on 'the home front' (in response to the ongoing challenge of terrorism alongside cyber and hybrid attacks). As one former NATO official remarked in 2019, this combination of problems was probably 'unmanageable'. In dealing with it, NATO faced the distinct 'danger [of] strategic overload'.[14]

The Roots of the Problem

How has NATO found itself in this position? What internal and external factors have led the Alliance to a point where it is straining at the seams?

NATO as an Institution

NATO has displayed a feature common among complex organizations: that of 'mission creep' or 'competence creep'.[15] Scholars looking at this phenomenon have often attributed it to the power of organizational bureaucracies.[16] This is not really relevant in NATO's case: its administrative cadre is too small and the power of the allies too great. As we shall see below, it is the allies who have loaded NATO with increased responsibilities. But why has the Alliance been susceptible to these demands in the first place? An important part of the answer here lies in the 'institutional assets' referred to in the introductory chapter. In general, institutional survival and continuity require adaptation to external circumstances: striking a 'balance between exploring new possibilities and exploiting existing capabilities'.[17] In NATO's case, there have certainly been ample opportunities for repurposing. The Alliance's traditional mission has not gone away, as evident in the tense relationship with Russia, but in addition it has had to deal with myriad other problems: identity-based violence, terrorism, pandemics, environmental degradation, food shortages, organized crime, cyber attacks and large migration flows. During the Cold War, such issues were side-lined by the imperative of superpower competition. The Soviet Union's demise along with the acceleration of globalization has dissolved that suppressant. The upshot has been the spread of 'a variety of threats [. . .] global in scope [. . .] more serious in their effects [and] inherently more difficult to measure, locate, monitor and contain'.[18] In this world of uncertainty, the very notion of 'threat' for some has lost its relevance. It is rather 'risks', unbound by time or space, that have proliferated. Risks cannot be eliminated, only managed, and bodies such as NATO have had to engage accordingly in an unending task of risk management.[19] Doing so has not turned the Alliance into a general-purpose organization akin to the UN or regional bodies such as the EU, the African Union or the Association of Southeast Asian Nations (ASEAN). NATO's political, scientific and other functions remain very much secondary to its security imperative. And here, it possesses a number of distinct advantages.

First, NATO has an authoritative legal basis in the shape of the North Atlantic Treaty. It is not unique among international organizations in this regard – just think of the Treaties of the European Union or the European Convention on Human Rights of the Council of Europe. But the NATO treaty has the benefit of concision (it is a mere fourteen articles long) and flexibility. Its key provisions – Article 5 on collective defence and Article 10 on the admission of new members – are open to interpretation, but precisely because of this, according to James Goldgeier, they 'provided the alliance with its purpose and scope' during the Cold War and have 'enabled [it] to move forward in the decades [since]'.[20]

Second, NATO is the location of unrivalled command and force structures. During the Cold War, it met its match in the Warsaw Pact, but that body disappeared in 1991. Contemporary multinational alliances (the Russian-led Collective Security Treaty Organization, for example) have integrated military structures, and international organizations such as the EU, the OSCE and the UN have military and civilian bodies that oversee the tasks of peacekeeping and conflict management. But none of these come close to NATO's sophistication and scope. The Alliance is possessed of two strategic commands based on either side of the Atlantic: Allied Command Operations (ACO) in Mons, Belgium, and

Allied Command Transformation (ACT) in Norfolk, Virginia. These sit above a number of multinational headquarters at the 'operational and component levels of command, distributed geographically and commonly funded'.[21] Since the early 1990s, NATO's command structures have been refashioned several times as well as being subject to a significant downsizing of personnel. Nonetheless, they have proven both resilient and adaptable – illustrated most recently by decisions in 2018 to establish two new Joint Commands and a Cyberspace Operations Centre. NATO's force structures, meanwhile, consist of air, land, maritime and special operations forces and local headquarters held by allies (individually or in multinational format) available for assignment to NATO's Supreme Allied Commander Europe (SACEUR), the commanding officer of SHAPE located at ACO. Taken together, command and force structures oversee NATO operations, force deployments and exercises. They are complemented by an array of integrated military resources (air and ballistic missile defence, an airborne warning and control system or AWACS, alliance ground surveillance, joint intelligence, surveillance and reconnaissance), training and educational establishments (the NATO-accredited Centres of Excellence, the NATO Defence College and NATO School) and specialized agencies (on science and technology, security of communications, standardization and procurement).

Third, NATO is characterized by robust force generation and defence planning processes. The former has had to keep pace with the growing number of NATO missions and the increased number of allies and partners participating in them. The latter, meanwhile, has had to accommodate NATO's enlarged membership and increasingly complex capability requirements. But both processes, Christian Tuschhoff has shown, 'have been confirmed, refined, and enhanced by continuing practice'.[22]

While we have highlighted the accumulation of tasks as a problem, NATO at least has the institutional wherewithal to absorb them. But that has become a problem in itself. NATO's institutional flexibility has meant it has been less than discriminate in the tasks it has taken on. It has become the 'garbage can' into which allies dispose all manner of problems confronting them.[23]

NATO's Politics

NATO's institutional character provides only a partial explanation for the acquisition of new tasks. Its development has also had an expressly political dynamic. Allied governments, politicians and the Secretary General have all, in different ways, argued that NATO's relevance and credibility require it to do new things or do existing things differently. Failure to do so, it has often been claimed, puts the very survival of the Alliance at stake.

This 'self-preservation challenge'[24] was evident even in NATO's finest hour, at the end of the Cold War. With the Alliance having completed its mission of facing down a potential Soviet aggressor, was it time, the journalist (and later Clinton administration official) Strobe Talbott asked, to think about NATO's retirement?[25] Such views were not confined to journalists. West German Foreign Minister Hans-Dietrich Genscher indicated in early 1990 a preference for the Conference on Security and Cooperation in Europe (CSCE) as a pan-European solution to Europe's post-Cold War security relations. French President François Mitterrand argued similarly in favour of a 'European Confederation'. Neither proposal had much time for NATO. Such schemes proved unacceptable, however, to the US and many of the other allies (Canada and the UK in particular), as well as to the West German Chancellor, Helmut Kohl, all of whom lobbied forcefully in NATO's favour. American advocacy of NATO would win the day. President George H.W. Bush argued that NATO was the most effective vehicle for ensuring American's continued presence in Europe, for containing a reunified Germany and for projecting 'a renewed Western vision for the future of Europe'.[26] The EU, the CSCE and the Western European Union, Bush made clear, were partners of but not substitutes for the Alliance. That position, encapsulated in NATO's historic London and Rome Declarations (issued in July 1990 and November 1991, respectively), effectively positioned the Alliance as Europe's principal security institution. But as one observer noted at the time, NATO would not now be able to duck a whole range of new security issues arising from instability in Eastern Europe and the Balkans.[27]

And so, during the 1990s, arguments on NATO's relevance continued. Republican Senator Richard Lugar warned in 1993 that the Alliance needed to go 'out-of-area' or it would go 'out-of-business'.[28] Zbigniew Brzezinski, former National Security Advisor in the Carter administration, suggested similarly that if NATO did not enlarge it would die.[29] By the mid-1990s, the Clinton administration had fixed upon a firm position to beef up the Alliance – hence the moves toward enlargement, new partnerships and conflict management in the Balkans. The specifics of each policy were debated long and hard, but they were conjoined by a common logic. As noted by Robert Hunter, the US Ambassador to NATO throughout much of the period, the Alliance needed to 'justify itself', show that it was 'strong, relevant and able to act' after the Cold War.[30]

The debate on NATO entered an entirely new phase following the 9/11 attacks on the US. In response to this unprecedented act of terrorism, the Alliance activated for the first, and still only, time Article 5 of the North Atlantic Treaty. Secretary General George Robertson would later comment that this was a transformative moment for the Alliance.[31] But many commentators at the time were not so convinced. NATO played only a marginal military role in the initial US response to 9/11 (it was not involved in the overthrow of the Taliban in Afghanistan in late 2001), ended up deeply divided over Iraq in 2002/3 and appeared ill suited to tackling a security agenda of terrorism and counter-proliferation whose primary focus was outside of Europe.[32] Largely under American influence, NATO's 'historic' Prague summit of November 2002, which concentrated on this new agenda, was billed as having 'fundamentally transformed the Atlantic Alliance'.[33] But even a positive spin on NATO's position in the post-9/11 environment saw it as facing daunting existential challenges, requiring a further reinvention or reimagining.[34]

The most marked expression of that shift was NATO's involvement in Afghanistan. Precisely because the mission there was so demanding, it soon emerged as yet another test of relevance – a test that much more significant because the NATO-led ISAF was where the Alliance meshed with Washington's desire to give it a 'global' outlook. For sure, that vision was not equally shared. The UK, the Danes and the Dutch enthusiastically supported the ISAF mandate. NATO's new entrants in Eastern Europe, however, wanted to keep the focus on Russia. And the Mediterranean allies – France, Italy and Spain – were sceptical of a mission that was so obviously geared to American rather than European interests. Yet whatever their differences, the allies settled on ISAF as NATO's principal concern. And having made that commitment, so, according to US Secretary of Defence Robert Gates, 'the credibility of NATO, and indeed the viability of the Euro-Atlantic security project itself', came to depend on how well that mission performed.[35]

NATO's priorities shifted decisively again in 2014. Russia's annexation of Crimea and incursion into eastern Ukraine caught the Alliance on the hop. With NATO having dedicated itself to expeditionary missions after 9/11, the Russian action demonstrated that a more pressing danger was situated much closer to Europe. What had happened in Crimea, a report of the UK parliament's Defence Committee suggested, presaged possible action against 'a NATO country'. '[T]he future existence of NATO', it concluded, meant the Alliance had to be ready to act 'against common threats' and to hold 'a collective view of Russian actions'.[36] A narrative of Russian threat was soon matched by concrete actions (see Chapter 4) – what the NATO Secretary General would describe in October 2015 as 'the biggest reinforcement of collective defence since the end of the Cold War'.[37]

But no sooner had NATO elevated Russia to priority status than other issues intervened. Converging in what would be dubbed NATO's 'southern' agenda, these included civil war and violence in Iraq, Syria and Libya, the rise of ISIS and the Mediterranean migration crisis of 2015. NATO's response was the concept of 'Projecting Stability', formally adopted at the Warsaw summit in July 2016. Coupled with deterrence and defence, a new 'conceptual operating framework' emerged for NATO – a '360 degree' approach that responded to both the concerns of the Alliance's eastern members (whose priority was Russia) and those of countries such as Italy, France, Spain, Turkey and Greece who cared much more about instability nearer to home.[38] But what of the US? The election in 2016 of Donald Trump meant NATO governments saw the need to align themselves with Washington's priorities – counter-terrorism and burden-sharing, most notably, and, as evident from the 2019 NATO Leaders' Meeting, China. Further, and to counter Trump's NATO scepticism, a more general sense of ambition was accorded the Alliance. Keynote NATO declarations of the early Trump period – much like those of the 1990s and 2000s – were thus replete with claims to transformation and keeping NATO relevant for the future.[39]

America's Foreign Policy Priorities

NATO, as an inter-governmental organization, enjoys functional flexibility by virtue of its institutional features. But the allies determine in which direction it moves. For reasons we consider in Chapter 2, the US stands head and shoulders above the others. NATO has consequently mirrored American priorities more often than not. And that is relevant here because US foreign policy has historically been expansive, indeed global, in scope.

That impulse was especially evident in the 1990s. President George H.W. Bush had already imagined a reconfiguration of global politics – a US-led 'new world order' – as the Cold War came to an end and the US assembled a military coalition in early 1991 to reverse Iraq's invasion of Kuwait. Bill Clinton, upon assuming office in 1993, was initially hesitant to take on the mantle of global leadership, but by its end his was an administration characterized by 'global hyperactivity', premised on a claim that the US was the world's 'indispensable nation' committed to global democratic enlargement, the spread of free trade and, where necessary, military intervention to promote regional order.[40]

Bush and Clinton are generally remembered as multilateralists, pursuing international cooperation for noble purposes. Yet both were clear that in foreign policy an American interest had to be served and that international organizations should be subordinate to that purpose. Such a proprietorial attitude was informed by a view that the Canadian and European allies were unwilling and unable to lead. Clinton's reported views on Bosnia are instructive here. Concerned by 1995 that NATO was paralysed by crisis in the Balkans, 'Clinton and his advisors decided', one official noted, 'that the only way to end the disagreements among the allies was to stop listening to them.' American officials 'would settle on a course of action' and then expect the allies to fall in line.[41]

After 9/11, American foreign policy shifted to the self-declared 'global war on terror'. The so-called 'Bush Doctrine' that emerged in response was premised on 'tak[ing] the fight to the enemy before they can attack us [. . .] confront[ing] threats before they fully materialize [and] advanc[ing] liberty and hope as an alternative to the enemy's ideology of repression and fear'.[42] Such ideas lay behind the overthrow of the Taliban in Afghanistan, the invasion of Iraq in 2003, the US rendition programme and American counter-terrorist measures in places as far afield as the Philippines, Pakistan, the Horn of Africa and Yemen. Much of this activity was clandestine and unilateral. Where it did involve partners, it was often done ad hoc through coalitions of the willing. Insofar as NATO mattered, it was through the development of capabilities and doctrine that would support American efforts. US Secretary of Defence Donald Rumsfeld thus demanded in September 2002 that the allies develop expeditionary and rapid response forces. NATO's answer was the 2002 Prague Capabilities Commitments, the development of the NATO Response Force, a major command structure reform and the 2002 Military Concept for Defence against Terrorism. ISAF, as we have seen, would be the signature mission that bore NATO's commitment to this new global agenda, but NATO also mounted a training mission in Iraq and lent its support to the African Union in Somalia and Sudan.

The Obama administration came to power with the intention of getting America off its war footing – emphasizing diplomacy over intervention, and coalition building over unilateral endeavour. To its supporters, Obama's foreign policy was characterized by caution, patience and empathy. Obama committed the US to the Paris Agreement on climate change and the Iran nuclear deal, opened up relations with long-time foes such as Cuba and 'reset' relations with Russia.[43] Yet for all this, Obama remained committed to American exceptionalism and global military primacy. Distancing itself from Bush's war on terror, the administration still managed to pursue an extensive policy of targeted assassinations and drone strikes. A desire to curtail overseas commitments was also only partial. The US drew down its forces in Iraq but changed tack in 2014 in order to counter the threat from ISIS. And in Afghanistan, while NATO's combat mission was terminated in 2014, the smaller Resolute Support mission was committed to the country for the long term. Within this context, Obama expected much of the allies. All US administrations have bemoaned the problem of burden-sharing (see Chapter 3) and Obama, too, was clear on this point. If the US was to pour its energies into local crises, then it would do so, in the words of the 2015 National Security Strategy, by 'mobiliz[ing] allies and partners to share the burden and achieve lasting outcomes'.[44] Yet deferring to allies was good only insofar as America's partners had something to offer. On matters of collective defence in Europe, the US remained as essential as ever. NATO's Readiness Action Plan launched in the wake of the 2014 Ukraine crisis brought significant European and Canadian resources to the fore but was overshadowed by the US-led Operation Atlantic Resolve and the European Reassurance Initiative (which, despite the name, was an American effort).

Obama's successor Donald Trump struck an intemperate attitude toward NATO. But even in the face of Trump's criticisms, the Alliance was unable to break the spell of American leadership. The allies under pressure from Washington recommitted to increased defence spending and re-emphasized NATO's role in countering terrorism. Insofar as the Trump administration could claim to have a signature foreign policy, it was to balance regional and global challengers – Russia and China (and, of a lesser order, Iran) – in a new era of great power competition. Alliances such as NATO were seen as material to that effort.[45] In the case of Russia, that sat well with NATO's traditional mission. But a policy for China (alluded to at the 2019 NATO Leaders' Meeting) took the Alliance off into uncertain territory. Trump's suggestion that NATO expand its mission and membership to the Middle East was even less well defined.[46]

Liberal Ideas and Liberal Order

NATO's task expansion has been made possible by alliance institutions, given shape by allied politics and driven by American ambition. Allied calculations here are best understood as 'interests'. But interests co-exist with ideas – the beliefs which provide the broader setting of action, a desirable end state in its grandest sense and, linked to that, a roadmap that provides answers to why and how a particular course of action should be taken.[47] Measuring the influence of ideas upon policy is a complex business, but in NATO's case the task is made a little easier because the Alliance has explicitly articulated an ideational rationale for its endeavours.

The relevant ideas have been described by commentators as 'Atlanticist' or 'multilateral', but 'liberal' is the term which has stuck. In the Cold War, NATO's liberal identity was, in part, a projection of the allies' domestic democratic systems. But it was also defined in juxtaposition to NATO's communist 'other', the Soviet bloc. The end of the Cold War's ideological divide meant the liberal appellation became fuzzier. In its political (as opposed to economic) formulation, it has revolved around a belief in the sanctity of rights and the related position that such rights are universal and should be both protected and promoted – a view that goes back to the formation of the UN in 1945 and the adoption of the Universal Declaration of Human Rights in 1948. During the Cold

War, NATO's defence of liberal values was very much symbolic (hence the toleration of some distinctly non-democratic members among NATO's ranks). But the seeming victory of 'freedom, democracy, human rights and the rule of law' at the Cold War's end opened up new historic possibilities.[48] The Clinton administration took the view that NATO, through enlargement and partnerships, should assume a new liberal mission of democracy promotion. This, moreover, would have geopolitical benefits. Democracies were viewed as essentially peaceable in their relations with each other. As NATO membership spread, therefore, so, too, would inter-state peace.[49] Subsequent enlargements stuck to this narrative. The 'big bang' enlargement of 2004 sat explicitly with President George W. Bush's 'Freedom Agenda'. Obama commended Albania and Croatia's entry in 2009 as contributing to domestic reform and regional stability.[50] The Trump administration, not known for its support of democracy abroad, welcomed the entry of North Macedonia (NATO's most recent member) in similar terms.[51]

NATO's promotion of liberal values has also occurred through more direct intervention. Operation Allied Force of 1999 provided the template in this regard. As UK Prime Minister Tony Blair argued at the time, the mission was necessary to reverse Serbia's ethnic cleansing of Albanian Kosovans – it was 'a just war based not on any territorial ambitions but on values'.[52] David Cameron and Barack Obama provided similar justifications a decade later for the NATO intervention in Libya to stop attacks by the Qaddafi regime on its civilian population.[53] In between sat the long NATO mission in Afghanistan. Here, the connection to liberal values was more obscure. But alongside its counter-terrorism and counter-insurgency rationale, ISAF was also justified as improving 'governance, and economic and social development'.[54] In that sense, it was of a piece with NATO's earlier efforts in the

Balkans – in Sten Rynning's phrase, at 'the heart of a wider liberal order' of nation-building, humanitarian standards and stabilization.[55]

However noble its motives, the upshot of this liberal impulse has been a lack of restraint. The abstract quality of values or ideas gives them a universal and expansive application. NATO has attempted to instantiate those ideas through expeditionary nation-building, the management of global security and the spread of liberal market democracy. In consequence, Patrick Porter suggested in 2010, NATO had become unbound, cast loose from its traditional 'demarcated sphere' of activities, and facing the world with a sense of unlimited responsibility.[56]

NATO's Treadmill of Problems

There are powerful reasons, then, why NATO has taken on more tasks. But the manner and scope of that adaptation has brought with it real problems. Some of these we consider below. In doing so, our analysis is not structured around NATO's big topic agenda items: terrorism, Russia, the Afghan conflict and so on. Rather, we examine four categories of dysfunction that underlie the concrete challenges the Alliance faces: a reluctance to make hard choices; imprecise policy goals; a thinning of commitment; and division among the allies.

Hard Choices

An expanded agenda means there is simply more for NATO to do, and many of its tasks are exceptionally difficult to execute. NATO has assumed an almost heroic quality: it claims to have taken whatever action necessary to keep the allies and their one billion citizens safe, and accepted the necessary price of that effort in blood and treasure.[57] But such a view is too forgiving. NATO is not simply a victim of circumstances. Some of the problems it faces have followed from the particular choices it has made.

Afghanistan provides a telling example. It was not inevitable that NATO would end up in an open-ended commitment to the country. The Taliban had been overthrown before NATO took charge of ISAF in 2003 and at that point Afghanistan was reasonably stable. However, within a short space of time, a regrouped Taliban had dragged NATO into a counter-insurgency war, which by 2006 was already described as 'unwinnable'.[58] Yet the NATO/ISAF mandate was extended time after time, and eight years would elapse before the Alliance ended its combat mission, with the Taliban no nearer to defeat. NATO, for sure, operated under exceptionally testing circumstances. Afghanistan is one the world's poorest countries, and the government of Hamid Karzai which the Alliance partnered for many years was both manifestly inept and corrupt. The nation-building mission thus proved next to impossible to execute despite huge inflows of financial aid. As for the military dimension, the Taliban (aided by clandestine support from Pakistan) proved a tenacious opponent. NATO was reasonably adept at tactical innovation and made a valiant effort to train national Afghan armed forces. Despite well-reported political divisions among the allies, at its peak in 2011, some 130,000 personnel were under ISAF command – drawn from all NATO's then twenty-eight nations alongside over twenty partner countries. This was no mean feat of political and military will. The positive impact on Afghanistan itself was less marked, however. Official statements portrayed ISAF in a positive light right up to the end of its mission in 2014.[59] But such optimism was belied by the release in late 2019 of classified documents which revealed persistent doubts among American civilian and military officials at the wisdom of policies they themselves had been overseeing.[60] By that point, the US had spent over $750 billion on the military effort in Afghanistan plus some $130 billion on civilian projects. It had also endured nearly 1,900 fatalities and over 20,000 casualties. The UK, for its part, had suffered over 450 deaths, a figure by 2010 already higher than in the Falklands War. The number of total war dead in Afghanistan, meanwhile, was estimated at 147,000, including 38,000 Afghan civilians.[61] And yet the Taliban insurgency showed no sign of abating. The US government's own reporting estimated that insurgent activity in 2019 was higher than at any time since 2001.[62] This was the context within which NATO's Resolute Support mission then operated. Post-ISAF, the Alliance had clearly retreated from the ambitious agenda of its first ten years in Afghanistan, but to what strategic end and over what time scale remained an open question. NATO had committed at the 2018 Brussels summit to fund assistance to the Afghan security forces until 2024, in pursuit of 'long-term security and stability'. But a survey of Afghan specialists in February 2018 had already noted that alliance and American aims were 'largely unachievable and Afghanistan's future [is] only partly salvageable'.[63] In 2009, the US had appointed Richard Holbrooke as its first Special Representative for Afghanistan and Pakistan. Holbrooke soon concluded that counter-insurgency in Afghanistan was failing. Efforts by the Obama administration to open talks with the Taliban, however, proved half-hearted.[64] Trump took a more decisive approach, but the upshot was a deeply controversial agreement (pp. 89–90).

Russia provides another example of the consequences of hard choices. Here, tensions have been an all-too-predictable downside of enlargement. The arguments mobilized in favour of the policy may have been powerful and the benefits to new members tangible and real. But Russia objected to the policy from the outset. Critics in NATO countries echoed these concerns: George Kennan, the architect of America's Cold War strategy of containment, warned in 1997 that enlargement could prove 'the most fateful error of American policy in the entire post-Cold War era'.[65] For some, he was proved right. As we show in Chapter 4, efforts at NATO–Russia partnership failed to blunt Moscow's opposition, and once the Alliance chose to support Georgian and Ukrainian membership, things spiralled downward. Both the Russo-Georgian war of 2008 and Russia's annexation of Crimea in 2014 can be seen as pre-emptive moves by Moscow to forestall Georgia and Ukraine from joining NATO. Russia, particularly in Crimea, is in clear violation of international law, but whatever the legal position, as John Mearsheimer has pointed out, 'anyone with a rudimentary understanding of geopolitics should have seen this [crisis] coming. The West was moving into Russia's backyard and threatening its core strategic interests.'[66] Russia's 'backyard' also includes the three Baltic States – Estonia, Latvia and Lithuania – all of which were once incorporated into the Soviet Union. Russian officials in the 1990s indicated that there, too, NATO membership for these countries was 'categorically unacceptable'.[67] NATO went ahead regardless. Moscow did not respond with active intervention, but the armed build-up in Russia's Western military district since places the Baltics in a position of huge vulnerability. Most studies conclude that NATO would be unable to defend them in the event of a Russian attack.[68]

Imprecision

NATO has found itself in hot water over enlargement, in part, because of a reluctance to define the policy's limits. Admittedly, here it has faced a real predicament. Had NATO been too restrictive on enlargement's scope after the Cold War (or even eschewed the policy altogether) it would have been accused of abandoning Eastern Europe, and plunging the region into a 'grey zone' of strategic uncertainty. The course it chose instead was expansive but ambiguous. The Alliance's position on enlargement is formally subject to Article 10 of the North Atlantic Treaty, a clause that affords the possibility of membership to 'any [. . .] European State'. NATO, having now taken in a number of Balkan countries, much of former communist Eastern Europe and the Baltic States, has an 'open door' that hypothetically extends to the whole of the former Yugoslavia, European neutrals and the former Soviet republics of Transcaucasia (including Georgia), as well as Moldova, Belarus, Ukraine and even Russia. Within this elastic geopolitical context, NATO has exercised choice by imposing political, military and geostrategic preconditions. But conditionality has, in effect, entrapped the Alliance. Entry can be delayed, but it has denied itself the ability to foreclose membership as a matter of principle.[69] This has given rise to some real predicaments. Georgia especially has taken every opportunity to solidify its relations with NATO. Its troops have served in Afghanistan and Kosovo, it has units assigned to the NATO Response Force, and its armed forces are engaged in all manner of NATO-approved defence assistance packages. Georgia has 'nothing else left to prove', according to the former commander of the US army in Europe.[70] Yet, fearful of Russian reaction, the allies have been unwilling to provide Georgia with a Membership Action Plan (MAP). Enlargement, at least in this case, is at a 'geopolitical impasse'. NATO remains formally committed to the process but unable or unwilling to execute it.[71]

NATO's partnership policies have exhibited a similar ambiguity. Since the early 1990s, the Alliance has developed relations with over forty states, drawing upon a menu of some 1,400 separate partnership activities. These have undoubtedly had some benefits. PfP helped prepare post-communist states for NATO membership and fashioned close working relations with neutral states such as Finland and Sweden; the 'strategic partnership' with the EU has facilitated practical cooperation on issues such as cyber defence and military mobility; and individual partners have made important contributions to NATO exercises as well as to operations in Afghanistan, Libya and Kosovo. But some obvious failings have also been evident. NATO's umbrella scheme, the Euro-Atlantic Partnership Council, has become too unwieldy to be useful, and regional initiatives such as the Mediterranean Dialogue and the Istanbul Cooperation Initiative have proven largely ineffectual. The Alliance's attempts to rationalize its partnerships' portfolio, meanwhile, have had only limited success. The overall impression is still one of unchecked institutional proliferation: 'an accumulation of partly unconnected, partly overlapping formats' sits alongside 'antiquated practices'; new formats have failed to displace old ones; and multilateralism competes with special bilateral relationships or minilateral sub-groups.[72] Partnership schemes also require coordination across several agencies. The sheer scale of that effort has exacted a significant toll upon NATO's human and financial resources. Partnerships in the round, one former alliance official has suggested, have become 'close to unmanageable'.[73]

Thin Commitment

NATO's orientation to new tasks has been driven by the need to demonstrate relevance. The Alliance has, however, struggled to add substance to some of its high-level political commitments. Counter-terrorism (CT) policy provides a good example. On the one hand, NATO can point to some concrete progress following its mission reorientation after 9/11. Many of the relevant measures have already been noted, but it is worth emphasizing that NATO's two longest missions – ISAF/Resolute Support in Afghanistan and Operation Active Endeavour/Sea Guardian in the Mediterranean (launched in October 2001 and ongoing as of 2020) – have their origins in CT action. NATO has also been busy creating institutional capacity (a Terrorism Intelligence Cell was set up in 2017), agreeing CT Policy Guidelines and action plans for the allies (first adopted in 2012), embedding CT training in partnership programmes and exchanging expert knowledge with allies and partners through the Science for Peace Programme, the Emerging Security Challenges Division and the work of the Centre of Excellence for Defence against Terrorism based in Ankara. In mid-2017, NATO became a formal partner in the Global Coalition to Defeat ISIS. But despite these efforts, the Alliance has fared poorly in coordinating its actions with those of other bodies, notably the EU. It also lacks many of the tools essential to CT efforts: it has no ability to apply sanctions, block terrorist funding, police the borders of its members or liaise with national civil authorities dedicated to homeland security. NATO, in contrast to the EU, also still lacks its own CT Coordinator.[74]

NATO's CT efforts have become increasingly associated with its Projecting Stability agenda, working with partners 'to build stronger defence institutions, improve good governance, enhance [. . .] resilience and [. . .] more effectively contribute to the fight against terrorism'.[75] Projecting Stability has been favourably compared to NATO's eastern strategy of the 1990s, where a similar 'preoccupation with the shape of an entire geopolitical system' gave rise to a sense of strategic priority.[76] But the differences are also clear. PfP, the Alliance's signature partnership policy of the 1990s, was geared toward eventual NATO membership for many of its participants. Such is not the case with NATO partnership schemes focused on the MENA region. The influence that a membership perspective can bring to bear on local military and political transformation has thus been absent. The problems in the MENA region are also on a scale greater than the post-communist east. Most states of the region are characterized by 'challenging demographic developments, [. . .] a stagnant economy, illegal migration, violent forms of political Islam' and the negative effects of climate change (involving water shortages and crop failures).[77] COVID-19 has only exacerbated these problems.[78] Further, MENA is home to powerful non-state actors (Hezbollah, ISIS and groups representing the Kurdish populations of Turkey, Syria and Iraq), regional rivalries and proxy competition. Iran, Russia, Turkey, Saudi Arabia, Israel and the US have all, in various permutations, competed for influence, so exacerbating violence in Iraq, Yemen, Libya and Syria. Within these very difficult circumstances, NATO's positive influence has been limited. Its defence reform and capacity-building programmes have been beneficial to a handful of countries in the Persian Gulf and North Africa (Jordan and Tunisia, for instance). The Alliance has also adopted a partnership 'Package for the South' (endorsed at the NATO summit of July 2018) and stood up a Strategic Direction-South Hub in Naples and a Regional Centre in Kuwait. But overall, as a NATO Parliamentary Assembly report concluded in 2018, the Alliance's efforts have proven 'insufficient to address the multifaceted threats emanating from its Southern flank'.[79]

NATO's standing in the region has also not been helped by the legacy of its intervention in Libya in 2011. (That mission overthrew Qaddafi but did not stick around to help with the transition to a new political order. Libya has been in a state of civil unrest ever since.) But lurking behind this is a much bigger issue of purpose. NATO's Military Committee has drawn up a Military Concept for Projecting Stability, but, according to Jeffrey Larsen, still lacks 'a strategy that articulate[s] clearly [the Alliance's] ultimate goals, as well as adequate funding and the political support of member states'.[80] NATO is internally divided over what to do in MENA and cooperates poorly with organizations such as the UN and the EU that are better suited to operating there. Following the draining experience of Afghanistan, and wary of the pitfalls of Syria and Iraq, many allies have simply preferred to keep NATO out of the region. The Alliance has thus become victim to its own raised expectations: claiming an important role in the region but lacking the appetite to do much of any significance. NATO is, in institutional terms, too 'thin'. It lacks the capacity to address the problems it has identified and has suffered a loss of credibility as a result.[81]

Fragmentation

NATO also suffers from internal division. Alliance unity or 'cohesion', Patricia Weitsman has suggested, is 'relatively easy to generate and maintain' where there is 'a mutual desire to contain a mutual adversary'.[82] But NATO no longer has this singular focus. It has taken on more responsibilities and so there are more points of disagreement. The Alliance has also acquired more members, so making the problem worse. Just how bad things have become does need some qualifying. Weitsman points out that NATO has become an alliance that fights. Its missions in Bosnia, Kosovo, Libya and Afghanistan have all occasioned significant internal disagreement: over war aims, variable levels of commitment among the allies and the utility of force. But none of these operations has proven fatal to the Alliance. NATO's collective resolve has held, and whatever the wisdom of the missions themselves, staying the course 'suggests', according to one view, 'that the Alliance can adapt to difficult circumstances'.[83]

In fact, NATO suffers from a more deep-seated politico-strategic problem. As we have seen, post-Cold War threats impinge differently on the allies. NATO has responded to this problem by trying to accommodate as many viewpoints as possible. An expanded agenda, while not optimal for all allies, does at least have the benefit of 'satisficing', generating a minimal level of agreement on a shared interest. Further,

NATO allies often have powerful secondary reasons for tacking toward security issues that do not affect them directly: a desire to be associated with the US (a factor for many allies who took part in ISAF) or for upholding solidarity as part of a broader commitment to multilateralism and transatlantic relations (one reason for Canadian involvement in NATO's defence of the Baltic States). But while NATO has a good track record of accommodating division, the problem of fragmentation remains serious. Indeed, in 2017, NATO commissioned a project to study alliance unity, on the assumption that 'without cohesion', 'NATO can and will fail'. Again, the main problem was identified as 'differential threat assessments',[84] a problem compounded, in turn, by the erosion of liberal democratic values among some NATO allies (Hungary and Turkey most notably).[85] Such divisions have had debilitating effects. Defence plans drawn up in 2016 for NATO's eastern and southern flanks were later blocked by American and Turkish objections. This caused a big row at the 2019 NATO Leaders' Meeting. As one analyst observed at the time, a failure to 'retain [. . .] cohesiveness in an environment where threats have proliferated and diversified' might indeed 'confirm that NATO is comatose'.[86]

Conclusion: Walking and Chewing Gum

NATO has staked its claim to relevance on an expansion of both its membership and agenda. Up to a point, that has worked. The Alliance has adapted rather than ossified and answered the demand for action in the face of multiple challenges. But it has also, as a result, taken on too much. As one official suggested in the margins of the 2014 summit, NATO 'must be prepared for every challenge the world throws at us'; it must 'multi-task, while remaining proficient at every task'.[87] The intervening years have demonstrated the folly of such ambition. NATO's position in Afghanistan has gone from bad to worse, its southern strategy has proven irrelevant to the conflicts in Syria and Iraq, and enlargement has foundered over questions of what to do about Georgia and Ukraine. The Alliance has become more impotent and more divided as its range has been extended. On some issues, it might have proven its worth (the military response to Russia's annexation of Crimea could only have been effected by NATO), but the high tide of allied efficacy has seemingly been reached. If NATO is to avoid a future forever over-promising and under-delivering, it needs to take a hard look at its strengths and weaknesses, and to discriminate between the impossible and the achievable. That is the job of task discretion, a theme we turn to in Chapter 5.

CHAPTER TWO

Weary or Wary? The Problem of American Leadership in NATO

A vigorous debate on the broad direction of American foreign policy has been ongoing since the end of the Cold War. The power and resources at America's disposal and the consequences of its actions for the rest of the world have meant such debates have been cast in sweeping terms. NATO has figured prominently, giving rise to three questions of critical importance. Is NATO a necessary and essential component of any American grand strategy? Is the US capable of leading the Alliance materially and temperamentally? And are the European and Canadian allies still willing to follow the American lead? During the Cold War, such questions would have been answered affirmatively with only minor qualifications. That is no longer the case on either side of the Atlantic. For the US, leadership of NATO has been subject to a logic of decreasing returns as American interests have been increasingly threatened in regions beyond Europe. European interests, meanwhile, continue to be defined regionally as much as globally. A transatlantic divergence has consequently developed, undermining the basis of Euro-American security cooperation.

If the Americans are indeed weary of leading NATO, and the Europeans increasingly wary of following the US, can the Alliance survive? This chapter addresses that question in three steps. First, it considers the long-standing tensions inherent within the 'transatlantic bargain' and, related to this efforts to redistribute tasks and responsibilities in NATO after the Cold War. Second, it identifies some of the inherent barriers to collective action among the allies. And, third, it assesses how American leadership of NATO sits with the evolution of thinking on foreign policy and grand strategy in the US. These issues are presented as problems for NATO. They are real and have deep roots. In Chapter 6, we address them by reference to a countervailing set of assumptions and a set of foreign policy choices more amenable to transatlantic cooperation.

The Transatlantic Bargain: Coming Unstuck Again

During the Cold War, the transatlantic bargain had two reinforcing components: the economic and the military-strategic. The first, Stanley Sloan has suggested, entailed US support for European economic recovery (most obviously in Marshall aid) in return for coordination by the Europeans so as 'to use the assistance most effectively'. It would help give rise to European economic integration, the precursor to the European Economic Community and later the European Union. The second component meant a US commitment to defend Western Europe on the assumption that the Europeans would assist the American effort by organizing themselves 'to help defend against the Soviet threat'. That assumption would help give rise to NATO.[1]

The transatlantic bargain was strained even during the Cold War. Article 3 of NATO's founding treaty encapsulated well its military quid pro quo: that the allies would through 'effective self-help and mutual aid [. . .] develop their individual and collective capacity to resist armed attack'.[2] The problem for the US was that the shared defence burden sat far too heavily on its own shoulders. Some European allies, meanwhile, reflecting the extent of their dependency, worried periodically that the US would abandon them in a crisis. But the military bargain still held. Nearly 300,000 US military personnel were stationed in West Germany throughout most of the Cold War and NATO's strategy of 'flexible response' (rolled out from the 1970s) also saw intermediate-range nuclear weapons being stationed in the country. This approach meant a Soviet attack on West Germany would engage American forces in significant numbers and be as much an attack on the US as on the host nation. NATO's collective defence mission thus acquired a 'special meaning': as a 'source of reassurance' to allies and as an expression of the dependability of American leadership.[3]

The economic component proved seemingly more fragile. In the early 1970s, it became clear that the US could not defend the dollar-centric fixed exchange rate system. The economic rise of Japan, the emergence of a German-dominated Europe and the seeming collapse of American manufacturing in the late 1970s also cast into doubt the continuing financial sustainability of the US security guarantee. It became commonplace at that time to assume that American hegemony was in decline and that the Nixon administration had initiated a 'retreat from empire'.[4] The administration of Jimmy Carter provided little to contradict this perception. The American withdrawal from Vietnam saw East Asia dominated by communist regimes in China, Laos, Cambodia and Vietnam itself. Throughout Africa and Latin America, leftist governments came to power aligned with either the Soviet Union or Cuba, and the final year of Carter's presidency saw the Soviet invasion of Afghanistan and an Islamist revolution overthrow America's long-time ally the Shah of Iran.

The administrations of Ronald Reagan and George H.W. Bush were based on correcting American decline by standing up to the Soviet Union and re-energizing American leadership of NATO. The great reversal of the Cold War's end was a seeming vindication of this approach. A sense of forward momentum also informed European sentiment. In 1992, the

Treaty of European Union signalled movement toward the next stage of European integration. In NATO, meanwhile, the talk was of a 'European pillar' that would ease the burden of American responsibility. Yet for all this seeming optimism, forging a post-Cold War transatlantic bargain would prove far from straightforward. Since the early 1990s, that bargain has narrowed to its military component (the economic aspect being much transformed in light of economic globalization and the emergence of the EU as an economic power). It has been revisited on at least five occasions.

The first of these involved differing responses to post-communist transition. The Europeans gave priority to 'soft' threats to security (for instance, decaying nuclear reactors and environmental degradation in the former Soviet Union), while the US took on responsibility for military-related assistance (military reform in Central and Eastern Europe and securing nuclear weapons and weapons-grade materiel in the former Soviet Union). As for NATO, transatlantic differences quickly emerged. The administrations of George H.W. Bush and Bill Clinton oversaw significant force withdrawals from Europe and indicated they were turning their strategic attention to the Asia-Pacific region. This was a perhaps inevitable consequence of the global shift of economic and military power to China, but it stoked concerns in Europe that the favoured status of the continent in American foreign policy had come to an end. Despite such fears, however, the US retained its hold on the Alliance. Washington was thus reluctant to support what became known as the European Security and Defence Identity (ESDI), worried (if French ambitions were anything to go by) that the initiative would slip out of NATO's control.[5]

The second iteration of the post-Cold War transatlantic bargain was conditioned by events in the Balkans. The US was initially criticized for inaction. Over Bosnia, French President Jacques Chirac memorably declared that the post of leader of the free world had become 'vacant'.[6] The NATO interventions in both Bosnia and Kosovo, when they came, would show just how reliant the Europeans still were on US firepower, much to the consternation of the American military, who bemoaned the Europeans' military shortcomings (the British excepted). Both conflicts also highlighted political problems. In the Kosovo campaign, for instance, the need to maintain consensus among NATO's members often took precedence over operational decisions on how best to prosecute 'the basic logic of warfare'.[7] A number of lessons were drawn in the US: that European capabilities were not sufficiently interoperable with the American military; that European governments lacked resolve in a crisis; and that only America could lead the Alliance.

After 9/11, therefore, the US took a hard look at NATO's value. Intra-alliance divisions over Iraq (Germany and France were strongly opposed to intervention in 2003) meant NATO was bypassed in favour of a US-led 'coalition of the willing'. Yet the US was determined to repurpose NATO for the long war on terror. In 2002, the Alliance adopted the Military Concept for Counter-Terrorism. The 2006 Comprehensive Political Guidance (CPG) noted a need to respond to the challenges of terrorism 'from wherever they may come'.[8] As the UK House of Commons Defence Committee noted, 'If NATO limits itself to a regional role in defence of the territory of the North Atlantic area alone, its value will be diminished, particularly to the United States, and its future will be in doubt.'[9] But not all the European allies were convinced. French Foreign Minister Michèle Alliot-Marie argued that a global NATO would 'dilute the natural solidarity between Europeans and North Americans in a vague ensemble' consisting of Pacific powers and other rising powers to be named at a later date.[10] German Chancellor Angela Merkel insisted that NATO should focus 'principally [. . .] on the collective security of the

North Atlantic partners'.[11] American leadership, it seemed, still remained dependent on Europeans' insistence that their security interests take precedent.

A fourth effort to strike a sustainable transatlantic bargain was undertaken during the two terms of Barack Obama's presidency. The US during this period became increasingly concerned with China. Secretary of State Hillary Clinton put the issue into stark relief in a widely cited article in 2011 that argued for a US 'pivot' to Asia to protect American strategic interests.[12] The corollary was that the Europeans assume a greater share of responsibility in NATO for their own security – hence the notion that the US would 'lead from behind' in interventions such as that then unfolding in Libya.[13] Such considerations were set aside by the 2014 Ukraine crisis as the Obama administration reaffirmed its commitment to a NATO fashioned to deter Russia.

These efforts were continued by the Trump administration, but other issues remained in play. Growing US–Chinese rivalry became *the* determining feature of foreign policy under President Trump. The Chinese Communist Party, Secretary of State Mike Pompeo declared in January 2020, is 'the central threat of our times'.[14] NATO's status, in Trump's view, accordingly diminished. We noted his view of NATO's obsolescence in the introductory chapter. Trump displayed a marked ambiguity on Article 5. Having omitted reference to collective defence at his first NATO summit in May 2017, he seemingly committed to it in a speech in Warsaw in July.[15] Trump was evasive, however, on how the US might support the Baltic States if threatened by Russia and questioned the wisdom of defending one of NATO's newest members, Montenegro. Trump also made the defence of NATO allies conditional: demanding that the more wealthy reimburse the US and suggesting that America might exit NATO if the allies failed to increase their military spending. In June 2020, he announced a withdrawal of US troops from Germany on the grounds that Berlin was 'tremendous[ly] delinquen[t]' in meeting NATO's defence spending targets.[16] In parallel, Trump struck a mercurial note on Russia. The administration's Russia policy, it is true, involved sanctions, diplomatic expulsions, the reinforcement of Eastern Europe as well as withdrawal from the Intermediate-Range Nuclear Forces (INF) Treaty following charges of Russian non-compliance – measures all within the NATO mainstream. That said, Trump showed an indulgence toward Putin's Russia at odds with the approach of most NATO allies. A joint press conference with Russian President Vladimir Putin in July 2018 was described by Senator John McCain as 'one of the most disgraceful performances by an American president in memory'.[17]

Prompted by such behaviour, German Chancellor Angela Merkel and French President Emmanuel Macron drew the conclusion that the US was no longer a reliable ally, that NATO, in consequence, had been hollowed out and that European 'strategic autonomy' through the EU had to be taken much more seriously.[18] Even the normally loyal UK was flustered. British Prime Minister Theresa May temporarily suspended intelligence sharing in May 2017 after Trump seemingly passed on classified materials in a White House meeting with the Russians. Disquiet in Europe was made worse by Washington's broader foreign policy trajectory. The US and its allies were at odds over Washington's unilateral withdrawals in 2017 from the Paris Agreement on climate change and the Joint Comprehensive Plan of Action on Iran, and the imposition of tariffs on European products (including iron, steel and cars). Trump's impeachment trial in early 2020 – although leading to acquittal by a Republican majority in the Senate – stoked further anxieties. Trump had, after all, been called out on an issue of direct interest to the allies: that US military assistance (in this case to non-NATO Ukraine) could be made subject to political conditions.[19] And as the COVID-19 crisis enveloped the world in 2020, the Trump administration adopted a distinctly national position, eschewing any role in coordinating a global response, providing no assistance to afflicted countries (in contrast to China) and closing borders to European countries, without prior consultation.

Trump, in short, had undermined the axioms of statecraft that had underpinned NATO since its founding: the desirability and sustainability of American leadership; a European willingness to follow the American lead in exchange for policies that served the interests of the Alliance broadly defined; and the provision by the US of global public goods. As the US geared up in 2020 for the presidential election, the prospect of a second Trump term filled many NATO watchers with dread – fearing it would usher in an irreversible loss of trust in US leadership and 'the very real possibility' of the US withdrawing from the Alliance.[20]

To summarize, during the Cold War, the transatlantic bargain developed within a predictable context; its terms set by the joint (if unequal) effort of balancing the Soviet bloc. Since the early 1990s, that bargain has had to be rethought amidst unremitting disruptions, ranging from the wars in the Balkans to jihadist violence, to the Russian annexation of Crimea, to the global COVID-19 pandemic. Each has produced a new category of threat. But striking a sustainable bargain has been complicated by a growing divergence of interests. After 9/11, a focus on international terrorism led the US to invade Iraq – a war that occasioned NATO's deepest division since the 1956 Suez crisis. The economic and military rise of China, more recently, has posed existential questions for the transatlantic relationship. The US views China as a threat to the strategic status quo in Asia and as its only global peer competitor. Views in Europe are diverse. The EU has branded China a 'systemic rival', but many European countries nonetheless see relations with Beijing as an economic opportunity largely free of strategic importance for Europe.[21] These divergences make a bargain difficult to sustain. They also make collective action harder to achieve.

The Difficulty of Collective Action

NATO's future depends upon the credible provision of security to its members. Throughout its history, there has been an ongoing dispute as to how that provision is shared. While an unevenness of contributions is to be expected in an alliance where the US is the superior military power, Americans have complained repeatedly that they have had to shoulder too much. We explore the mechanics of burden-sharing in more detail in Chapter 3. It is relevant here because it has implications for America's willingness to lead. Disputes over burden-sharing can become a barrier to collective action if the majority of allies shirk their responsibilities and the leading power is unwilling to make up the shortfall.[22] As we have seen, Donald Trump cast this issue in especially blunt terms. But Trump is not alone. Successive US administrations have warned that America's patience with its NATO allies is not limitless. The problem of collective action is, therefore, of long standing. By one reading, the Alliance has evolved precisely to deal with bargaining among allies over who should do what for the common defence.[23] But in so doing it has tolerated, even encouraged, free-riding: that is, the ability of allies to partake of the benefits of shared security while doing too little by way of providing for it. Crudely put, in NATO the allies have benefited from something akin to a public good stumped up largely by the US.

Public goods have two characteristics: they are non-excludable (available to all and not to be denied to those who might be regarded as undeserving) and they are non-rivalrous (the enjoyment of a good by some does not reduce its availability to others). Obvious public goods include street lighting, universal free health care and open access to information. They might also include the provision by the state to its citizens of homeland and national security, and in relations between states, the protection afforded by a great power or superpower to its allies. In an alliance, the 'publicness' of such goods is subject to an important caveat: the benefits are first and foremost enjoyed by members: public goods are actually club goods. But if NATO is a club, it is an unusual one. Members must meet certain criteria in order to join, but once inside they can duck the responsibilities of membership. An ally who under-contributes to the common defence still retains the benefits of security provided by others as NATO has no formal mechanism for expelling or sanctioning its members. During the Cold War, this state of affairs was accepted because the American interest in containing the Soviet Union far exceeded any concern about asymmetry of effort. In the post-Cold War period, however, American tolerance has diminished. At the same time, NATO's collective action problem has worsened. Why is this the case?

First, NATO has seen a rapid increase in its membership, from sixteen allies at the end of the Cold War to thirty in 2020. These states have joined the Alliance to consume rather than produce security. With a few exceptions (Poland, for instance), the small size of their armed forces means they make only a marginal contribution to NATO's collective defence and other missions. Many of them are also very vulnerable (think of the Baltic States' exposure to Russia), so adding to NATO's burdens.

Second, the proliferation of threats has exacerbated the problem of free-riding (something we explore in more detail in Chapter 3). NATO has taken on more tasks to respond to these threats, but this has shone a light on those allies unable or unwilling to stump up their fair share in NATO operations. We encountered this problem above when discussing NATO's Balkan interventions of the 1990s. In Libya in 2011, the problem was equally apparent. Only fourteen of NATO's then twenty-eight members provided military assets for Operation Unified Protector and only six European allies (the UK, France, Belgium, Italy, Norway and Denmark) took part in strike missions.[24] The US, who had looked to France and the UK to provide leadership, reluctantly escalated its own involvement, prompting criticism from both Secretary of Defence Robert Gates and President Barack Obama at the lacklustre European effort. Gates warned at the time that NATO had become a 'two-tiered alliance' in which some members were not willing to 'pay the price and bear the burdens of alliance commitments'.[25] President Trump would later make similar claims about NATO's role (or lack of it, as he claimed) in counter-terrorism.[26]

Part of the problem here is that allies disagree on the nature and urgency of threats, and how to respond to them (a version of the fragmentation problem we encountered in Chapter 1). Many European states have a marked preference for addressing the underlying sources of conflict outside Europe with civilian instruments of statecraft, whereas the US appears to be more inclined to rely upon military solutions. This is one reason why most European allies were unwilling to join the US in fighting in Iraq in 2003 and why only a handful of NATO allies, other than the US, were prepared to commit to combat (with attendant fatalities) in Afghanistan.

Divergent assessments of threats are to be expected in an alliance as geographically, politically and economically diverse as NATO. The assumption held in Washington that it enjoys the ability (even the right) to set the Alliance's agenda is bound, therefore, to be frustrated. Such an assumption may have been sustainable in the Cold War when the allies faced a single, relatively undifferentiated threat. But that world – as we pointed out in Chapter 1 – no longer exists. Three snapshots – migration, the militarization of the High North and hybrid warfare – illustrate how security impacts differently on NATO members.

- Irregular migratory flows after the NATO operation in Libya and during the Syrian civil war created a crisis for the Schengen system of the EU. It also placed heavy burdens upon Turkey, Greece and Italy as transit countries, and Germany as the preferred final destination for migrants. In 2015–16, Germany accepted 424,905 Syrian asylum seekers while Greece had given temporary shelter to one million displaced Syrians. Italy accepted 630,000 African migrants transiting through Libya between 2011 and 2016, and as of the end of 2018, Turkey was home to 2.8 million Syrian refugees.[27] These inflows caused considerable political difficulties for the governments concerned, and contrasted with the almost total refusal of certain allies – Hungary and Slovakia, for instance – to admit refugees. Poland, interestingly, welcomed very large numbers of Ukrainian migrants but was openly hostile to Syrians and Yemenis. As for the US, under Trump it, too, was reluctant to welcome large numbers. In fiscal year 2019, just 30,000 refugees entered the US. For fiscal year 2020, the cap was set at a mere 18,000.
- The High North is of increasing strategic importance for NATO in light of climate change and growing Russian and Chinese interest in the Arctic. Longer periods of ice-free seas will extend the seasonal opening of sea lanes, so facilitating the rapid redeployment of naval forces from the Atlantic to the Pacific theatre and lessening the cost of shipping goods from Asia to Europe. Freedom of navigation in the Arctic Ocean approximates a public good for the Alliance, but

the costs of patrolling the Arctic fall almost entirely upon Canada, Norway, the US and, to lesser degrees, the UK and Denmark. These countries consequently bear the brunt of territorial, resource and governance conflicts with the Russian Federation.[28]

- Hybrid warfare has been defined as 'the coordinated [use of] military, political, economic, civilian and informational instruments of power' by malicious actors to exploit 'specific vulnerabilities across the full spectrum of societal functions'.[29] It involves election meddling, malicious interference with cyber networks and disinformation campaigns undermining citizen confidence in national or multilateral institutions. As the Russian annexation of Crimea illustrated, it can also scale up to involve military intervention accompanied by propaganda efforts, the mobilization of proxy forces and diplomatic denial. The established democracies within NATO enjoy a certain resilience in the face of hybrid warfare, although they are not immune to the problem, as demonstrated by Russian interference in the 2016 US presidential election and the Brexit referendum. The newly established democracies are more exposed and harbour vulnerabilities of alliance-wide significance. The presence of sizeable Russian-speaking minorities in Estonia and Latvia, meanwhile, makes these two Baltic countries especially susceptible to Russian subversion aimed at undermining political stability and casting doubt on the readiness of NATO to come to their defence. Despite such consequences, the allies decided in 2018 that 'the primary responsibility for responding to hybrid threats or attacks rests with the targeted nation'.[30] NATO has recognized that hybrid warfare could constitute an Article 5 contingency, but there is neither an agreed upon 'red line' that could trigger it nor a clear articulation of what form such a response would take.

Each of these issues creates vulnerabilities focused on and around Europe. While some of NATO's European members – Italy and Turkey to the south or the Baltic States to the east – have been acutely affected, the US, by virtue of distance, is less directly impacted. This adds to transatlantic divergence; it also reinforces the argument that Europeans need to attend to their own security. Yet this presumption is one the US has been reluctant to acknowledge, at least in regard to NATO. The Alliance, consequently, has proven ill suited to the task of generating European leadership. This provides a further reason for NATO's collective action problem. The US jealously guards its primacy in NATO while paradoxically also calling for greater European effort.

Options beyond NATO, meanwhile – those which would serve to balance the US role in the Alliance – have only limited possibilities. If the ability to supply international public goods is a necessary condition of leadership, a European role would require the effective aggregation of capabilities and an institutional mechanism ensuring that the European allies could act dependably in concert. A partner with whom the US could share leadership and, by extension, fully contribute to the production of security might be realized in one of two forms: the emergence of the EU as an integrated defence actor, a development immediately elevating Europe to the status of a superpower; or a concert of the major European states capable of eliminating the imbalance between the American and European contributions to security.

Currently neither option is viable. The EU has made remarkable strides toward achieving a meaningful security profile, but as we make clear in Chapter 6, it still has very limited prerogatives on matters of mutual defence. Contemporary EU security policies have favoured polices of self-insurance (police and judicial cooperation, control of migration and external borders), self-protection (preventive engagement in regions abutting Europe) and risk-pooling (mutual assistance provisions), consistent with its Treaty-based policy prerogatives.[31] Policies that require a military component have remained, by and large, under NATO's purview and consequently closely tied to the US. Such a state of affairs should perhaps not be surprising. The US has global responsibilities and interests that require a formidable military capability and presence, whereas the Europeans have more parochial regional interests that can be effectively managed with the civilian instruments of statecraft. In Europe, only France and the UK have pretensions to be full-spectrum military powers, and the UK, at least, has long conceded that such a role can only be carried out in alliance with America.

The alternative to the EU is a leadership concert on matters of conventional and potentially nuclear defence and deterrence. Such an arrangement might be formed, for example, by the UK, France, Germany and Italy (Europe's four main military powers) or exist as a duopoly involving either the UK and France, or France and Germany. But the concert option is also an unlikely substitute for American leadership of NATO. For starters, the smaller European allies would hardly be enthusiastic supporters. Why would Poland, Croatia or Denmark want to replace American leadership in NATO with German or French leadership outside it? A European concert would also not find favour in the UK. The British have developed meaningful military relations with their European neighbours, both bilaterally with France and Germany, and multilaterally through the UK-led Joint Expeditionary Force (JEF). But these are all viewed as reinforcing or compatible with NATO. A concert option would be different, and would be perceived as a rival to the Alliance and to good relations with the US.

To summarize, the collective action problem in NATO can be boiled down to a core, connected set of issues. The US is the only power in NATO capable of providing leadership; that leadership is welcomed by some (notably 'Atlanticist' states such as the UK, Poland and Denmark), accepted by the majority and openly questioned by only a few (France in particular). The US, however, has increasingly diverged from its European allies on the relevance and urgency of contemporary security threats, has regarded NATO as of declining significance in consequence and has railed against the allies for their reluctance to share its worldview and contribute to the common defence. Hence, the increasingly toxic US complaints about free-riding.

NATO has always been seen as the main institutional expression of the transatlantic relationship. Its collective action problem is, therefore, one that reflects a growing separation of the US and Europe. How US foreign policy has addressed – indeed, contributed to – that dynamic of separation is considered next.

Grand Strategy, American Foreign Policy and NATO

In Chapter 1, we already encountered the determining influence American foreign policy has had on NATO's development. Here we repackage that discussion, showing how big foreign policy ideas – containment during the Cold War and neo-Wilsonianism after it – have become exhausted, so bringing US leadership of NATO into question. In their place a more unilateral, transactionalist, even isolationist view of America's place in the world has gained traction. Such a position, seen in raw form in the Trump administration, is at best ambiguous on the value of NATO and at worse openly hostile to the idea of alliances.

Throughout the Cold War, the US defined its national security interests by reference, primarily, to the Soviet threat.

The collection of policies it adopted in response – the grand strategy that guided its actions, in other words – was that of containment. Aimed at preventing the spread of communist rule, containment morphed into a global competition for influence waged against the Soviet Union and its allies (which for a period included China). It justified American involvement in wars in Korea and Vietnam, the support of anti-communist client governments (including autocracies in Pakistan, Iran, Egypt, Chile and Zaïre), the active destabilization of leftist governments throughout the developing world and the massive build-up of American nuclear and conventional military forces. It also gave rise to the creation of a global network of allies. By the mid-1950s, the US enjoyed treaty-based bilateral or multilateral security arrangements with forty-two countries spread across Asia, Latin America and Europe. Described as 'containment through collective defence', this network found its most sophisticated and enduring expression in NATO.[32] Other multilateral arrangements proved fragile. The South East Asia Treaty Organization (SEATO) was dissolved in 1977, the Middle East Treaty Organization (METO) came unstuck two years later and the ANZUS Treaty was dealt a severe blow in 1986 when the US effectively suspended the participation of New Zealand. NATO, by contrast, was as relevant and central to US objectives in 1989 as it was when it was formed in 1949. Throughout those four decades, the US, by providing for the conventional and nuclear defence of Western Europe and Turkey, backed by a formal treaty guarantee, had overseen a NATO that was among the most effective of all its formidable policy instruments for keeping Soviet influence in check.[33]

The Alliance also proved to be an effective instrument of American leadership. NATO was established as a means by which European countries, severely weakened by World War II, could access an ongoing US (and, of a lesser order of magnitude, Canadian) military commitment to

Europe. The necessary price was an acceptance of US political as well as military dominance. The preponderance of American military power meant the allies (with the significant exception of France) resigned themselves to the reality of 'America's hegemonic embrace in a US-dominated Atlantic Community'.[34] Two consequences followed: first, West European military integration outside of NATO was held in check; and, second, the institutions and procedures of the Alliance came to entrench US influence. During the Cold War, two of NATO's three commands (Europe and Atlantic) were permanently held by American officers. (The third, less significant command, centred on the English Channel, was held by a British officer.) The formulation of NATO strategy and the military planning that followed was consequently reliant on direction from US commanders 'directly linked to the Pentagon and the White House'.[35] Politically, NATO was multilateral in character, symbolized by the principle of consensus decision-making. But this, too, simply reinforced the American position. Consensus, one of NATO's foremost historians suggests, was usually 'achieved by a willingness on the part of the allies to accept the judgments of the senior partner'.[36]

Underlying these essentially power-political dynamics within NATO was a sense of moral purpose. Successive American leaders – most eloquently John F. Kennedy and most directly Ronald Reagan – described NATO as an alliance of democracies, a guardian of the values of Western civilization. These claims we might want to take with a pinch of salt given how the US supported some obviously undemocratic causes in the name of containing the Soviet Union. The crucial point, however, is that the US relied on NATO to reference its case. The Alliance was used as an instrument to keep at bay those communist states who did not share democracy's values and who, by definition, were antithetical to the community NATO represented.[37] NATO during the Cold War was thus the object of what Michael Brenner has described as 'an imperfect, yet effective intertwining of liberalism's internationalist strand with [a] distinctive US brand of realism'.[38] That the Alliance straddled both these currents of American foreign policy meant it attracted a refreshed sense of purpose at the Cold War's end. Containment may have appeared redundant as Soviet power collapsed, but the liberal strand in US foreign policy remained.

As a substitute for containment, the Clinton administration eventually landed on the conjoined ideas of engagement and enlargement – a blend of realism and 'hints of neo-Wilsonian idealism'. [39] The latter drew heavily on a current of thought dating back to President Woodrow Wilson's vision of a peaceful and stable international order. Based on a presumption of amity between democratic states and the stabilizing effects of international law and international organization, the Wilsonian outlook meant for the Clinton administration an emphasis on free trade, democracy promotion and the strengthening of alliances – particularly those such as NATO where the US was in the ascendant. As we saw in Chapter 1, the upshot of this approach for the Alliance was partnerships (including with Russia), an enlargement of membership and humanitarian interventions in the Balkans. In all cases, the US executed a shift in NATO's mission in line with its own evolving vision of international order. A similar pattern was repeated under George W. Bush. The Wilsonian democracy promotion impulse remained, dressed up in the guise of regime change, the preventive use of force and the war on terror.[40] And while the Bush administration was certainly much less sympathetic than Clinton to working with formal alliances, NATO still figured large in its robust approach to national security. Hence, America's crucial support of the 2004 'big bang' enlargement and the repurposing of NATO for expeditionary missions. With Bush's departure, the White House in Barack Obama acquired an occupant seemingly well disposed to the liberal cause. However, his eight years in office – a period which witnessed the 2008 financial crash, the unresolved conflicts in Syria, Iraq and Afghanistan and a major deterioration of relations with Russia – were not good ones for Wilsonian principles.

Donald Trump then placed such already challenged principles in total eclipse. The Trump administration's foreign policy, both by accident and by design, also ceded the idea of American leadership. The upshot was an emptying of credibility from American foreign policy.[41] This did not mean that Trump's foreign policy was entirely without substance. His administration articulated a strategic vision of 'principled realism'; held firm in trade talks with China; sought a political accommodation with the Taliban in Afghanistan; exited the Trans-Pacific Partnership; and kept campaign promises on Iran, climate change, Israel (recognizing Jerusalem as the capital) and Cuba (by tightening sanctions). Some accounts of the Trump period note these as examples of 'actual policies' with real objectives.[42]

What animated this approach? While no intellectual or student of history, Trump had expressed admiration for the seventh US President, Andrew Jackson. (Jackson's portrait was placed in the Oval Office once Trump took up residency.) 'Jacksonian' thus tended to be the descriptor applied to Trump's foreign policy. The Jacksonian tradition is rooted in a notion of an American 'folk community'. By extension, it assumes the US has singular interests in the world and neither international organizations nor international laws are necessary vehicles for sharing those interests with others.[43] It also combines economic nationalism (and so a scepticism regarding free trade, open borders and technological, scientific and commercial cooperation) with a view that international

expenditure and to 'move towards' the two per cent guideline 'within a decade' (by the end of 2024, in other words).[5]

In what follows, we look in more detail at the troubled issue of NATO burden-sharing. The analysis supplements that already provided in Chapter 2, where unequal burden-sharing was seen as an obstacle to collective action. While NATO's problems are often viewed through the lens of allied defence spending, this alone is too narrow a perspective. This chapter, therefore, considers also the military capabilities which such spending provides and the operational purposes to which those capabilities are put.

Defence Spending in an Era of Fiscal Austerity

Allied defence spending has declined precipitously since the end of the Cold War. This trend has affected all allies. Between 1989 and 2018, US defence spending fell by just under 42 per cent. The combined defence spending of America's European allies declined by some 51 per cent in the same period (see Table 3.1). Falls in spending were at their greatest in the 1990s. US spending experienced a significant upward reversal after 9/11. Aggregate European spending continued to decline, albeit at a slower rate. Not until 2014 did European spending turn a corner. Between 2014 and 2019, as a share of GDP, it expanded by just over 4.5 per cent. These increases were not evenly distributed. France, Spain and the UK were spending roughly the same GDP share in 2019 as in 2014; Germany and Italy had registered marginal increases; bigger increases were evident in Canada, Poland, Romania, the Slovak Republic and Turkey; Bulgaria, Latvia and Lithuania, meanwhile, had more than doubled the share of their national wealth dedicated to defence. In 2014, just three allies met the NATO's 2 per cent of GDP target; nine did so in 2019.[6]

Table 3.1 Change in defence expenditures as share of GDP (%), 1989–2018

	1989–2018	1990–2001	2001–14	2014–18
US	−41.53	−47.46	21.42	−9.90
NATO-Europe	−51.42	−33.33	−27.91	4.45
Canada	−38.31	25.00	−59.65	22.31
Germany	−35.09	−46.43	−21.29	4.53
France	−50.88	−30.56	−27.21	−0.12
Italy	−49.99	−13.04	−45.88	6.26
Netherlands	−51.64	−40.74	−29.17	19.48
Poland			−2.49	10.48
Spain	−55.53	−33.33	−23.66	1.95
UK	−47.51	−39.02	−13.46	−0.53

Source: NATO, 'Information on Defence Expenditures', 25 June 2019, at: *https://www.nato.int/cps/en/natohq/topics_49198.htm.*

These increases in GDP share were mirrored in absolute and real-term figures for the period 2014–19.[7] NATO Secretary General Jens Stoltenberg reported in November 2019 that Canada and the European allies would, by the end of 2020, have added $130 billion to their combined defence budgets compared to the 2016 figure.[8] These increases, however, cannot mask the preponderant share of NATO spending still accounted for by the US. As of 2019, America remained by far the world's greatest military power. Its defence expenditure was as much as the next eleven largest military spenders combined, nearly four times as much as China's (the second largest military spender) and eleven times greater than Russia's.[9] Within NATO, the US accounted for approximately 70 per cent of total defence spending.[10] And the gap between it and the allies had widened. Prior to 2001, the European and Canadian share of NATO defence expenditures equalled almost 44 per cent of the total, roughly equivalent to the combined economic weight of these allies. By 2019, the non-US allies accounted for nearly 50 per cent of total NATO GDP, but only about a third of total NATO defence spending. Further, increases in European defence spending had not, as noted above, embraced some of the major allies. Budget projections for Germany, France, Italy and Spain suggested that none of these countries would hit NATO's 2024 defence spending target.

Alongside the 2 per cent GDP target, in 2014 NATO also adopted a related ambition that allies spend at least 20 per cent of their annual defence budgets on equipment and related research and development. Progress here has been more encouraging. Seven allies met the benchmark in 2014; fifteen did so in 2019. The US, nonetheless, still accounted for approximately three-quarters of NATO procurement.

The evidence would thus seem to support American claims about inadequate European defence spending. Future increases are, however, unlikely. Table 3.2 places in context declines in national defence expenditure over the period from

Table 3.2 Change in government expenditures (%), 1995–2017

	Central government expenditure	Defence	Health and social protection
Europe*	−10.94	−29.41	7.11
Germany	−19.74	−28.57	0.38
France	3.10	−28.00	13.73
Italy	−5.7	0.00	20.96
Netherlands	−20.86	−42.11	0.43
Poland	−14.20	−29.17	0.48
Spain	−7.45	−35.71	15.31
UK	5.97	−32.14	14.72

*Eurozone countries only.
Source: Eurostat, 'General Government Expenditure by Function (COFOG)', at: *https://ec.europa.eu/eurostat/statistics-explained/index.php/Government_expenditure_by_function_%E2%80%93_COFOG.* Authors' calculations.

1995 to 2017. These figures show a general decline in central government expenditure and an accompanying squeeze on defence spending in order to accommodate significant increases in health and welfare provision. Even before the COVID-19 pandemic, those expenditure categories were projected to increase significantly over the coming decades. Ageing populations will have a particular impact. Credit Suisse estimated in 2013 that between 2010 and 2060, aggregate 'age-related' expenditures (public pensions and health care) in the EU would increase from 20.3 per cent to 24.5 per cent of GDP.[11] Similar trends apply to the US and Canada also, but in certain European countries – Belgium, Denmark, Germany, Lithuania, Romania – the trend is especially notable, with increases of between 5 and 8 per cent in age-related spending up to 2060.[12] Fiscal rules for members of the Eurozone (thirteen of whom, including France, Germany, Italy and Spain, are in NATO), meanwhile, have, since the late 1990s, aimed to limit budget deficits and government borrowing. For governments wanting to meet pressing social and economic priorities, it is defence that is squeezed.[13] EU fiscal rules have often been ignored or relaxed, but not for reasons of defence. The COVID-19 pandemic in 2020, for instance, resulted in a suspension of EU deficit limits. Across all EU and NATO countries, the pandemic ushered in a severe economic downturn and with it historic levels of government borrowing. It seemed inevitable as governments grappled with the virus that defence would enjoy a lesser priority following recovery and that debt servicing would significantly impinge upon discretionary spending. One estimate suggested that European defence spending would fall by 20 per cent up to 2025.[14]

Military Capabilities and Force Projection Shortfalls

NATO in recent decades has pursued an ongoing process of force structure reform and military transformation. The end of the Cold War initially put paid to a focus on territorial, collective defence. In the 1990s and 2000s, the Alliance adapted to conflict management, 'out-of-area' operations and expeditionary and counter-insurgency warfare. The deterioration of relations with Russia following the Georgian and Ukraine crises of, respectively, 2008 and 2014 shifted attention back to deterrence and preparing for collective defence – all the while with a need to attend to other contingencies relating to hybrid, cyber and terrorist attacks as well as possible stabilization operations. These multiple demands upon NATO have been played out against debates on capability development and shortfalls, and the deployability, sustainability and interoperability of allied armed forces.

Capabilities

David Yost has defined the 'capabilities gap' between the US and its allies as adding up to a quantitative and 'sometimes qualitative' imbalance in the possession of military assets. The position, Yost wrote in 2003, is that the US 'is currently superior to any combination of its European allies in its ability to plan, conduct, and sustain theatre-wide expeditionary operations'.[15] A later, 2018, report of the International Institute for Strategic Studies (IISS) noted, similarly, that without the US, European military forces would be hard pressed to conduct peace enforcement missions in their neighbourhood.[16] The situation wasn't much better when looking at Europe's own defence. Another IISS report noted that in a conflict with Russia, NATO would be entirely reliant on certain capabilities that are 'unique to the US' (in electronic warfare, 'upper-layer' missile defences, early warning systems and large-scale command and control systems) and highly dependent on others (naval frigates, submarines, fighter aircraft, surface-to-air missiles) where European assets were few in number.[17]

US military superiority is an established fact in NATO. Calls for greater European effort are aimed not at replacing the American contribution (this would only be relevant in the event of a US withdrawal from the Alliance) but rather at the achievement of a greater balance of effort. As Yost has noted, capability gaps have been the 'backdrop for burden-sharing debates, which have been virtually continuous since the founding of the Alliance'.[18] During the 1990s, these gaps rose to prominence as American force superiority became manifest in Operation Desert Storm and in the NATO interventions in Bosnia and Kosovo. The Alliance's response was the Defence Capabilities Initiative (DCI). Launched in 1999 at American prompting, the DCI was meant to 'enable the European allies to make a stronger and more coherent contribution to NATO'.[19] The scale of the task was evident in the fifty-eight separate areas identified for improvement. Subsequent capabilities programmes and commitments suggest that very little progress has been made. The North Atlantic Council Defence Ministers' Report (2001) and the Prague Capabilities Commitments (2002) enjoined the Europeans to reduce their dependence on US intelligence, surveillance, target acquisition and reconnaissance (ISTAR) assets. The 2006 CPG focused on the need to acquire capabilities that would allow the European allies to achieve information superiority, protect cyber space, cope with asymmetric threats and terrorism and conduct urban operations in 'demanding geographical and climatic environments'.[20] The 2011 Lisbon Capabilities Package and 2012 Connected Forces Initiative (CFI) identified ten areas requiring immediate attention, half of which were first identified in the DCI. At the 2014 Wales summit, meanwhile, the allies identified four broad capability shortfalls: the deployability, sustainability and interoperability of allied forces; the acquisition of enhanced intelligence, surveillance and reconnaissance capabilities; the strengthening of cyber and information systems security; and the enhancement of command and control capabilities across a broad spectrum of military tasks.[21] At the 2016 and 2018 Warsaw and Brussels summits, these shortfalls remained a source of concern, but a renewed emphasis was placed on air-to-air refuelling and interoperability.[22] A report of the UK House of Lords prepared just before the 2019 NATO Leaders' Meeting noted that the Alliance had identified twenty-one capability shortfalls, 'many of which are the result of NATO European members not having the necessary capabilities to contribute to the Alliance's collective defence'.[23] Below we provide snapshots in four areas identified in the DCI and successive capabilities' programmes. In some instances, US predominance has declined. The point, however, is that NATO still remains heavily skewed toward American capabilities.

The first set of forces concerns strategic assets – nuclear, early warning and space-based. Of these, nuclear weapons have a quality all of their own. The US is the world's only nuclear power which justifies the size of its arsenal by reference to extended deterrence: that is, the protection of allies as well as of itself.[24] Deterrence is effected by intercontinental nuclear weapons based at sites in the US, ballistic missile submarines on patrol and forward-deployed nuclear bombs located at bases in Europe. The latter, for use on so-called 'dual-capable aircraft', remain, the NATO website explains, under the 'absolute control and custody' of the US.[25] The US offers positive security guarantees to its NATO allies, meaning it would be prepared to offer assistance (up to a counter-strike) to non-nuclear weapon states that are subject to an act (or threat) of aggression involving the use of nuclear weapons. Although France and the UK are themselves nuclear powers, these guarantees apply to them also. French and British nuclear weapons, meanwhile, are not insignificant in number. Their combined warheads (approximately 515 in total) are a small fraction of the 6,000-plus possessed by both the US and Russia, but almost double those held by China (280). France also holds more submarine-launched missiles than the US. French and British nuclear weapons, NATO points out, 'have a deterrent role of their own and contribute significantly to the overall security of the alliance'.[26] NATO's nuclear strategy and posture has changed little since the end of the Cold War and the US has no interest in farming out responsibilities for nuclear defence in the Alliance. To do so would mean encouraging nuclear proliferation, limiting the advantages that nuclear predominance gives the US in alliance management and imposing a significant extra cost on just two allies: France and the UK.[27]

The US also possesses the bulk of other strategic assets, although in some areas allied acquisitions have been notable. As of 2017, a NATO Parliamentary Assembly report noted, seven allies other than the US were able to contribute to the Alliance's satellite communication (SATCOM) capability.[28] The EU, meanwhile, has developed Galileo, an alternative to the US Global Positioning System (GPS) – although NATO still remains locked into the American system.[29]

The second set of capabilities concerns air combat and enabling assets. Figures from 2019 show that the US possessed 2,657 fixed-wing combat aircraft compared to a combined figure of just over 1,800 for the other NATO allies. The 5,400 US combat helicopters, meanwhile, compared to the 2,848 held by the allies.[30] The non-US allies also possessed a much smaller share of unmanned aerial vehicles (or drones) and aircraft dedicated to intelligence, surveillance and reconnaissance (ISR), electronic and signals intelligence and airborne early warning. In some of these cases, there have been improvements in the absolute levels of commitment outside of the US, but parallel increases in American procurement mean these have not necessarily yielded a greater share of total NATO assets.

Turning to maritime assets, here (and befitting its global ambition) the US has a significant advantage in force projection capabilities – aircraft carriers and cruisers most notably. The French and British navies have some, much lower, force projection abilities through aircraft carriers and submarines. Overall, however, the NATO European, Canadian and Turkish navies are preoccupied with coastal and regional maritime tasks – hence, combined, the allies outweigh the US when it comes to frigates, mine warfare and coastal patrol vessels. Canada, France, Italy, the Netherlands, Spain, the UK and Turkey also possess significant amphibious forces (naval assets capable of projecting force onto hostile territory), but here, a 2019 RAND study noted, even in European scenarios (conflict with Russia especially), American forces would still be needed to ensure mission success.[31]

The strategic, air combat and maritime assets considered so far provide a mixed picture of the transatlantic balance of capabilities. There is a much more obvious imbalance, however, in air support. Air-to-air refuelling has been repeatedly singled out as an area of concern in NATO (and, indeed, EU) capability programmes. Refuelling is essential for sustaining aircraft in flight on missions where ground support is unavailable. In both the NATO interventions in Kosovo in 1999 and Libya in 2011, European and Canadian forces were heavily reliant on American assets. As the Belgian Defence Minister pointed out in 2018, the problem appeared to be entrenched as the US then accounted for over 90 per cent of NATO's air-to-air refuelling capacity.[32] Only eight allies possessed any capability in this area, with France and the UK accounting for over 50 per cent of those assets. Similar shortfalls also exist in airlift capabilities. European and Canadian forces are well provided in tactical lift (aircraft able to move personnel and equipment *within* theatre) but significantly short in strategic lift (the ability to transport *to* an operational theatre). At the beginning of the 2000s, critical shortfalls had become clearly evident from the missions in the Balkans and Afghanistan. Many participating nations in ISAF, for instance, had to lease or charter commercial aircraft (including from Russia and Ukraine) to get their personnel in theatre. A variety of initiatives were instigated in both NATO and the EU to remedy this situation, with procurement programmes (for the A400M airbus) launched in the UK, France, Germany, Spain and Canada. Analyses published in 2019, however, noted that an 'airlift deficit' remained and that the allies remained 'heavily dependent' on the US.[33] For this reason, according to Adam Thompson (the UK's former NATO ambassador), the US remained Europe's 'indispensable ally.'[34]

Force Deployment

Capability issues have overlapped in NATO with discussions on deployability and sustainability. The US has warned since the mid-1990s that capabilities count for little if they cannot be sent to where they are needed. Responding to that concern, the 2006 CPG stated that 40 per cent of individual allies' land forces should be ready for deployment at any given time. (The figure was subsequently increased to 50 per cent.) These ambitions became an important feature of coordinated defence planning among the allies and for some smaller nations such as Denmark and the Netherlands were a welcome prompt to restructure their militaries. Other allies, however, were less nimble. Germany, in particular, has struggled. Years of low defence spending and slow restructuring have meant the German armed forces have obtained a reputation for unreliability. These forces have been criticized for their lacklustre performance in NATO's mission in Afghanistan, and Germany's own Parliamentary Commissioner for the Armed Forces noted in 2018 that they were 'not deployable for collective defence'.[35] This is more than a hypothetical issue. Germany is the lead NATO nation for the enhanced Forward Presence (eFP) mission in Lithuania and the moving force (as we shall see in Chapter 7) behind NATO's Framework Nations Concept.

Deployability is linked to interoperability – what NATO defines as 'the ability [of] Allies to act together coherently, effectively and efficiently to achieve tactical, operational and strategic objectives'. It does not require that the allies operate always with identical equipment, training procedures or command and control mechanisms, but it does mean that national militaries when working together should be able to effectively 'interact, connect and communicate'.[36] Interoperability became especially important after the Cold War as the allies (and key partners) engaged together in more and more missions. Yet even though NATO has comprehensive arrangements – including so-called 'standardization agreements' (STANAGs) – to foster this quality, problems have persisted. These fall into a number of categories, some of which – such as overcoming differences of national military doctrines and subsuming national military formations into multinational operations and commands – are fairly routine. A further, growing, problem has arisen from technological disparities. A long-term American superiority in high-tech investment and research and development led Hans Binnendijk and Richard Kugler to warn back in 2002 that NATO faced the 'ultimate risk' that its European and American forces could soon not be able to fight together.[37] A 2008 report of the NATO Parliamentary Assembly identified the policy conundrum facing the US: '[W]ould US national interests be better guarded by providing advanced military technology to allies [. . .] or should the US keep these technologies and rely solely on its overwhelming superior technology to win future wars and conflicts without the substantial help of allies?'[38] It appears that the US has opted for the second alternative: European efforts to gain sufficient access to American network-connected warfare technologies have been severely circumscribed.

NATO actions to redress the interoperability gap have nonetheless been rolled out. These include the 2002 NATO Network-Enabled Capabilities initiative, Smart Defence projects launched in 2011, the 2012 CFI and NATO Forces 2020. The NATO Joint Forces Training Centre (established in 2004) has also conducted annual Coalition Warrior Interoperability Exercises dedicated to enhancing interoperability and identifying problem areas. Tangible progress has been registered against each of these initiatives, but problems remain. NATO nations make individual decisions on equipment purchases, something that results in 'stovepiped' inventories with different operating standards and often with the US way out in front in terms of technological prowess.[39]

NATO Military, Stabilization and Reconstruction Operations

NATO's defence spending targets and associated capabilities can be regarded as 'input' measures by which the allies' commitment to the shared defence can be judged. The allies have repeatedly given such measures their political seal of approval and so they have acquired a special significance in internal debates on burden-sharing. Yet there has been a recognition that these benchmarks need supplementing. NATO Secretary General Jens Stoltenberg has referred to the importance of looking at 'contributions' to operations and missions as well as the more standard 'cash [and] capabilities' measures.[40] Following that cue, here, too, it can be seen just how dependent NATO has been on US military and political leadership. Our primary focus below is on Libya and Afghanistan – two NATO operations which have ongoing implications for how the other allies might act if and when American leadership and commitment are moderated.

Libya

What happened in Libya was in some ways informed by NATO's earlier missions in the Balkans. As noted in the previous chapter, US preponderance in Operations Deliberate Force (Bosnia, 1995) and Allied Force (Kosovo, 1999) generated America's disillusionment with the reliability of its allies. The takeaway from both was that while some allies (France and the UK most notably) were involved with competent and committed air forces, ultimate success was dependent on US involvement. The peacekeeping forces that deployed in Bosnia and Kosovo after these initial interventions did show a somewhat different pattern of commitment: the US was responsible for the largest numbers, but the UK, along with middle powers such as Canada, Denmark, the Netherlands and Norway, committed higher percentages of its active duty personnel.[41] Yet it was the contribution to the combat phase that rankled in Washington. In Bosnia and Kosovo, the US undertook over 65 per cent of strike operations.[42] And so in Libya the Obama administration resolved from the outset that it would encourage greater allied involvement. This was not initially a difficult case to make as in early 2011 both French President Nicolas Sarkozy and British Prime Minister David Cameron had signalled a determination to use air strikes that would deter the Qaddafi regime from carrying out attacks on Libyan civilians. When NATO's Operation Unified Protector (OUP) concluded in October 2011 after five months, it was heralded by some as 'a model intervention'.[43] The operation had prevented a civilian massacre in Benghazi, had removed the widely despised Qaddafi from power, had enjoyed a legitimacy afforded by UN Security Council resolutions and had involved the military participation of local partners (Jordan, Qatar and the United Arab Emirates).

Important for the current discussion, OUP had also entailed, according to two high-ranking US and NATO officials, a 'sharing [of] the burden among the alliance's members', so 'demonstrat[ing] that [NATO] remains an essential source of stability'.[44] The US had initially conducted its own air strike mission (Operation Odyssey Dawn) but handed over to NATO in the belief that the allies would be willing to conduct the 'front end' of the operation given their 'profound self-interest' in Libya.[45] This gave rise to what one Obama official described as 'an innovative hybrid approach', 'tightly scoping American involvement' to the provision of 'unique capabilities' that supported, but did not directly engage in, air strikes.[46] In the end, the US still flew more sorties and strikes than any other ally, but France and the UK together provided over 40 per cent of such flights, and these were supplemented by significant contributions by the air forces of Belgium, Canada, Denmark, Italy and Norway. The US adopted a similar position on the naval operation, where, according to one analysis at the time, it 'attempted to scale back its commitments as early as it could'.[47] France, Italy, Turkey and the UK provided significant naval forces and the mission broke an important precedent, being 'the first time in recent history [that] a major coalition combat operation was conducted without the presence of a large-deck US aircraft carrier'.[48]

Yet for all this, NATO's reliance on the US was still acute. Nicole Koenig points out that 'approximately 90 percent of the military actions against the Libyan regime would not have been possible without the support of the US'.[49] Michael

Clarke, the Director of the Royal United Services Institute, noted that without the US, the allies struggled to 'get their act together in a convincing way, even over a comparatively small operation against a weak and crazy opponent'. 'The greatest military alliance the world has ever known', he continued, 'was made to look puny in what it could really deploy.'[50] We have already referred to America's near monopoly of air-to-air refuelling in the operation. In addition, the US was almost entirely responsible for the destruction of Libya's air defence system (through cruise missile strikes), provided most of the ISR information and targeting data and ended up replenishing allied weaponry for air strikes as supplies ran short during the campaign. To make matters worse, some allies stood completely aside from the operation. Political consensus was maintained in NATO, but the Czech Republic, Germany, Hungary and Poland played no role in the operation and openly criticized it.[51]

Although short-lived, the Libya operation was important for a number of reasons. First, it took place not far from Europe. OUP was different from the NATO mission in Afghanistan or the coalition operation in Iraq – campaigns waged at distance. In Libya, NATO's victory was never in doubt, given allied military superiority and local advantage, and the Qaddafi regime's international isolation. Second, America's signal that it expected European leadership made Libya an ideal candidate for a new sort of NATO mission. As it turned out, the combined allied contribution was relatively greater than that made to the Bosnian and Kosovan interventions. But a mission involving some of the world's most advanced militaries still relied on the US for key capabilities. That reliance, third, also had a political dimension. Having pursued a mission which resulted in regime change, NATO undertook no subsequent effort aimed at stabilizing Libya, and so in the years that followed the country descended into civil war and ungovernability. The US had always made clear that it did not intend to lead such an effort. (The Obama administration was too preoccupied with Iraq and Afghanistan.) Samantha Power, special adviser to the US President at the time of OUP, reflected later that the Obama administration had 'expected our European allies to take the lead on helping the Libyans manage the aftermath'.[52] But for all the bravado of British and French military action, little thought was given in London or Paris to Libya's longer-term future – no follow-on mission was executed through NATO or, taking advantage of French and British (and, indeed, German) influence, through the EU or the UN either.

These problems are not of mere historical importance. In Chapter 5, we argue that NATO needs to be far more serious about engaging with its southern periphery. The Libya intervention did not set a good precedent. And this, moreover, was a reasonably propitious case. Libya, Christopher Chivvis notes, 'was militarily weak [. . .] tactically and strategically inept' and lacking Russian or Chinese protection.[53] Further, the NATO intervention had purportedly been based on a humanitarian argument. UN Security Council Resolution 1973 passed in mid-March 2011 (and used by the allies to legitimize their actions) had invoked the language of Responsibility to Protect – the resolution's aim being the protection of 'civilian and civilian-populated areas under threat of attack' by Qaddafi. That initial aim was satisfied. But that humanitarian impulse proved temporary and NATO squandered the international goodwill it had garnered over the Libya intervention to assist a long-term and stable transition.[54]

Afghanistan

The NATO mission in Afghanistan was very different from the Libya operation. Yet it yields some similar lessons on how the Alliance conducts itself in operations. The most straightforward charge is that the allies again failed to pull their weight and that the US has shouldered a disproportionate share of the mission costs. Secretary of Defence Gates, interviewed in January 2008, described many allied forces as poorly trained and unsuitable for the Afghan theatre of operation.[55] He told NATO defence ministers in March 2011 (at a point when the US was 'surging' its own troop contribution) that there was 'too much discussion of exit and not enough discussion about continuing the fight'.[56]

Certainly, in terms of absolute figures, the US is a case apart. As we saw in Chapter 1, the fatalities and casualties it has endured, as well as the money it has poured into the military effort, are exceptional. Troop contributions also place the US well ahead. ISAF was at its largest in 2011; at that point, two-thirds of the mission's forces were American. The situation was similar for ISAF's successor, Operation Resolute Support (ORS). As of June 2020, the US was providing half of all personnel to the mission.

These figures, however, do not tell the full story. If we take the ISAF mission as a whole (2003–14) and look at the size of a country's deployment relative to the size of its army, population and GDP, then some allies – Bulgaria, Canada, Denmark, Estonia, Lithuania, Poland, Romania and the UK – come out in a much more favourable light. The same can be said for exposure to risk. As a proportion of the number of troops deployed to Afghanistan, the level of fatalities and casualties was especially high for forces from Canada, Denmark, Estonia, the Netherlands, Romania and the UK, deployed to face the Taliban insurgency in Afghanistan's eastern and southern districts.[57]

With this in mind, the problem for NATO in Afghanistan was the disproportionality of effort *among* the non-US allies not *between* all allies and the US. Surveying the Afghan mission, a number of studies have identified the great variation of effort, with some (Belgium, France, Portugal and Spain) singled out as free-riding on the efforts of others (the US, Canada and a handful of European allies).[58] Hew Strachan has observed that some in NATO were guilty of deploying token contingents, imposing national caveats on what their forces were permitted to do and withdrawing their forces precipitously in response to domestic political considerations.[59] Such behaviour was the cause of frustration not just in Washington. The UK and Canada, for instance, were disappointed at the tight restrictions under which German personnel carried out their duties. (Forces from Belgium, Spain and Turkey also operated under similar constraints.)[60] Canada's own record of commitment, however, was mixed. In 2011, it unilaterally ended all combat operations in Afghanistan, requiring the US to substitute for Canadians in Kandahar province. The Dutch had done the same in Uruzgan province in the summer of 2010. France, meanwhile, unilaterally withdrew from combat in Afghanistan at the end of 2012.

Such defections from the ISAF mission suggested that when calculating the risks and costs of deployment, domestic political considerations counted for more than loyalty to partners and allies[61] – a dynamic that occasioned no neat transatlantic line of division or burden-sharing gap. That said, ISAF (and the point applies equally to the follow-on ORS) was, nonetheless, dominated by the US. The allies entered Afghanistan after 9/11 initially as part of an American-led coalition. From 2003, NATO oversight of ISAF sat alongside a separate US operation (Operation Enduring Freedom – Afghanistan) and chain of command. These two arms were integrated from the mid-2000s, but American personnel, 'double-hatted' to both US military authorities and NATO, effectively called the shots on the broad objectives of the in-country counter-insurgency and training missions. US (not NATO) counter-insurgency doctrine, meanwhile, shaped thinking on mission objectives and operational planning. And at NATO HQ, it was the Americans, with the UK, France and Germany in supportive but subsidiary roles, who led on policy decisions relating to the campaign.[62] The big strategic decisions meanwhile were taken in Washington. The timetable that led to the termination of ISAF in 2014 was worked out by the Obama administration. And it was the Trump administration which brokered a deal in 2020 with the Taliban. NATO organizationally was significant. The US could not have aggregated allied effort over such a long period in Afghanistan without the Alliance. By the same token, most allies would have been unable to deploy and operate in the country if not for the logistics, communication, command and shared intelligence funnelled through NATO.[63] But the inescapable conclusion is that the US chose to go to war in Afghanistan and the allies then followed it. Equally, the US has driven the timetable for NATO's exit. The US–Taliban agreement signed in February 2020 provided for the removal within 135 days of 5,400 of the 14,000 American troops in the country. Other NATO forces would, in parallel, be reduced 'proportionally' and a withdrawal of 'all military forces of the United States, its allies, and Coalition partners' was envisaged within fourteen months. Many pointed to the fragility of the agreement. Its negotiation had not involved the Afghan government yet foresaw an intra-Afghan dialogue; it contained assurances that the Taliban would not permit groups such as al-Qaeda to use Afghanistan 'to threaten the security of the United States and its allies', yet was silent on the conditions under which the US/NATO troop withdrawal could be reversed or suspended.[64] For many observers, the agreement was little more than a means to extract the US from Afghanistan whatever the consequences.[65] In October 2020, Trump tweeted that American forces would be out of Afghanistan by Christmas, even though negotiations between the Afghan government and the Taliban had only just begun and violence remained endemic across the country.[66] Significant in the current context is that this flawed deal, envisaging a NATO retreat, had been engineered by the US; the allies were consulted but had no material role it.

This dynamic of leadership and followership has a number of longer-term consequences for the Alliance. In the previous chapter, we noted the draining effect of Afghanistan on NATO, and the argument we will make in Chapter 5 is that expeditionary warfare at such scale and distance is both unlikely and unwelcome for the foreseeable future. Yet, in NATO's neighbourhood, smaller but nonetheless complex and sustained military operations, perhaps involving counter-insurgency, should not be ruled out over the next two decades or so. '[O]nly two entities in the world', Seth Johnston suggests, 'are capable of running a large-scale multinational military campaign: the United States and NATO.'[67] But as the Afghan (and Libyan) case illustrates, take the US out of NATO and the allies struggle.

Conclusion: Learned Helplessness

The detail in this chapter has repeated a theme found elsewhere in the book: namely the material and political dominance the US exerts in NATO. That dominance is actually a mixed blessing for the US. It gives Washington considerable influence, but has fostered a condition of dependency among the allies. The US is able to bend NATO to its purposes, but it can't necessarily rely on the allies to provide the material resources to lighten the load of leadership. This is not to say the Alliance is simply an appendage of American foreign policy. The security NATO affords to the allies (evident, not least, in the reorientation to eastern defence from 2014) means it is a crucial component of their own national security policies. Perhaps because of this, dependency is widely accepted. But such a lopsided relationship is not always beneficial to the allies themselves. As the Libya case illustrates, the desire to orientate NATO in ways that allowed them greater autonomy ran foul of individual capability limitations and entrenched American influence in allied command structures. Whether this condition is unalterable – a case of 'learned helplessness' – or whether it can be addressed is the subject of Chapter 7.

CHAPTER FOUR

NATO and Russia: Cold War Redux

Throughout the Cold War, NATO's principal mission was to deter Soviet military power. The NATO–Warsaw Pact military balance thus came to define Europe's division. With the collapse of the Soviet Union in 1991, NATO's focus shifted necessarily, but the geopolitical significance of Russia as the post-Soviet 'continuing state' means the country has consistently functioned as NATO's most significant 'other' on the international stage.[1] Developing some kind of functioning relationship with Moscow has thus been imperative. But that relationship has been far from straightforward. The failure to establish what a 2010 joint statement referred to as the goal of a 'true strategic partnership'[2] has meant one of the key variables of European security has remained unsettled some three decades after the Cold War's end.

NATO–Russia Relations in the 1990s

As the Cold War wound down, the initial assumption among both the NATO allies and an increasingly beleaguered Moscow was that the Soviet Union would be accommodated in a restructured European 'security architecture', an arrangement (reflecting a strong American preference in particular) in which NATO was central. The Soviet position during 1990–1 had evolved into acceptance that NATO was a necessary means for anchoring a reunified Germany in Europe's security structures. President Mikhail Gorbachev had initially anticipated a formal dissolution of NATO and the Warsaw Pact, and the creation of some kind of ill-defined pan-European construct, but came round to the NATO option once it was obvious that the George H.W. Bush administration was adamant about the Alliance's survival and the new Germany's place within it. The Soviet collapse did not render these issues any less important. Russia emerged as a formidable international actor in its own right. Led by the mercurial Boris Yeltsin, it inherited the Soviet Union's diplomatic privileges as well as much of the Soviet military (including its nuclear arsenal) and established itself at the head of the Commonwealth of Independent States, a loose organization of most of the former Soviet Union Republics.

During Yeltsin's tenure as Russia's President, from 1991 to 1999, two key issues overshadowed all efforts to develop a stable relationship with NATO. The first was enlargement. Moscow claimed that the Soviet leadership had been persuaded to accept a unified Germany within NATO in return for a 'no enlargement' pledge. The unearthed historical record tends not to support the Russian argument,[3] but that did not stop Yeltsin from making it central in the mid-1990s to the Russian case against 'the possibility of [the] expansion of the NATO zone to the East'.[4] The Russian military, meanwhile, was quick to point out that 'the expansion of military blocs and alliances' was 'to the detriment of the interests of the Russian Federation's military security' and one of the 'basic existing and potential sources of military danger' to the country.[5]

Such views could not hide the fact that enlargement was a humiliation for Russia, demonstrating as it did the country's diminished position in post-Cold War Europe.[6] To compensate for its reduced standing, Moscow demanded special relations with NATO. In what might be termed a form of 'co-binding', it aimed to secure the institutional means of preventing the Alliance from doing things that Russian leaders did not support. As second best, Moscow wanted at least consultative rights with NATO, so that Russia's voice would be heard in relevant deliberations. NATO's own emerging approach, meanwhile, was based on something similar. Co-binding and mutual restraint, it was hoped, would supplement Russia's putative embrace of liberal democracy and market economics as first steps toward its integration with the West.[7]

The Permanent Joint Council

A formal decision to proceed with a first round of post-Cold War enlargement was taken at NATO's Madrid summit in July 1997. At that point, the allies and the Russian leadership both wished to manage the process so as to prevent a terminal rupture in their hitherto hesitant and largely uninstitutionalized relationship. Six months before the summit, negotiations got underway aimed at some kind of accommodation. The resulting 'Founding Act on Mutual Relations, Cooperation and Security between NATO and the Russian Federation'[8] was lengthy and detailed but proved open to competing interpretations on both sides.

In some regards, the document did give the Russians a good deal. It referenced restrictions on future nuclear and conventional force deployments on the territory of new NATO members in East-Central Europe, and a commitment that NATO's 'new missions of peacekeeping and crisis management' would be conducted 'in support of the United Nations and the OSCE – two bodies in which Russia played important roles. A new 'Mechanism for Consultation and Cooperation' was also established: the 'NATO–Russia Permanent Joint Council' (PJC). This was to meet regularly at either ministerial or ambassadorial level and, to that end, Moscow was to establish a mission at NATO Headquarters led by an ambassador. Russia's formal representation would thus be almost on a par with the allies themselves and superior to that of other non-NATO members.

There were two key caveats, however. First, it was stated that the 'provisions of this Act do not provide NATO or Russia [. . .] with a right of veto over the actions of the other nor [. . .] infringe upon or restrict the rights [. . .] to independent decision-making and action'. Second, the scope of the PJC was restricted in that NATO members could exclude any agenda item they did not wish to discuss with their Russian counterparts. With these restrictions in mind, some in Russia interpreted the Founding Act as a defeat. The newspaper *Izvestia* argued that 'Russia seems to have bidden farewell to [. . .] any illusions that it could stop the military alliance from drawing closer to its border. [The Act's signing ceremony] evoked the picture of a country parting with the role of a great power.'[9] Countering such an interpretation, the Yeltsin government argued that everything depended on how the Founding Act worked out in practice, with NATO and Russia, according to the President's press secretary, at 'the beginning of the struggle [to] interpret [. . .] the agreement'.[10] By this logic, the lack of prior agreed understandings might actually work to Russia's advantage, if it could establish a more assertive and influential role than NATO members had originally envisaged.

Concerns in NATO about precisely this possibility were soon evident. In the lead-up to the signing of the Founding Act, the emphasis had been on how far NATO–Russia relations might develop. By late 1997, however, the mood was already becoming more restrictive. Testifying to the Senate Foreign Relations Committee, one Clinton official noted:

> The PJC is a consultative mechanism, and [. . .] consultation in diplomatic parlance means just that, talking together. It does not mean a situation in which you are obliged to negotiate. It does not mean you are in a situation where you are

> obliged to make a decision [. . .]. In cases where the Russians might suggest subject matter on which there is no NATO position, it is clearly provided that NATO is not required to undertake any such discussion and certainly can, if it wishes and chooses to make such a discussion, first agree among itself, its members, as to what its position is.[11]

In the Founding Act, no provision was made for NATO members to 'pre-cook' positions in this way before taking them to the Russians. But neither was such a manoeuvre expressly ruled out. Yet Russian leaders could be forgiven for thinking that the apparent hardening of the US stance indicated bad faith. Equally, there were grounds for doubting whether the Russians themselves were prepared to engage constructively and substantively. The first meeting of the PJC in July 1997 had to be postponed because Russian representatives raised last-minute objections to the chairing arrangements. Thereafter, Russian officials threatened to walk out several more times. Their government also showed a persistent reluctance to finalize agreement on the opening of a NATO Military Liaison Mission in Moscow, something expressly provided for in the Act.

Despite these problems, there were early indications that the PJC was showing promise. Colonel General Leonid Ivashov, Director of the Russian Defence Ministry's Chief Administration for International Military Cooperation (and a noted NATO sceptic), described a PJC defence ministers' meeting of June 1998 as having been 'highly appraised by both sides in terms of substance and transparency'.[12] Six months later, Russian Foreign Minister Igor Ivanov declared that NATO–Russia relations had 'come a long way, from distrust to mutual understanding'.[13] Public assessments on the NATO side were similarly upbeat.[14] This burgeoning optimism would be rudely curtailed, however.

The Kosovo crisis

Up until the late 1990s, the Balkans had been a venue of nascent operational cooperation between NATO and Russia. Following the 1995 Dayton Peace Accords, a Russian contingent had been deployed (with special command and control arrangements) as part of the NATO-led peacekeeping operation in Bosnia. For the first time, NATO allies and Russia had agreed to work together within a single overall military framework. The PJC also emerged as a useful framework for NATO–Russia consultations on other Bosnian issues.

However, OAF against Serbia dealt a severe blow to the NATO–Russia relationship. Yeltsin accused NATO leaders of violating the terms of the Founding Act and announced the suspension of Russian participation in the PJC. The Russian President had some solid grounds for concern. According to the Act's provisions, both NATO and Russia had pledged to respect 'the primary responsibility of the UN Security Council for maintaining international peace and security', yet NATO had launched OAF without a UN mandate. To add insult to injury, the provision in the Founding Act for consultations at times of crisis was simply ignored. The PJC did not convene to discuss NATO's intervention, neither was Moscow informed of the action beforehand. Against these arguments, NATO members suggested that emerging international humanitarian law provided sufficient legal cover and that Russia's threat of a veto at the UN Security Council had, in effect, forced the Alliance to bypass the body. The latter argument proved persuasive to outside observers;[15] indeed, even to some Russian officials, who subsequently criticized the inflexibility and narrow-mindedness of their own country's diplomacy during the build-up to the crisis.[16] Whatever the disagreements, it was clear that the PJC had not lived up to its initial promise and that it had failed to function as a mechanism of consultation. That failure was perhaps most graphically illustrated at the end of NATO's air campaign, when the Russian 'dash to Pristina' in June 1999 appeared to threaten direct military confrontation between Russian and NATO forces being deployed into Kosovo.[17]

Yet the Kosovo crisis alone had not torpedoed the PJC. In retrospect, it was apparent that the body was already floundering. As noted above, NATO members had regularly been caucusing in advance of meetings and presenting their Russian interlocutors with pre-agreed positions. In consequence, the PJC had become, in the words of one contemporary critic, 'a talking shop for rather stale dialogue'.[18] NATO members also stood accused of being unwilling to discuss the 'main political issues' favoured by the Russians, preferring instead to confine the PJC to narrow, lower-level, technical concerns.[19] Overall, at the end of the 1990s, it was clear that no binding sense of 'partnership' or 'community' had emerged between the NATO allies and Russia. The record of the PJC indicated that neither a common interest, nor a sense of reciprocity had developed in the relationship. When faced with its first real-world test, the PJC had proven almost entirely ineffectual.

NATO–Russia Relations in the Putin Era

If the rupture over Kosovo drew attention to the absence of a shared strategic or normative understanding, both sides nevertheless recognized the need to repair the relationship. Russian leaders accepted that they would have to learn (again) to live with NATO. Foreign Minister Ivanov conceded that, 'like it or not, NATO is a reality in today's international arena, primarily in Europe but also in the world in general'.[20] One immediate consequence was a return to pragmatic cooperation. Following the tension and high drama of the Pristina incident, NATO and Russia concluded a Bosnia-style agreement facilitating Russian troop deployments with KFOR, the NATO-led stabilization mission in Kosovo. Russian forces would go on to remain in Kosovo and Bosnia until 2003. A similar spirit of flexibility was evident on the NATO side. In February 2000, Secretary General Lord George Robertson made the first high-level NATO official visit to Russia since the Kosovo crisis. Meeting with new President Vladimir Putin, he agreed to 'intensify [. . .] dialogue in the Permanent Joint Council [. . .] on a wide range of security issues'.[21] Robertson was careful to maintain a sense of perspective, stating that this agreement merely indicated that 'we've moved from permafrost into slightly softer ground'.[22] Indeed, the two sides had essentially just restored the *status quo ante bellum*.

The NATO–Russia Council

A significant qualitative enhancement would not occur until after 9/11. Putin's offer of practical Russian assistance in support of US-led military operations against al-Qaeda and its Taliban sponsors in Afghanistan prompted a political and diplomatic response on the NATO side. On a visit to Moscow in November 2001, Lord Robertson described how a different set-up might work. It would

> [i]nvolve Russia having an equality with the NATO countries in terms of the subject matter and [it] would be part of the same compromising trade-offs, give and take, that is involved in day-to-day NATO business. That is how we do business [. . .] we get compromises. We build consensus. So the idea would be that Russia would enter that. That would give Russia a right of equality but also a responsibility and an obligation that would come from being part of [a] consensus-building organization.[23]

From these remarks, it was apparent that the NATO side was still influenced by the co-binding rationale, with any new arrangement serving to socialize the Russians into NATO's institutional *modus operandi*. The new forum was called the NATO–Russia Council (NRC). It gave the Russian government formal co-decision-making responsibilities with the NATO allies in nine areas, including military crisis management, counter-terrorism, non-proliferation and missile defence. Once again, however, important provisos were included. One was the so-called 'safeguard' mechanism, which reportedly allowed any NATO member to veto discussions on specific issues.[24] It was also left unclear as to whether NATO members would retain the option of pre-cooking positions in advance of meetings.[25]

As the NRC was getting established, Russian analyst Alexander Goltz suggested a useful yardstick for measuring its effectiveness:

> [W]e can come to mutual understanding and mutual decisions even without this body. [. . .] [W]hat Russia needs is the opportunity to participate in a decision-making process when [there's] some problem, some controversial issues, something like war in Yugoslavia. [It's] not a problem to reach an agreement when you have the same points of view. The problem is to reach an agreement and to come to a consensus when you have different views on the same problems. That is the task.[26]

As with its predecessor, the NRC's early months and years were positively appraised on both the NATO and Russian sides. In November 2002, President Putin sent Foreign Minister Ivanov to Prague to participate in an NRC ministerial meeting. This was part of NATO's Prague summit programme, at which further eastern enlargement was a key item on the agenda. Notwithstanding this apparently inauspicious backdrop, Ivanov, according to Secretary General Robertson, 'offered a glowing assessment' of the NRC's work during its first six months.[27] Perhaps more significantly at the time, the fledgeling Council was not deflected by the Iraq crisis of 2002–3, notwithstanding Russian opposition to the use of military force against the Saddam Hussein regime. The NRC's durability contrasted with the collapse of the PJC in 1999. NATO Secretary General Robertson commented:

> I think that the existence of the NATO–Russia Council has prevented differences over Iraq from becoming a crisis, like the NATO–Russia relationship suffered during Kosovo in 1999. It has brought about a new maturity. It has created a new equality and a new respect for each other, so that we are now capable of disagreeing without falling out, of having different opinions without walking out of the room. [. . .] [T]he NATO nations and Russia [. . .] have established a working relationship of such durability that it can survive and move on from even passionately held differences of opinion.[28]

On the face of it therefore, Goltz's test for the new Council seemed to have been met. But the parallel with Kosovo was not entirely accurate. Over Iraq, the NATO allies were themselves at loggerheads and the Alliance was not responsible for mission oversight. There was no sense, therefore, that Russia had staked out a position of principle at odds with one taken and being acted upon by the Alliance as a whole. That said, Robertson's remarks were gracious and of note because he was prepared to concede that cooperation remained the presumption of NATO–Russia interaction.

More was to follow. During its first half-decade, the NRC developed significantly in terms of the number and range of activities nested within its structural and institutional framework.[29] Alongside the continuing operations in Kosovo, this included the participation of the Russian navy in NATO's Operation Active Endeavour: anti-terrorism patrols in the Mediterranean Sea by multinational maritime task forces drawn mainly from the NATO allies. These patrols had been ongoing since 2001 and were important because their origins lay in the invocation of Article 5 of the NATO treaty after 9/11. More significant in overall security terms were the NATO-led stabilization operations in Afghanistan from 2003. Consultation with Russia in the NRC yielded important practical cooperation here too, including agreement on transit rights for materiel for ISAF through Russia, and cooperation in counter-narcotics training.

Thus, it was somewhat premature to write off the NRC during its formative years as being 'merely a low-key technical-cooperation workshop operating at NATO's side'.[30] Having said that, some of the cooperation established under its auspices would prove to be vulnerable to political differences. Russian naval contributions to Operation Active Endeavour, for instance, were sporadic and limited, and would be terminated altogether at the outset of the Russo-Georgia war in August 2008. Further, there was little evidence of any emerging cooperative 'spill-over' from 'low' to 'high' politics. Instances of ongoing practical cooperation did not, in other words, stimulate broader normative, strategic or diplomatic rapprochement. In consequence, the NATO–Russia relationship remained subject to disagreement over contentious 'big picture' issues. As the April 2008 NRC communiqué candidly acknowledged, issues which bedevilled the NATO–Russia relationship remained unresolved. The final status of Kosovo, the treaty on Conventional Forces in Europe (CFE), US missile defence plans and NATO enlargement were all listed.[31] At least it could be argued that these matters were being aired and none at that point had been the cause of a dramatic reversal of relations. But that reversal was in the offing.

The Georgia crisis

It was disappointing but scarcely surprising that, when confronted with the outbreak of conflict in Georgia, the NRC in August 2008 proved to be as fragile, ineffective and deficient as the PJC at the time of the Kosovo crisis nine years earlier. As with its progenitor, the NRC failed to function either as an early warning mechanism or as a venue for crisis management consultations.

Although the immediate triggers of the conflict were bilateral disputes between the Russian and Georgian governments,[32] there was a clear and important NATO dimension involved. Of the four major unresolved disputes between NATO and Russia noted above, each had a distinct Transcaucasian aspect or resonance in the region. Most pertinent was NATO enlargement. By 2008, Russian opposition to any intention or plan to include Georgia (or Ukraine) in NATO was well established. The Russian military intervention in Georgia in August of that year can thus be seen as a vivid 'red line' warning to NATO against any future Georgian accession. In this context, it is worth recalling the timing of the Russian action. It occurred mid-way between a NATO summit in Bucharest in April 2008 and a follow-up meeting of allied foreign ministers scheduled for December. At Bucharest, the allies declared that:

> NATO welcomes Ukraine's and Georgia's Euro-Atlantic aspirations for membership. [. . .] We agreed today that these countries will become members of NATO. [A] MAP is the next step for Ukraine and Georgia on their direct way to membership. [...] We have asked Foreign Ministers to make a first assessment of progress at their December 2008 meeting. Foreign Ministers have the authority to decide on the MAP applications of Ukraine and Georgia.[33]

Despite French and German scepticism about NATO's commitment to Georgia and Ukraine, the Bucharest declaration was remarkably robust. Its language was meant to fudge the timeline on offering MAPs to the two countries. Granting such programmes was a step up the escalator toward membership for which no NATO consensus existed.

The clear reference to the goal of future membership, according to one senior US official, thus overly indulged Ukrainian and Georgian hopes. At the same time, it indicated to Putin 'a course he saw as an existential threat'.[34] The intra-NATO wrangling at Bucharest had been intense and protracted. Condoleezza Rice described it as 'the most heated that I saw in my entire time as Secretary [of State]'.[35] It had left NATO leaders and officials with little time or inclination to focus on how their eventual decisions might play with *external* audiences – Russia most obviously. Such complacency rested on the assumption that the Russian government either could not, or would not, act decisively to try to block any decision on future enlargement, as indeed it had not in the case of previous enlargement rounds during the 1990s and early 2000s. 'Red lines' previously established by Moscow – over the Baltic States, for instance – had been breached by NATO with little sign of Russian counter-measures. When Russia did act (suspending participation in the CFE Treaty, for instance, in December 2007), the measures were seen as indicative of its subsidiary place in the European pecking order and not as a signal of a new type of assertiveness.[36] Russia's military intervention in Georgia therefore caught the NATO members 'utterly unprepared'.[37]

The Russian invasion took place four months after the Bucharest declaration. Having driven Georgian forces out of the disputed enclave of South Ossetia, the Russian army proceeded to occupy towns and military bases elsewhere in the country, in the process systematically destroying or looting military equipment, much of which had been supplied by the US. NATO's accession criteria stipulated that candidates should be able to contribute militarily to the Alliance and its missions. Russia's actions thus seemed purposely designed to degrade efforts to demonstrate Georgia's suitability for membership. The same could be said of the subsequent Russian decision to recognize South Ossetia and the similarly contested territory of Abkhazia as independent states. A further NATO criterion has been that prospective members should have no unresolved territorial disputes, either internally or with their neighbours. Since August 2008, Georgia has effectively had both.

In 2008, the NRC clearly failed the Goltz test. Indeed, it has been suggested that the Council might even have got in the way of effective crisis consultation and management. James Sherr has argued that '[t]he elaborate architecture of NATO–Russia "cooperation" and the focus on "programmes" and process substituted for negotiation, blunted warnings and marginalised analysis of Russian policies and plans.'[38] This recourse to process pointed to the limited political will on both sides to develop a pragmatic, results-orientated ethos. At their meeting in December 2008, NATO foreign ministers had also declared that '[i]n a partnership based on common values, the lack of a shared commitment to those values must naturally cause the relationship and the scope for cooperative action to suffer.'[39] This statement glossed over the fact that the NATO–Russia relationship had never actually been a partnership based on values in the first place.

The Ukraine crisis

In the NATO states, most media and political attention in the period leading up to the 2008 Bucharest summit had been on Georgia. Ukraine was strategically more important, but its desire to align with NATO much less obvious. Opinion in Georgia favoured membership; that in Ukraine was very much divided.[40] On the Russian side, however, it was a different story. President Putin allegedly told US President George W. Bush at the NRC summit in Bucharest that 'Ukraine is not even a state.' He warned that moves to associate it with NATO could lead to Russian intervention to 'protect' ethnic

Russians, particularly in Crimea and mainland eastern Ukraine.[41] In public comments, Putin declared: 'We view the appearance of a powerful military bloc on our borders [. . .] as a direct threat to the security of our country.'[42] He stuck to that view thereafter. In a 2014 public address justifying the Russian annexation of Crimea, Putin reprised what he had said in Bucharest. NATO, he claimed, 'remains a military alliance, and we are against having a military alliance making itself at home right in our backyard or in our historic territory. I simply cannot imagine that we would travel to Sevastopol to visit NATO sailors.'[43]

The Ukraine crisis was precipitated by a dispute over whether the government in Kiev should sign an association agreement and develop closer institutional relations with the EU. This was not initially a dispute with NATO. Since the Russo-Georgia war, NATO and its members had announced no further significant policy initiatives vis-à-vis Ukraine. Additionally, nobody familiar with the jealously guarded institutional autonomy of the EU would have given credence to the idea that it was acting as some kind of stalking horse on behalf of the Alliance or the US. That Russian leaders and officials evidently believed otherwise is testimony to the depth of distrust that had developed by that time, and the failure of the NRC, amongst other forums, to mitigate it in any significant way.

As an object of NATO–Russian disagreement, the Ukraine crisis had deep roots. It had become apparent soon after the Russo-Georgia war that any prospect of either Georgia or Ukraine being invited to join the Alliance had been closed off, even if this position had not been set out in official statements. This turned out to be an important omission. By never formally revising the Bucharest declaration, NATO members effectively, though perhaps unintentionally, ensured that Ukraine and Georgia remained objects of contestation with Russia. As Eugene Rumer noted, 'As long as the West [was] not prepared to consign these states to the Russian sphere, they [became] the arena for East–West competition.'[44] Abandoning enlargement, however, would have conceded the point that NATO was unwilling to stand up to its declared commitments and so would have severely dented alliance credibility in consequence. Handling this dilemma meant delaying movement toward NATO membership for Georgia and Ukraine but keeping up the pretence that it was a desired outcome. This effectively left the two countries in a state of strategic and diplomatic limbo, so aggravating unresolved constitutional and territorial issues that lined Russia and NATO up on opposing sides.

Issues relating to Ukraine had animated Russian political and cultural leaders ever since the break-up of the Soviet Union. Crimea was viewed as particularly important. (The region had been transferred from Russia to Ukraine in 1954 when both were Union Republics of the Soviet Union.) Ukraine also engendered tensions between President Putin and George W. Bush's administration following contested (and eventually re-run) presidential elections during the so-called 'Orange Revolution' in late 2004. Those events also impacted upon Russia and Europe. The victory of Viktor Yushchenko (and defeat of the pro-Russian Viktor Yanukovich) resulted in a new package of EU assistance to Ukraine, something that, in turn, soured the relatively benign view held in Moscow of the EU's pre-accession and engagement programmes. EU and NATO processes were, of course, separate, but in the Russian leadership's view both converged in a process whereby Russia was diminished and pushed to the fringes of Europe. That Ukraine was the crucible for that slight should never have been in doubt. As noted earlier, Putin had long insisted that Russia and Ukraine 'are one nation'.[45] Any serious analysis of Russia's national security thinking should thus have concluded that Ukraine really was a red line which NATO crossed at its peril. Unlike the Baltic States (also once part of the Soviet Union), Ukraine had been conjoined to Russia demographically, culturally, religiously and territorially for centuries. As Anatol Lieven had noted as early as 1995, the prospect of Ukraine joining the Alliance would thus 'be regarded by Russians as a catastrophe of epochal proportions', which would likely 'involve a complete collapse of cooperation with the West'.[46]

In such circumstances, the NATO–Russia partnership proved marginal at best. Between 2009 and 2014, the NRC remained operative and NATO–Russia relations did improve (helped, in turn, by the Obama administration's 'reset' of relations with Moscow). This rapprochement yielded some tangible results – chiefly a new agreement on military transit rights to Afghanistan to support the NATO-led ISAF operation. Tellingly, however, there was no reference to either Ukraine or Georgia in the statement issued at the end of an NRC summit in Lisbon in November 2010, at which the Afghan agreement was announced.[47] In fact, up to 2014, the NRC failed to engage with the issues connected to Ukraine and Georgia in any substantial way. All told, by the beginning of 2014, the NRC had run out of steam. It had become, according to Heidi Reisinger, 'a kind of institutionalized Potemkin village' lacking traction on issues of substance. Blame for this was laid at Russia's door. Policy proposals in the NRC were a 'one-way street' with 'almost all initiatives for military cooperation com[ing] from Brussels'. 'Russia', Reisinger suggested, 'is not in the least interested in becoming or being seen as a "normal partner" of NATO.'[48] Unsurprisingly, Russian leaders blamed NATO for this situation. In the aftermath of the annexation of Crimea in March 2014, Defence Minister Sergei Shoigu dismissed the NRC as largely irrelevant. 'We all talk and smile at each other', he suggested, but 'joint work is not being carried out, and our concerns are not taken into consideration'.[49]

Wherever blame lay, the net effect was that, once again, the NRC proved to be ineffectual in a crisis. In the initial wake of Russia's annexation of Crimea (followed, in short order, by Russian support of rebel groups in eastern Ukraine), the allies declared that '[w]e intend to engage with Russia in the NATO–Russia Council.'[50] On the face of it, this suggested that NATO members were seeking to bring pressure to bear on Russia through proactive diplomatic engagement. However, that position was soon reversed. NATO foreign ministers decided in April 'to suspend all practical civilian and military cooperation between NATO and Russia'. The exception would be NRC meetings at ambassadorial or ministerial level, although the essentially pro forma nature of this was readily apparent. The NATO ministers declared that this single institutional channel of communication would be kept open in order 'to allow us to exchange views, first and foremost on this crisis'.[51] Such a function was hardly likely to be productive, however, as leaders and officials on both sides had by then adopted entrenched positions.

Conclusion: The NATO–Russia Deep Freeze

After 2014, there was no meaningful revival of the NATO–Russia relationship within the NRC framework. Neither was any effort expended on creating an institutional alternative. NATO–Russia relations, in other words, had become deadlocked. Two years after the Ukraine crisis, NATO's Warsaw summit declaration suggested that the allies had little expectation that the relationship with Russia might be revived, putting the onus clearly on the Russian government to make the first move. However justifiable in principle, this looked unrealistic in the circumstances prevailing at the time. In the words of the NATO members:

> [W]e continue to believe that a partnership between NATO and Russia, based on respect for international law and commitments, including as reflected in the NATO–Russia Founding Act [. . .], would be of strategic value. We regret that despite repeated calls by Allies and the international community since 2014 for Russia to change course, the conditions for that relationship do not currently exist. The nature of the Alliance's relations with Russia and aspirations for partnership will be contingent on a clear, constructive change in Russia's actions that demonstrates compliance with international law and its international obligations and responsibilities. Until then, we cannot return to 'business as usual'.[52]

This formulation was repeated several times thereafter, accompanied by an ever- lengthening list of NATO complaints at Russian behaviour. The Brussels summit declaration of July 2018 took Russia to task not only for its continuing interference in eastern Ukraine and 'continued military build-up in Crimea', but also for the 'violation, non-implementation, and circumvention of numerous obligations and commitments in the realm of arms control and confidence and security-building measures', a build-up of conventional and nuclear forces, 'malicious cyber activities', electoral interference in NATO states and a chemical weapons attack on British soil.[53] NATO's 2019 London declaration blamed Russia for the demise of the Intermediate-Range Nuclear Forces (INF) Treaty (the Trump administration had served notice of its withdrawal in February of that year in response to alleged Russian violations) and went on to note that 'Russia's aggressive actions constitute a threat to Euro-Atlantic security'.[54] NATO had also long complained about Russian support for the Assad regime in Syria. In June 2020, moreover, Secretary General Stoltenberg criticized Russia's military involvement in Libya.[55]

Russia, for its part, was equally critical of NATO. In announcing a modernization of Russia's nuclear forces in March 2018, President Putin justified the initiative as a response to US missile defence deployments (in part on the territory of NATO allies in Central Europe) and the 'bringing of NATO's [conventional] military infrastructure closer to the Russian border'.[56] In November 2019, the Russian President added that NATO now also had plans 'to militarize outer space'.[57]

NATO by this point had, in fact, already taken a series of robust military measures. At their first post-Crimea summit meeting, in Newport, Wales, in September 2014, the allies set in train plans to create the eFP consisting of two elements.[58] The first would involve rotational military deployments at battle-group strength overseen by the US, UK, Canada and Germany, stationed in four separate deployments in Poland and the three Baltic States. The second element was the creation of a small multinational military unit modelled on the Allied Command Europe Mobile Force (AMF). Originally formed in 1960, the AMF was intended for deployment at short notice to wherever a potential military threat was developing. The AMF was too small to resist a serious Soviet assault. Rather, the thinking behind it was that an aggressor could never be sure whether attacking NATO troops – drawn from a cross-section of allies – would trigger an Article 5 collective defence response. The AMF thereby contributed to overall NATO deterrence. This so-called 'tripwire effect' was revived with the creation in 2015 of the NATO Very High Readiness Joint Task Force (VJTF), for potential rapid deployment wherever needed but with an eye principally to Poland and the Baltic States.[59] Alongside, NATO ramped up its programme of military exercises, initiated a set of Force Integration Units across the Alliance's eastern members and in 2017 established a tailored Forward Presence (tFP) in the

Black Sea region (focused on Romania and Bulgaria) with both land and maritime components. These developments were supplemented by a significant commitment by the US (initiated by President Obama and continued by President Trump) under the umbrella of Operation Atlantic Resolve and the European Deterrence Initiative (see Chapter 6).

NATO has repeatedly stressed the small-scale and rotational nature of these deployments (so claiming not to have breached the prohibition in the Founding Act against *permanent* conventional force infrastructure in new NATO members). It justified them as a defensive response to heightened perceptions of a potential Russian threat, especially to the small and vulnerable Baltic States.[60] Russian leaders saw things differently and responded by enhancing the scale and intensity of military exercises conducted in their western military districts: that is, those closest to, or bordering, NATO member states. A 2017 exercise code-named Zapad-2017 provoked particular concern amongst NATO political and military leaders. Vostok 2018, meanwhile, although staged in Siberia, was also worrying given it was the largest Russian exercise since the Soviet period and entailed the participation of the Chinese military. This, a NATO Parliamentary Assembly report noted, 'underscore[d] a growing strategic partnership between Moscow and Beijing'.[61]

By the time of NATO's London meeting in December 2019, the Alliance and Russia were not cooperating in any substantive way. A report of the NATO Parliamentary Assembly noted that 'the current relationship between NATO and Russia can be described as one of high tensions and confrontation'.[62] The relationship appeared to have sunk into a classic 'security dilemma': a condition of mistrust in which actors take military measures to enhance their security only to find that resultant counter-measures make their circumstances even more precarious. Further measures follow, leading to a spiral of escalation and increasing tension.[63] Getting out of this mutually damaging position is very difficult, and so as NATO–Russia relations entered their fourth decade in 2020 the future looked bleak. The Cold War was long over, but the promise of recasting the old East–West relationship had seemingly failed to materialize. How this situation can be retrieved is the subject of Chapter 8.

Part II

Treatments

CHAPTER FIVE

Task Discretion: Doing Less but Better

In Chapter 1, we saw that NATO had got itself into trouble by over-promising and taking on too many tasks. The problem of overload requires greater discretion on the part of the Alliance, avoiding new commitments where the potential pitfalls are too great and rowing back where prior commitments have become unrealistic. The argument in favour of discretion once seemed unusual, but no longer. Arguments mobilized in the 1990s and 2000s to justify greater responsibilities for NATO have been replaced by more sober reflection on how the Alliance can concentrate its strengths. Several options have emerged from these debates, some of which entail a radical rethink of NATO's mission. But just as an expansion of the Alliance's mission can bring problems, so, too, can a rapid curtailment. A prudent way forward, therefore, has to be alert to the problems of doing too little (or even nothing at all) as well as the problems of doing too much.

Matching Means to Ends

For an organization facing an unsustainable increase in its responsibilities, there are two stark alternatives: either increase resources or reduce the number of tasks.[1] The first course of action is one NATO has been wedded to for decades – hence the demands upon allies (most loudly voiced by the US) to increase defence expenditures. If all allies were to meet existing defence spending obligations (NATO's 2 per cent of

GDP target), significant revenues would be generated (some $114 billion in 2018 alone). But does this solve the overload problem? As we discussed in Chapter 3, the persistence of the 'guns versus butter' dilemma means there are limits on how far defence budgets can be increased. Since 2015, the aggregate defence spending by the NATO allies has gone up significantly, but by 2019 it was still (when adjusted for inflation) below 2012 levels. With a few exceptions (countries such as the Baltic States and Poland, for instance), the sense of national priority that attaches to defence is insufficiently compelling to elevate the issue up the national political agenda. This is especially true among NATO's big military powers. France and the UK have registered only modest real-term increases in spending since the adoption of NATO defence spending pledge in 2014. The GDP percentage, meanwhile, has been static. German spending increases have been greater, but the country's Defence Minister conceded in November 2019 that achieving the 2 per cent ambition had been pushed out to 2031 (well beyond the NATO target date of 2024).[2] Even the US has experienced pressure on its defence commitments. The real-term increase in its defence budget between 2014 and 2019 was the second lowest of all the NATO allies; the GDP percentage the US spent on defence in this period actually fell.[3] As the COVID-19 pandemic gripped the world in 2020, increasing defence spending slipped still further down the political agenda.

In addition to these constraints, there are three other qualifications to any resource-based fix to NATO's problems. First, even if spending increases, it will be wasted unless accompanied by a clear sense of how to match resources with shifting strategic priorities. Such reorientations can take years, if not decades, to achieve. Second, spending more doesn't necessarily deliver better results. This is something we have seen in NATO's own operations – the billions spent in Afghanistan have not resolved that country's problems. Equally, large defence budgets may simply compound inefficiency. The German case is again instructive. While the country fails to meet NATO's spending target, it is nonetheless NATO's third largest defence spender (behind the US and the UK). Yet its armed forces are in a parlous condition – 'dramatically bad', according to an official report of the German parliament.[4] Extra spending on a military which is widely regarded as badly managed and poorly motivated won't deliver a more able and deployable armed force until these deeper problems are tackled. That may take many years – indeed, may even prove impossible, as Germany's ruling political parties have shown little interest in the country's military failings.[5]

A third qualification concerns the setting and estimation of costs. Coordinating defence budgets more effectively, and spending those budgets wisely, has been the narrative and practice in NATO for most of its history (something we take up further in Chapter 7). Currently, through the NATO Defence Planning Process, the Alliance has a sophisticated methodology for establishing capability requirements and identifying shortfalls. Military planners at SHAPE, meanwhile, oversee operational requirements for NATO's missions, exercises and force deployments. Work such as this is part of the ongoing routine of alliance management. Within its purview, it is possible to specify the force requirements and attendant costs of collective defence and even time-limited scenarios that arise from conflict management. But with geographically and politically imprecise projects such as partnership, Projecting Stability and 'open door' enlargement there is no obvious answer to the question: what spending for what purpose? One of the basic requirements of strategy – to align resources with objectives – is, therefore, left hanging.

The Need for Prudence

Increasing resources is thus not an entirely reliable approach to dealing with overload. The alternative – cutting back on tasks – accepts that resources are limited, that ambition is bounded and that priority-setting is essential. This is an approach informed by prudence: an 'understanding of the possible, the probable, and the appropriate' when confronted with multiple demands and finite ways of achieving them.[6] Prudent decision-making is not blind to ideas and values (these might condition the types of action taken), but as we pointed out in Chapter 1, the problem is that ideas often run ahead of what is achievable or feasible. To be prudent guards against that danger; it is to take practical action in specific circumstances aware of both the risks of doing nothing or acting beyond one's competence and capability.[7] To be prudent is to strike the middle ground in-between. That said, the middle ground may have already moved. In circumstances of over-commitment, prudence would, therefore, suggest a course correction: that due attention be given to restraint so as to mitigate prior problems of excess and over-commitment.

The case for restraint has been popularized by the leading figures of American realist thinking. Their concern is not NATO as such but the over-extension of the US in international affairs. The remedy, as they see it, is to disentangle the US from costly overseas commitments, and to recognize that liberal ideas, and the associated quest for 'liberal hegemony', do not translate into an effective foreign policy. The irony of these arguments for NATO is that American restraint could actually mean *more* responsibility for the Alliance if the US were to offload its overseas commitments onto its European and Canadian allies.[8] Many of those obligations the allies would be unable or unwilling to take on. Restraint, if it is to work in the NATO setting, must, therefore, be an alliance-wide adjustment – one commensurate with shifts in American foreign policy, with an understanding of appropriate European and Canadian responsibilities and with a shared strategic awareness of NATO's modified mission. Such an adjustment is eminently possible given shifts in thinking among the allies, first and foremost the US.

We suggested in Chapter 1 that NATO's ambition had, in many ways, been driven by the goals of American foreign policy. This was most evident in the Clinton and Bush Jr years, but the Obama and Trump administrations, too, viewed the Alliance as, in the words of the 2017 US National Security Strategy, a means to 'increase [America's] strategic reach'.[9] That reach has found its limits, however. Obama and Trump had many and obvious differences, but their foreign policies were both characterized by a scepticism about nation-building projects and draining military interventions.[10]

The other allies have followed America's lead in curtailing NATO's level of ambition. For the majority, signing up to conflict management and expeditionary missions was a luxury affordable only because it occurred within the NATO framework and under American leadership. As we saw in Chapter 3, countries such as Denmark, the Netherlands, Norway and Canada, and even a small state such as Estonia, made significant contributions to the mission in Afghanistan and structured their forces for out-of-area missions accordingly. But this was not because Afghanistan was a priority. Their actions, rather, reflected a desire to be associated with NATO's strategic purpose and to show fealty to US foreign policy priorities. The payback, it was hoped, was influence in Washington and a reciprocal commitment by the US to NATO's collective defence guarantee. But as the pendulum in NATO swung back to collective defence following the 2014 Ukraine crisis, so these states became willing partners in reconfiguring their efforts 'to deter and defend against Russian aggression in Eastern Europe'.[11]

Larger European allies, too, moved toward a more focused NATO. This was hardly a surprise when it came to Poland, a country whose national security strategy is preoccupied with Russia. Germany, meanwhile, had always been uncomfortable with NATO's more expansive missions. The 'Red–Green' coalition did support OAF in 1999 (persuaded by the humanitarian case for stopping Serb aggression against Kosovo). But German involvement in Afghanistan was qualified (battlefield restrictions or national 'caveats' upon Germans in ISAF were amongst the most restrictive of all allied contingents) and the country shunned involvement in NATO's 2011 mission in Libya. Berlin has long been sceptical about extending NATO membership to Georgia and Ukraine. Not surprisingly, therefore, it has been an enthusiastic supporter of NATO's post-2014 reorientation. Germany has been the lead nation of the eFP in Lithuania, in 2019 it took leadership of the VJTF and in September of that year a new NATO Joint Support and Enabling Command began operating in the German city of Ulm. While Germany's long-time Chancellor, Angela Merkel, has given her backing to 'strategic autonomy' for the EU, her government has expressed a continuing support for a NATO concentrated on 'European defence'.[12]

France is also more comfortable with an alliance centred on Europe. In Chapter 1, we noted President Charles de Gaulle's support of a global role for the early Alliance. But this should be regarded as idiosyncratic. Paris, sceptical about grand designs that promote American influence, has historically steered to 'a traditionally minimalist vision of NATO'.[13] This has meant an enthusiasm for the development of EU military capabilities and a preference for bilateral or ad hoc alliances (with the UK and the US especially) to support its own interventions in Africa, Iraq and Syria. None of this means France has shunned NATO. It rejoined the Alliance's integrated military structures in 2009 after a forty-year absence, took a lead role in the Libya intervention and sent troops to Afghanistan (although it withdrew them unilaterally in 2012). But France's own ambitions to be a global actor and military power do not translate into support for NATO as a vehicle for realizing that role.

In the case of the British, strategic thinking is wedded to the notion that the UK should be a 'tier-one' military power capable of mounting military missions around the world. Withdrawal from the EU has meant a continuing interest in talking up the UK's global military footprint. However, even though it is NATO's second biggest defence spender, the country has found it very difficult to balance a commitment to prestige capabilities such as nuclear weapons (and associated modern submarines), aircraft carriers and fifth-generation fighter aircraft with the more routine costs of maintaining a large defence estate, armed forces and reserve. Political pressures, too, have narrowed British options. Investment in the NATO mission in Afghanistan and the US-led coalition in Iraq came at a significant price both in lives lost and international credibility. The 'blunder' of Iraq meant an aversion to difficult foreign interventions – hence, parliament's vetoing in 2013 of a British military intervention in Syria.[14] The UK remains wedded to the idea that it will support US and NATO military interventions, but years of defence austerity mean the US itself is increasingly sceptical about British capability. Global power projection is still 'baked in' to UK military doctrine,[15] but British politicians, prompted by worries over Russia, have accorded greater priority to missions focused on defence and deterrence nearer to home.[16] Military deployments have reflected this shift. In 2014, the UK, along with partners in the Baltics, Scandinavia and the Netherlands, launched the JEF. Together with the UK presence in NATO's eFP, the development of the UK-led Northern Group and investment in a new fleet of maritime patrol aircraft, this initiative indicated a 'focusing [of] resources, leadership and activity on the High North, the North Atlantic and the Baltic'.[17]

NATO's Need for Strategy

The appetite, then, clearly existed among the major NATO allies to address the problem of overload. But what should be the priorities of a refocused NATO? And how can these be reconciled with the Alliance's legacy of ambition? Posing and providing answers to such questions is the purpose of strategy. But here we enter contested territory. 'Strategy', Hew Strachan has suggested, has become a term so over-used that it has been 'robbed [. . .] of meaning'.[18] Strategy also has an illusory quality. It is applied to circumstances that are too complex and unpredictable to produce the intended results; it requires rational foresight that is polluted by human bias, cultural blinders and political preference; and it is dependent on implementation through organizational structures that can be inefficient, inflexible and resistant to change.[19] In large organizations, these problems are compounded by administrative and political complexity. NATO, for instance, is required to reach agreement on strategy among thirty members. And that is only the beginning. Strategy needs to be translated into military doctrine and, in turn, into operational and tactical guidance across several 'functional and geographical issue areas'.[20]

There remain good reasons to retain the idea of strategy, however. Strategy is better than its alternatives: taking a 'shot in the dark', relying on abstract concepts such as honour and credibility or abjuring clearly specified goals as a guide to action.[21] Further, to pursue strategy is to embrace choice; to proceed from the conviction, Lawrence Freedman has suggested, 'that it is possible to manipulate and shape one's environment rather than simply become the victim of forces beyond one's control'.[22] But good strategy should be aware of its limitations – bounded, in other words, by an appreciation of what is possible and why the possible is desirable. Strategy starts, Freedman has suggested, 'with an existing state of affairs and only gains meaning by an awareness of how, for better, or worse, it could be different'. It is, in this sense, characterized by modesty. Strategy is about moving to a 'next stage' and not the attainment of some 'definitive and permanent conclusion'.[23] The actions that result give rise to one of the hardiest meanings of strategy: the need to articulate a set of specific goals and the means of their implementation. Strategy is thus about the employment of 'whatever resources are available to achieve the best outcome in situations that are both dynamic and contested'.[24]

Such fluidity of circumstance means strategy requires constant adjustment. The famous quip attributed to German Field Marshal Helmuth von Moltke that '[n]o plan survives first contact with the enemy' was an injunction on the need to adjust according to the moves of one's adversary. But for NATO the task is even harder: it is not simply reacting to the actions of a presumed enemy (be that Russia or the Taliban in Afghanistan); it has to take into account, as noted, a setting that is constantly in flux. And the need to adapt doesn't just follow from uncertainty; it may also result from an appreciation of limited success. If the likelihood of achieving strategic goals diminishes, new alternative courses of action hove into view.

Adopting alternatives can, however, prove difficult. 'Sunk costs' – the prior investment of effort, political capital and sometimes lives – may mean a particular set of policies is difficult to abandon or even modify lest these be seen as wrong or having been executed in vain. Strategic thinking can also be constrained by 'the power of habit': engrained beliefs that render decision-makers insensitive to changing conditions and dependent on 'traditional rationales' when weighing up choices.[25] These obstacles may not always be a bad thing. They can prevent sudden lurches in policy for which little preparation has been given. And they may also protect and stabilize a core consensus. It would be naïve, therefore, to imagine that shifts in strategy come either quickly or easily. But strategic awareness remains crucial. 'Plans are worthless', President Dwight Eisenhower once suggested, 'but planning is everything.'[26]

NATO's problem is not that it lacks strategy. Throughout its history, the Alliance has paid considerable attention to formulating and agreeing strategy, and then to planning its activities on the basis of guidance, concepts, directives and other statements of policy (or what is known in the military domain as allied joint doctrine). During the Cold War, NATO adopted four top-level Strategic Concepts (in 1949, 1952, 1957 and 1968) which finessed its core military task of defence against the Soviet Union and its Warsaw Pact allies. The end of the Cold War put paid to such strategic concision. The 'New' Strategic Concept of November 1991 affirmed NATO's relevance as the Cold War was ending. Its replacement of 1999 retained deterrence and defence as a 'fundamental security task' but, following NATO's active engagement in the Balkans and the emergence of enlargement and partnerships as core missions, gave due recognition to crisis management as well as partnership, cooperation and dialogue. The next revision was not until 2010, nearly a decade after 9/11 and several years into the Alliance's Afghan mission. NATO under US pressure did adopt the CPG in 2006, a document notable for its elevation of terrorism and the spread of weapons of mass destruction as 'the principal threats to the Alliance over the next 10 to 15 years'. The CPG retained an emphasis on crisis management, and collective defence was still specified as NATO's 'core purpose'. But the Alliance was enjoined to conduct multiple and simultaneous missions across this operational spectrum, and to do so without geographical limit – NATO, it was asserted, should be able to act 'on and beyond Alliance territory, on its periphery, and at strategic distance'.[27] The 2010 Strategic Concept, when it came, identified three 'essential core tasks' (collective defence, crisis management and cooperative security) largely detached from geography – a 'clear sign', according to one contemporary assessment, 'of a more global and political alliance'.[28]

The high aspirations of the 2010 Strategic Concept suggested that the constituency in favour of 'coming home' to focus on Europe mattered less than the American position, backed by key allies such as the British, in favour of a more global perspective. Commenting at the time on this internal debate, two Danish scholars noted that the balance of thinking in NATO would change should the Russian threat re-emerge or NATO face defeat (or, at least, a need for retreat) in Afghanistan.[29] Both eventualities subsequently materialized and so NATO embarked on a significant strategic reset evident in the package of measures endorsed by the Wales summit in September 2014 aimed at reasserting defence and deterrence, and transitioning the NATO force in Afghanistan away from combat. Further summit declarations at Warsaw (2016) and Brussels (2018) indicated the emergence of an overall strategic 'construct' or approach that gave prominence to collective defence, while retaining an attachment to other missions (counter-terrorism, conflict management) and geographical priorities adjacent to NATO's south as well as its north and east.[30]

A sense of focus was also evident in two classified documents adopted by the Alliance in early 2019: a new Military Strategy (NATO's first for 'over five decades', according to the commander of US forces in Europe [31]) and a Concept for the

Deterrence and Defence of the Euro-Atlantic Area, both of which placed greatest emphasis on Russia. What was missing, however, was a top-level political statement. In 2020, the Secretary General launched expert discussions on a 'forward-looking reflection process' alongside a broader consultation on a so-called '#NATO2030'. These initiatives were intended to inform recommendations to a NATO summit some time in 2021, although few believed there was consensus in the Alliance for a revised Strategic Concept to replace the dated 2010 document. The most authoritative NATO statement at this point was the checklist of priorities contained in the short 2019 London declaration.[32] NATO's London meeting, according to UK government sources, had organized around three 'baskets' or sets of priority: first, emphasizing transatlantic unity and so giving prominence to defence spending efforts; second, continuing the post-2014 reset and getting NATO 'match-fit' to deal with the twin challenges of Russia and terrorism (hence the new Military Strategy); and, third, preparing for the future by emphasizing space, technology, cyber and hybrid threats – all with an eye to China (which grabbed the headlines) but just as relevant to Russia given worries about the development there of cruise, hypersonic and AI weapon technologies. The sense of focus and consolidation this three-fold set of priorities implied was also evident in the absence of any reference to far-flung missions (with just a pro-forma mention of Afghanistan) as well as standard-issue language on partnerships and enlargement (without mention of Georgia or Ukraine). Reference to the '360 degree approach to security' and the importance of dealing with threats from 'any direction', meanwhile, clearly suggested that NATO's southern neighbourhood remained important. In essence, therefore, this was a NATO geographically concentrated on defending its territory and, if required, ready to assist in the stabilization of its periphery.

Table 5.1 What are the options for a more discretionary NATO?		
Retreat	Retrenchment and revival	Routine
Dissolution	Minimalist NATO	Continuing adaptation (official position)
Paper alliance	Region management	Smart incrementalism
Rump NATO		NATO re-calibration

Options for Consolidation

The case for consolidation had, then, clearly found favour among the allies and within NATO. But what might the necessary course of strategic prudence entail? Analysts and pundits have for some time weighed in with various options, often extrapolating these from NATO's own positions (or those of the US). Table 5.1 sets out three sets of options that summarize the debate. Each, in different ways, proceeds from the assumption that the Alliance is overstretched and needs to realign means to ends. Some options take the view that NATO's predicament is so bad that only a wholesale downsizing or even abandonment will suffice. That is not our view. Having surveyed the various alternatives, it will become clear that our preference sits in the middle column.

Retreat

As we saw in Chapter 1, winding up NATO and transferring its functions to other international organizations was a serious proposition at the end of the Cold War, but faded from sight once the US resolved to preserve the Alliance. Ever since, it has been a fringe position with none of the allies lining up behind it. The path to dissolution is still, however, conceivable. The Trump administration's occasional hostility was seen by some as presaging a collapse of the Alliance. Here, Trump's frustration at the allies was seen as likely to result in an American withdrawal and an implosion of NATO as the Canadians and Europeans would have found it impossible to provide the military resources and political leadership necessary for a post-American construct.[33]

An alternative scenario envisages the EU stepping into the breach, but as we noted in Chapter 3, capability gaps render such an outcome fanciful. Even a brief consideration of EU capabilities makes for stark reading. The EU's permanent operational headquarters, the Military Planning and Conduct Capability, launched in 2017, is made up of some 150 personnel; the NATO command structure, by comparison, comprises 6,800 across seven commands. EU Battlegroups, set up in 2005, have been described as having 'no self-contained capacity for deployment, sustainment, force protection, or manoeuvre against even modest ground-based opposition, quite apart from having no organic air power'.[34] These would be unable to mount the sorts of enforcement mission NATO has undertaken in Bosnia, Kosovo and Libya, let alone Afghanistan. And even if one accepts that the era of such missions is drawing to an end, EU capabilities are even less well suited to the core mission of territorial defence that remains. Should that function be thrust upon the EU, the effort would probably fail. Even if all European allies were to meet the NATO defence spending target by 2024 and sustain it beyond, and even if they were to invest that money in the right capabilities to substitute for those of the US, they would still not – even after ten to fifteen years, according to one estimate – have developed a credible and autonomous European capability that could be plugged into the EU for the sorts of Article 5 contingencies NATO is set up for.[35] And lurking in the background is the conundrum of nuclear defence. Bluntly stated, there is no substitute for US extended deterrence. Of Europe's two nuclear powers, one, the UK, has left the EU and the other, France, is no more likely to align its nuclear deterrent with the EU than it has been with NATO. Talk of a German or 'European' nuclear deterrent, meanwhile, is politically untenable and, under the terms of the Nuclear Non-Proliferation Treaty, certainly illegal.

EU-based defence also has other problems. It would sideline the non-EU British and Turks, and countries such as Poland would be likely to resist Franco-German leadership in favour of bilateral arrangements with the US. Worried by an incapable EU, Poland and the Baltic States would perceive themselves as even more exposed to Russia and, whatever Moscow's true intentions, may take national or regional measures of self-defence that ignite an arms race, entailing a spiral of mistrust and the possibility, even if inadvertent, of tensions escalating to war.[36]

For some, these risks are greatly exaggerated and so, the argument goes, an American retreat from Europe is precisely the political shock European states require to wean themselves off their military dependence on the US.[37] But shock therapy of this sort is more likely to kill the patient than to save it. Further, the Trumpian position that NATO is a one-sided drag on the US is itself misaligned – both with the substance of American policy itself (the US actually increased its commitment to NATO during Trump's presidency) and the balance of transatlantic interests. There may well be advantages to the US if it cuts loose from the Alliance (not bearing the cost of troop and other military commitments in Europe) but, as we point out in Chapter 6, there are many equally important benefits as well. NATO provides permanent access to European-based military facilities (useful for American force projection into MENA as well as the defence of Europe) and an institutionalized format for the exercise of US military and political leadership. Of course, none of this is a guarantee that some future American president won't pursue the withdrawal option to its conclusion. But the evidence of the

Trump administration – the most antithetical to NATO since the Alliance's foundation – is that criticism need not lead to the taking of that fateful step.

Rather than a wholesale abandonment of NATO, the US could instead chose to downsize its commitment. One option here is to relinquish the American military presence in Europe but maintain an attachment to the North Atlantic Treaty. 'Off-shore balancing' of this sort would preserve NATO but without the emplacement of a forward American presence: US land forces in Europe and the American contribution to NATO command structures would be withdrawn.[38] This position, too, lacks viability. It subtracts American leadership without any guarantee that an alternative is available; it removes the gravitational force of defence integration provided by the dominant military power; and it assumes wrongly that a power offshore can move back 'onshore' at will and at speed in a crisis.[39] Several decades of American-led coordination would, in other words, be undone. European and Canadian personnel might be able to substitute for Americans in NATO commands (they do, after all, already occupy significant positions), but the functional overlap between EUCOM and SHAPE (personified in American occupancy of SACEUR) would disappear. NATO in such circumstances would be reduced to a 'paper alliance'[40]: existing in name but marooned by an absence of American commitment.

Equally problematic is the suggestion that the US should downsize NATO through a pruning of America's European allies. The argument here is that some in NATO – the Baltics and Poland, for instance – are peripheral to American interests and difficult to defend against Russian aggression. The US should acknowledge this openly and reorientate NATO to the defence of those allies (essentially the core Cold War membership) where treaty commitments are more credible, and US political and economic interests more historically established.[41] This is certainly a bold proposal, but it is no way to fix NATO. Not only would it entail an historically unprecedented ditching of allies, it would also generate a grave sense of uncertainty among the rump who remained under the American (i.e. NATO) defence umbrella. It is also difficult to see how any such strategy could be translated into a NATO position given the organization's consensus-based way of doing things. It would require a series of US ultimatums and unilateral steps of such political toxicity that NATO would probably collapse and have to be remade to make them real.

The retreat options, then, all have fatal problems. They boil down to a set of American-imposed solutions, none of which has political traction in the Alliance. If the US did decide to take up one of these radical alternatives, the damage to NATO, and to European security relations more generally, would be grave. Rather than saving NATO, retreat is more likely to bury it.

Routine

Juxtaposed to retreat is what we have called the 'routine' option. This, in one sense, is the acceptable face of NATO reform and the stuff of much expert opinion. An awareness of the problem of overstretch has been a theme of NATO commentary for many years. NATO's fiftieth and sixtieth anniversaries in 1999 and 2009 led many to conclude the Alliance needed consolidation.[42] By 2019, NATO's seventieth anniversary year, such voices had grown louder.[43] Even though the range and complexity of security issues confronting the Alliance had not diminished, this line of thinking suggests that the most effective response is a tempering of ambition. Such a 'recalibration' of the Alliance is seen to entail: (i) political adjustment (recognizing that some issues are outside of NATO's purview); (ii) emphasizing NATO's 'comparative advantage' as a political–military alliance (able to deter military adversaries, act as a framework of joint defence planning and strategy making, and mount joint military operations); (iii) boosting partnerships with a focus on the specifically military domain (capacity-building, defence sector reform, joint operations) with more able non-members and enhanced cooperation with international organizations such as the EU, the UN or the African Union; and (iv) retaining the principle of 'open door' enlargement but recognizing that the accession of Georgia and Ukraine is currently unrealistic owing to an absence of consensus within NATO.[44]

Labelling such suggestions as 'routine' is fair in the sense that the proposals, even if individually far-reaching, are still, like NATO's own efforts at change, incremental in nature, informed by a set of well-rehearsed policy options and mindful of the policy preferences of the allies. A recalibrated Alliance is thus still one having to deal with the conundrums of the flawed relationship with Russia and how to balance the transatlantic relationship. These problems are not ignored; rather the premise is that a smarter set of choices on NATO's broader agenda creates greater scope for attending to them. But a fundamental challenge remains: however smart incremental thinking may appear, its very pragmatism can mean an absence of vision and the avoidance of a compelling rationale for change.[45] Such a rationale is essential if NATO is to strike a strategic balance between the interests of its members and justify the paring back of some tasks and the prioritization of others.

Retrenchment and revival

In this light, what remedies are on offer? Here we move to the middle column of Table 5.1. The first position here is that of a minimalist NATO. This asks not just what is NATO good at, but what is NATO *best* at? Attention then focuses on how to organize and prioritize Alliance efforts. The case for a 'slimmed-down NATO' focused on collective defence, Andrew

Wolfe argued in 2009, was one way of making the Alliance 'more manageable and its objectives more obtainable'. If 'current responsibilities cause problems', he suggested, 'then remove those burdens'.[46] But with NATO then ensconced in Afghanistan and with Russia still regarded as a partner not an adversary, such calls fell on deaf ears. That changed in 2014 with Russia's seizure of Crimea. As *The Economist* suggested at the time, with 'the first forcible annexation of territory in Europe since the second world war, it [is] clear that NATO is back in the business it was created for: collective territorial defence'.[47] NATO's seventieth anniversary year prompted a call for the Alliance to give even greater emphasis to 'defend[ing] the territorial integrity of its members', with '[e]verything else that NATO might do' as 'secondary' to this number one priority.[48]

A minimalist NATO of this sort has the benefit of clarity and focus. Gathering allied effort against Russia serves the principal security interest of some allies and is a powerful rallying cry for others to demonstrate solidarity. Countering Russia has thus provided NATO with a renewed sense of collective purpose which all the allies have bought into.[49] Further, dealing with Russia is the most suitable candidate for NATO's mission for years to come. The issues that bedevil the NATO–Russia relationship (enlargement, the military balance and a legacy of mistrust) are, whatever the remedies directed toward them (see Chapter 8), likely to be persistent.

A NATO narrowly focussed on Russia, however, does not pass the test of strategic balance. The US still regards the Alliance as having a broader purpose. Similarly, NATO's Mediterranean members, although sympathetic to the eastern agenda, possess a geopolitical orientation that looks south. This, of course, is one reason why NATO has adopted the '360 degree approach' to security. As we saw in Chapter 1, the 360 degree perspective and the attendant southern agenda have proven divisive and under-resourced. To give these initiatives greater meaning, while also striking a balance with NATO's eastern priorities, a more joined-up appreciation of NATO's regional responsibilities is required – a strategy of 'region management', in other words.[50] As a proposal for a more discretionary NATO, this exhibits features of both retrenchment and revival. *Retrenchment* because a regional focus makes clear where NATO's commitments lie and where withdrawal is possible from areas of over-extension. *Revival* because the achievement of task discretion means NATO is better able to provide an answer to the questions: against what should the Alliance defend and how should it marshal its military and political resources?

The underlying assumption of this approach is that territory and distance still shape security. Such an idea may seem misguided in an era when territorial borders have been dissolved by inter-continental nuclear weapons, cyber insecurity, the militarization of extra-terrestrial space and deadly pandemics. However, as Patrick Porter has argued, physical space (and the overlapping 'strategic space' of interactions between security actors) still matters greatly. Most wars are triggered by disputes between neighbours; internal wars are made worse by the interference of nearby rivals; and the spillover effects of conflict (refugee flows most obviously) bear down greatest on surrounding populations. Distance also acts as a constraint. A superpower such as the US has been able to sustain a cross-oceanic military relationship with Europe for decades, but this type of endeavour is an exception, not the norm. Power is much easier to project at short distances. By comparison, expeditionary warfare or military operations at distance are, as Vietnam, Iraq and Afghanistan clearly demonstrate, costly, difficult and uncertain of victory.[51]

What, then, does region management mean in practical terms? First, it helps demarcate NATO's strategic space.

Although the North Atlantic Treaty already holds to the idea of the 'North Atlantic area', this is too imprecise to direct NATO's energies. Important, rather, is what Alexander Mattelaer has referred to as NATO's 'representative geography' for defence and force planning.[52] Several recent measures already suggest that a geographical imperative has guided NATO action. These include the reinforcement of the Baltic States and Poland (the eFP) along with the Black Sea region (the tFP); the creation in 2018 of a new command for the Atlantic along with the Joint Support and Enabling Command to facilitate the movement of troops and equipment in Europe; the standing up of a Strategic Direction-South Hub in Naples; a series of large-scale military exercises focused on territorial defence; and the use of operating concepts such as the Maximum Level of Effort and the US European Commander's Area of Responsibility in coordinating planning for European-based contingencies.

Equally important is what Mattelaer refers to as a 'geography-inspired division of labour'. Here, the US continues its role as security guarantor of last resort but devolves a greater share of 'the defence burden to [America's] allies'. '[G]eographical frontier states – along the northern, eastern and southern edges of the alliance' – thus promote defence and stability in their own neighbourhoods. This allots roles to Norway, the Baltic States and Poland in Europe's north-east; to Romania and Bulgaria in the Black Sea region; to Italy, Greece, Albania and NATO entrants from the former Yugoslavia in the Balkans; to Italy, France and Spain in the Mediterranean; and to Turkey in the Middle East. Canada and militarily capable allies in Europe's more sheltered western part (the UK, France, Germany, Denmark and the Netherlands), meanwhile, are on hand to provide forces deployable to 'different regional contingencies'.[53]

Such an approach accords with the shifts in defence policy

already evident among key NATO allies. The emphasis on expeditionary warfare, counter-insurgency and conflict management – a signature of military force adaptation in the 1990s and 2000s – has since the mid-2010s been replaced by military preparations to deal with security threats in close proximity. There are significant differences of emphasis in how such threats are ranked and the response that follows. Concern at Russia is greatest among NATO's East European states. Other allies – the UK, Germany, Denmark, Norway and the US (as we shall see in Chapter 6, even under Trump) – have also shifted procurement, deployment and force planning to deal with Russia. By contrast, NATO's southern NATO members hold a much more benign view of Russia, as do some of NATO's Balkan members. Force configuration to NATO's eastern agenda has consequently been much less obvious. This pattern is most significant in the cases of France and Turkey, two allies with distinctive military preoccupations – respectively, counter-terrorism in the Sahel and the war in Syria. But what all these instances illustrate is that geography is key. The neighbourhood adjacent or proximate (as in the case of the Sahel) to the territory of NATO Europe is the focus of attention.

Region management offers a route to strategic consolidation for NATO, but it is not a miracle cure. In pursuing such a course, several key issues still need to be taken forward. The first relates to the level of ambition. Region provides a focus for activity, but the 'management' element is just as important. Insecurity is a defining feature of international politics. Most problems can only be managed, rarely solved. This need not be a counsel of despair; it is a recognition instead of the bounded nature of strategy. That recognition means an eschewal of the unachievable. One example: for NATO, region management ought not to be about democracy promotion. The spread of democratic government is rightly seen as promoting regional stability, and the Alliance has had some influence over its new members when the conditions of accession can leverage political reform. But NATO's neighbourhood is largely populated by non-democratic states without a membership perspective. Some of these (those of the Mediterranean Dialogue) are NATO partners, but even here the Alliance has proven inconsequential in prompting political reform. Only where NATO has had a long-term presence in-country (as in Afghanistan and Kosovo) has it had a political impact, and even then at great cost and with uncertain outcome.

Second, the complexity and multiplicity of issues at play in the neighbourhood mean NATO needs to continue to build relations with other international actors. The EU, for instance, is a much more significant player on issues of migration, development and cross-border cooperation. In the shape of the European Neighbourhood Policy, it has a dedicated set of policy instruments focused on the MENA region, and as of January 2020 had nine civilian and military missions there under the auspices of the Common Security and Defence Policy. Indeed, NATO's whole Projecting Stability agenda is as relevant to the EU and indeed the UN, and regional bodies such as the African Union and the Arab League, as it is to the Alliance. And even where NATO has a functional advantage, partnering remains important. The Alliance's defence posture to the east, for instance, has benefited directly from EU efforts to improve military mobility.[54] Equally, in Kosovo, Bosnia, Afghanistan and the seas off the Horn of Africa, places where both NATO and the EU have operated simultaneously, there has been an informal coordination of activities.[55]

And there is scope to do more, particularly in the shared southern neighbourhood. Such a regional partnership is, however, dependent on NATO first establishing its own credibility as an actor of consequence. The Alliance has articulated significant ambitions in the MENA region but has dedicated too few resources in their pursuit. NATO, one former Deputy Secretary General has argued, needs to approach the south with 'the same energy with which [it has] reinvigorated its posture in the east'.[56] To that end, NATO should: increase funding for defence capacity programmes; enhance its naval presence in the Mediterranean; elevate the Hub in Naples within NATO's command structure (giving it the status of a multinational divisional headquarters); identify a major regional ally (Italy, for instance) as a framework nation to coordinate NATO efforts; organize a greater number of exercises to deal with contingencies in the Mediterranean and MENA; and repurpose force initiatives such as the NATO Response Force and the 2018 Readiness Initiative for the Alliance's south as well as its east. New NATO deployments should also not be ruled out, although strict conditions should be attached. Any initial intervention should be limited in duration with a clear exit strategy or follow-on policy. This is not a recipe for cutting and running (as NATO was accused of doing following the Libyan intervention in 2011). The model here is Bosnia and Kosovo, where NATO intervened, created the conditions for political settlement and then policed it in partnership with the EU and the UN. The political and military efforts here have been significant and have stretched over many years. Prudence suggests that NATO must either intervene with commitment, as in these cases, or avoid intervention altogether.

Taking this agenda forward is about political will as much as strategic vision. The southern agenda, it is true, has acquired a distinct standing in the Alliance, but it has played second fiddle to the problem of Russia. The war in Syria has also led many NATO allies to keep their distance. NATO's southern allies, meanwhile, are at odds on what the Alliance can and should do. (In 2020, for instance, France and Turkey were backing opposing sides in Libya's civil war.) Divisions within the EU also matter as these feed mistrust in NATO where membership overlaps. The 2015 migration crisis, for example, saw France and Germany pitted against anti-immigration governments in Hungary, Romania and the Czech and Slovak Republics. In Italy, popular resentment at the large number of migrants from Libya arriving in the country was one factor in the formation of the Euro-sceptic, anti-immigrant coalition government in 2018.

These are not fortuitous circumstances for a revamped NATO approach. The possibility that it might emerge rests on a view that with NATO's reorientation toward Russia having become routine, the Alliance's political energies can be directed elsewhere. President Trump talked of a greater NATO role in the Middle East – and it is plausible that leadership and policy creativity on the issue from his successor, Joe Biden, could accommodate NATO's internal differences. Here Italy and France as key Mediterranean actors would need to be brought onside. The pivotal actor is, however, Turkey.

The strategic significance of Turkey to NATO is clear: it possesses NATO's second largest military after the US; Izmir is host to Allied Land Command; NATO AWACS aircraft participating in the anti-ISIS coalition have flown out of Turkey's Konya air base; radar for NATO's ballistic missile defence are situated at Kürecik; and some US nuclear weapons assigned to NATO are stored at Incirlik air base. As of June 2020, 600 Turkish personnel were serving in Afghanistan, making it the seventh largest troop-contributing nation to the NATO mission. Turkey is also geopolitically exceptional: it is the only NATO ally with shores on both the Black and Mediterranean Seas; it also straddles both the Middle East and Transcaucasia, having borders with Syria, Iraq and Iran, as well as with Armenia and Georgia.

Turkey's relations with the NATO allies have, however, often been fraught. In 1964, the White House warned Turkey off invading Cyprus by threatening not to honour NATO's Article 5 guarantee should the Soviet Union intervene. When Turkey did occupy northern Cyprus ten years later, it was subjected to sanctions by the US Congress. With the end of the Cold War, Turkey's strategic stock rose. It had occupied a flank position in the competition with the Soviet bloc but found itself in the early 1990s 'at a crossroads between several regions' and countries embroiled in conflict: the Balkans, Iraq and Transcaucasia.[57] During the ensuing decade, Turkey was a largely cooperative ally, lending its support to NATO enlargement, the allied operations in Bosnia and Kosovo and the establishment of ISAF in Afghanistan. Underlying tensions, however, remained. The US-led wars with Iraq in 1991 and 2003 prompted Turkey to request defensive assistance from NATO. On both occasions, the response was modest, stoking Turkish fears that the Alliance was not a credible partner. The election of the Justice and Development Party in 2002, meanwhile, prompted a turn toward national security concerns (with Kurdish separatism rising to prominence) and a more assertive promotion of Turkish interests in neighbouring regions. The Arab Spring and the subsequent war in Syria would then prove a decisive watershed. Ankara since has objected to US support of Syrian Kurdish militias to fight ISIS (a policy begun by the Obama administration and continued under President Trump) and to what it has perceived as a lack of American and European support for Turkey's elected government following a coup attempt in July 2016.[58] Doubts have also resurfaced as to the credibility of NATO's commitment. In 2013, the Alliance, at Turkey's request, deployed Patriot air and missile defences to the country, only to see the providing allies – the US, Germany and the Netherlands – remove their contribution soon after. Spain and Italy stepped into the breach, but the latter, in turn, withdrew at the end of 2019.

The allies, for their part, hold deep reservations over

Turkey's behaviour. Turkey's cross-border incursions into northern Syria to battle Kurdish militias have been seen as stoking the civil war. (Differences with the US on the issue led to the imposition of sanctions against Turkey in late 2019.) And while Turkey has accepted some 3.6 million displaced Syrians, it has also been accused of weaponizing these refugees by periodically allowing them to transit to its European neighbours. Concern has also been registered at Turkey's military interference in Libya; backing of Azerbaijan in the Nagorno-Karabakh conflict; obstruction of NATO partnerships with key neighbours such as Egypt and Armenia; assertion of territorial claims in the eastern Mediterranean; and decision to purchase a Russian S-400 air defence system.[59] Delivery of the latter began in 2019. Washington retaliated by blocking sales to Turkey of the F-35 jet fighter.

Strains with Turkey are not just an obstacle to region management in NATO's south; they impact also upon the Alliance's overall military and political cohesion. Turkey's military ties to Russia have been seen as incompatible with NATO membership and part of strategy by Moscow to split the Alliance. This has led to calls – including from some in the US Congress – that Turkey be expelled. No mechanism, however, exists for such a step. And even if it were possible, it would mean the irreversible loss of an important (if troublesome) ally. NATO's choices instead boil down to three other broad alternatives.

A first is to ride out the storm and await more amicable times. This is a hope premised on the self-correcting tendencies of the long, bumpy history of NATO–Turkey relations, and the assumption that Turkey's current circumstances are unparalleled. The war in Syria, it is assumed, will end, and President Recep Tayyip Erdoğan will eventually pass out of political life, so removing two major influences on Turkey's assertive foreign policy. Such a wait-and-see approach may well work but its outcome is uncertain. It only makes sense if supplemented by deliberate steps to shape Turkey's behaviour.

A second approach, therefore, seeks to manage the relationship through damage limitation. It assumes that the Kurdish and Syrian issues will set the course of Turkey's foreign policy for some time, that Turkey will retain authoritarian characteristics even after Erdoğan and that a pragmatic relationship with Russia based on military and energy ties will continue. Should these trends depart from the responsibilities of the Alliance (Turkey deepens its military and political ties to Russia, for instance), then the allies would have to conclude that Turkey posed too big an internal risk for cooperation in NATO to continue. As Turkey could not be expelled, other measures would have to be taken: for instance, the removal of NATO bases, the end to defence investment programmes and a curtailment of defence planning involving the country.[60] Ultimately, Turkey could be told that NATO's Article 5 collective defence obligation no longer applied.

Such measures are geared to incentivizing Turkey to move back toward the Alliance. They could, however, deepen divisions, by casting the country as a pariah. The alternative is to take a more accommodating line. This appreciates that Turkey's benefits to the Alliance outstrip the many problems and is sympathetic to the country's unique security circumstances. It also accepts that the Turkish–Russian relationship is not the beginning of some anti-NATO axis. The two sides are, after all, at loggerheads in Syria (Russia supports the Assad regime to which Turkey is opposed) and are rivals for influence in the Black Sea. In the long run, the 'conjunctural necessity' for Turkey to balance Russia will keep it anchored in NATO.[61] Turkey's purchase of the S-400 system seems untoward here, but even that has a certain logic, being a hedge against the perceived unreliability of America as an ally. In these circumstances, NATO's interest should be to preserve existing military ties with Turkey and keep the political relationship stable. Individual allies may have separate cause for complaint, but NATO as such should not seek to censure Turkey but rather to support it. For this reason, it makes good sense to honour Turkey's now frequent requests for consultations on its security situation under Article 4 of the NATO treaty and to continue with the measures of tailored military support in train since 2015. By this logic, the Alliance would have to be prepared to honour an Article 5 contingency – if Turkey ever found itself in direct conflict with Russia.[62]

Conclusion: A Strategic Centre of Gravity

Having to deal with Turkey should not stop the Alliance taking a more active stance toward its southern direction. In fact, accommodating the country ought to be part and parcel of region management in its own right. But settling on a geographical construct as a way of delineating a discretionary NATO raises questions beyond the status of this one, albeit important, ally. For starters, NATO's future-facing agenda – cyber, technology, resilient communications (and perhaps pandemic response) – is not geographically defined. One might argue, nonetheless, that region management provides NATO with a strategic centre of gravity. The Alliance is, therefore, better placed to attend to these other issues once that location is clear. The same might be said of NATO's position toward actors and issues beyond its neighbourhood. Does geography preclude an ongoing role for the Alliance in Afghanistan? It is stretching it to say that Afghanistan falls within NATO's neighbourhood. But Afghanistan is, in any case, a legacy commitment, and the subject of an American effort aimed at drawing down the NATO mission. More important in the longer term is China. Despite its geographical distance from all the allies, the country is making strategically significant inroads into NATO's neighbourhood. It thus falls within the Alliance's purview. China is one issue that will shape NATO's trajectory of development in the years to come. It is taken up in more detail in the concluding chapter.

CHAPTER SIX

American Leadership or European Autonomy?

In Chapter 2, we saw that America's commitment to NATO was cast into serious doubt by the Trump administration. The Trumpian position cannot simply be dismissed as idiosyncratic; it was the convergence of trends in American foreign policy and transatlantic relations that go back decades. Yet even under Trump, America's material support for NATO continued. We should not conclude, therefore, that the constructive aspects of the US–NATO relationship have disappeared. In this chapter, we focus on this more positive way of approaching the transatlantic link. NATO is open to a 'Goldilocks solution' – one, that is, which occupies the middle ground between two otherwise less satisfactory positions. For NATO, the satisfactory middle is a place where the US settles for the obligations of leadership (without the accompanying resentment that it is too burdensome) and the allies reciprocate with a more concrete commitment to European and transatlantic security (both through NATO itself and through EU partnership with the Alliance). Getting to that position is possible, this chapter suggests, for four reasons. First, public opinion in the US and Europe still shows a marked inclination to support NATO and, with it, American leadership. Second, the US, whatever the views of the Trump administration, derives significant benefits from NATO, and these provide an institutional anchor for a continuing and strong American commitment. Third, greater European effort (including within the EU) can be construed as being complementary rather than ill disposed to NATO and harmonious transatlantic relations. And, fourth, American foreign policy is not condemned by the exhaustion of the liberal or Wilsonian tradition to distance itself from NATO. Occupying this middle ground will not provide a permanent solution to the problems of American leadership identified in Chapter 2, but it does provide a means to render them tolerable and so ensure the transatlantic relationship continues on a sound footing.

US Leadership and Public Opinion: A Foundation for Optimism

At first blush, public opinion might not be the best way to assess (or predict) the direction of foreign policy. Governments often ignore the opinions of their electorates, and on many matters of foreign policy the public may be uninformed, disinterested or deeply divided. Yet, in democratic states, political leaders have a sense that public opinion matters – on issues such as how to react to terrorism; how long a costly foreign intervention can be sustained; how a crisis should be dealt with; and which countries should be given preference in foreign policy.[1] Public opinion, then, provides an important context within which policy decisions are made and so, in the case under consideration here, offers a proxy measure for comparing national attitudes toward American leadership of NATO and European satisfaction with it. The good news is that NATO has held up well in public estimation. Notwithstanding the policies of the Trump administration, that support is still underpinned by expectations that the US should lead the Alliance and that the European allies should follow.

Support for NATO

Publics among the allies have assessed NATO in generally favourable terms. In the US, support for the Alliance has shown a historical upward trend. Polling from 1974 indicated that 54 per cent of Americans wanted to maintain or increase the US commitment to NATO. The comparable figure stood at 60 per cent in 1990, rising to 76 per cent in 2002 (after 9/11) and a high of 78 per cent in 2014 (in the midst of the Ukraine crisis). Over the period 2002–14, clear majorities of Americans (ranging from 56 to 62 per cent in these years) regarded NATO as essential to their country's security.[2]

Views among the allies are diverse but generally supportive. Data from the German Marshall Fund indicate that Turks have been the most sceptical about NATO's value. Between 2004 and 2014, Turks who supported the idea of an 'essential' NATO ranged between 53 per cent (2004) and 49 per cent (2014), with a low of just 30 per cent in 2010. Elsewhere, only Greeks have registered a majority view ill disposed to NATO. In 2014, levels in favour of the Alliance ranged from bare majorities in Italy and Spain to 64 per cent among Germans, 68 per cent among the Portuguese, 70 per cent among the British and 81 per cent among the Dutch. European levels of support across the 2004–14 period as a whole largely paralleled those of Americans (being in a range of 55–61 per cent).[3] Among NATO's newer members, the picture is similarly varied, but generally supportive. A 2016 poll found that the publics of eleven new allies gave support to the idea that NATO should be regarded more as a protector of than a threat to their security (with support particularly high in Albania, Poland and the Baltic States).[4]

Support for NATO took a hit following Trump's election, a consequence, it appeared, of the US President's open criticisms of the Alliance.[5] Public support for NATO remained low in Turkey. Of greater significance was a drop in the Alliance's favour between 2017 and 2019 in France and Germany. However, there was also much for NATO to cheer. Favourable opinion of the Alliance in the US, according to the Pew Research Center, was no different in 2019 from levels registered during both the Bush and Obama administrations.[6] A poll carried out by the Chicago Council on Global Affairs found that support among Americans for NATO had actually *increased* under Trump.[7] Other data published in 2020 reported that 70 per cent of American respondents regarded NATO as either 'important' or 'very important' for their country's security.[8] Pew, meanwhile, found that in the cases of Canada, the UK, Poland, Italy and Spain, support for NATO either had remained constant or had marginally improved. Assessing its overall results, Pew reported, a 'median of 53 percent across 16 member countries surveyed have a favourable view of [NATO], with only 27 percent expressing a negative view'.[9]

Attitudes toward NATO's core mission of collective defence provide a further, albeit qualified, benchmark of support for the Alliance. In 2014, Pew found that 59 per cent of Americans felt this was a worthwhile task for NATO. In Europe, views were uneven. The Poles, the Dutch and the Portuguese were strong supporters; a majority of Italians, Greeks and French were opposed. But with the Germans, the British and the Turks also supportive, an overall majority of NATO publics surveyed supported the mission.[10] Such support endured during the Trump years. Data from 2020 indicated that 65 per cent of American respondents favoured US involvement in European security and defence.[11] More broadly, a YouGov survey among the publics in Denmark, France, Germany, Norway, the UK and the US found that sizeable majorities in all six supported retaining NATO's Article 5 commitment.[12] A Pew survey of sixteen allies that same year indicated that a majority of respondents in only five supported the deployment of their national armed forces to support an ally under Russian attack. In all sixteen, however, more supported than opposed the general principle that NATO writ large should use military force in such circumstances.[13]

American leadership

If the ability to lead and the legitimacy of leadership were solely dependent on asymmetries of power within NATO, then American leadership would be seemingly guaranteed into the future. Europe has a combined economic weight that matches the US (the GDP of the EU is roughly the same as that of the US) but European military equivalence is a distant prospect (in 2019, the US spent $730 billion on defence as compared to $309 billion spent by the remaining NATO allies combined).[14] American leadership would simply require that the US maintain its current military predominance. Yet leadership has a subjective as well as a material dimension: one party must be willing to provide direction, and the others must be willing to accept it. That relationship is a very complex one: it can be underpinned by a transactionalist logic (estimates of material benefit) but may be informed also by habit, cultural and political preferences, as well as perceptions of status, reputation and credibility. Our focus on public opinion here cannot deal adequately with all these factors. We use it simply to indicate a predisposition among American public opinion for international leadership and, in turn, a judgement among the allies about the desirability of followership.

Americans are generally divided on perceptions of their country's international standing. Gallup polling data going back several decades show a long-term decline in those who believe American power will increase year on year. In the early 1960s, before major losses in the Vietnam War, over 80 per cent of American respondents were positive about American power. That figure tumbled to 29 per cent in 1973. It then recovered rapidly and for the next three decades between 50 and 60 per cent believed American power would grow. A gradual tapering off of this view occurred after 9/11. In 2018, Americans were evenly split – 49 to 49 per cent – on the issue.[15] That division was reflected, in turn, in views of how the US should engage with the world. A 2019 Pew survey found a slight preference (49 to 44 per cent) for the view that the US 'should pay less attention to problems overseas' rather than 'be active in world affairs'. However, a significant majority (64 per cent) took the view that US engagement was beneficial – that, in other words, 'problems in the world would be even worse without US involvement'.[16] A separate 2019 poll found that 69 per cent of Americans felt the US should take 'an active part in world affairs' (with 30 per cent favouring 'staying out'). Most of these, moreover, felt that role should be in partnership rather than through the exercise of American dominance. Republican respondents were more likely than Democrats to favour unilateralism but, significantly, 61 per cent of Republicans still felt the benefits of an active role in the world outweighed the costs.[17]

These positions carried over into attitudes on NATO. Of those Americans questioned for the 2019 Pew survey, 77 per cent said NATO was good for the US, with high figures for both Democrats (82 per cent) and Republicans (71 per cent). Lower figures were registered on whether support for NATO should give rise to concessions on America's part. But a majority (54 per cent) agreed with the need for compromise in order to take account of the interests of allies (although this proposition found favour much more strongly among Democrats than it did Republicans).[18]

European followership

Favourable opinion of US leadership among NATO allies was dealt a severe blow by the Trump administration. Trump entered office with record low disapproval ratings in Europe for an incoming President, and his foreign policy initiatives and idiosyncratic behaviour generated 'a record collapse in approval for the US role in the world' by early 2018.[19] There was no subsequent improvement. Gallup polling in 2019 found that 59 per cent of Europeans disapproved of Trump's leadership (a disapproval rating the same as for Russian leader Vladimir Putin). Among the NATO allies, the publics in only four (Albania, Hungary, Poland and Romania) were more likely to approve than disapprove of American leadership.[20] The dent to US standing was reflected also in other measures. A 2018 Pew survey of publics in twenty-five countries found that 70 and 42 per cent of respondents, respectively, saw China and Russia's role in world affairs as having grown in the previous ten years (the comparable figure for the US was just 31 per cent).[21] A 2019 YouGov survey found that the publics in twelve NATO allies in Europe trusted the EU more than the US.[22] And in 2020, on the back of concerns at its handling of the COVID-19 pandemic, the publics in France, Germany and the UK indicated a significant deterioration of trust in American leadership.[23]

Such figures could easily be interpreted as showing an irreversible loss of support for the US among its key NATO allies. But other data point to a different view. There were also low levels of support for the US among European (and Canadian) publics during the George W. Bush years before a dramatic uptick during Obama's two terms in office. A resurgence of support for US leadership after Trump cannot, therefore, be ruled out.[24] Further, European sentiment has remained sympathetic to the underlying principle of American leadership.

Above, we noted that many Europeans took a dim view of deploying their armed forces in response to a Russian incursion against an ally. By contrast, all, according to 2019 polling, expressed a greater confidence in the willingness of the US to do so – notwithstanding Trump's own reservations on the matter.[25] A 2018 poll, meanwhile, showed that even among publics hostile to Trump (in France, Germany, the Netherlands, Spain and the UK), far more preferred the US to be the world's leading power than China.[26] COVID-19 may have damaged views of American leadership but it has also increased mistrust of Beijing. In 2020, Germans, for instance, ranked France as their most important international partner, but the US still came in second well ahead of China.[27]

The Institutional Sources of American Leadership

As we saw in Chapter 2, worries over the US commitment to NATO are of long standing and worsened significantly owing to positions adopted by the Trump administration. Yet a closer look suggests these worries may, in part, be misplaced.

In the first place, NATO has continued to enjoy broad bipartisan support in the US. In June 2017, the House of Representatives passed by a large majority (423–4) a resolution welcoming the accession of Montenegro and 'solemnly reaffirming' the commitment of the US to 'the principle of collective defence'. The NATO Support Act was passed by the House in January 2019 with a similarly large majority (357–22). Sponsored by both Democrat and Republican Representatives, this reaffirmed the principle of American membership of NATO and prohibited the President from appropriating funds for the purposes of leaving the Alliance. In December, the Bill was relayed to the upper chamber of Congress following a unanimous vote of the Senate Foreign

Relations Committee. The Senate, the previous October, voted 91–2 in favour of admitting North Macedonia into NATO. In April 2019, NATO Secretary General Jens Stoltenberg addressed a joint session of Congress – the first head of an international organization to do so.

Second, by some measures, the Trump administration actually *increased* American support for NATO and its European allies. Fiscal years 2018, 2019 and 2020 saw $4.8, $6.5 and $5.9 billion of funding, respectively, channelled to the European Deterrence Initiative.[28] (By comparison, Obama had requested $3.4 billion for 2017 to support the then European Reassurance Initiative.) In 2018, the US re-established the US Navy 2nd Fleet (mothballed in 2011) to focus on the North Atlantic and, in parallel, agreed to host a new NATO Joint Force Command at Norfolk, Virginia. The updated US Naval Strategy of 2018 and the 2019 Army Modernization Strategy, meanwhile, gave priority to investing in capabilities to support NATO's mission of countering Russia.[29] Other top-level documents – the 2017 National Security Strategy, the 2018 National Defence Strategy and the 2018 US Nuclear Posture Review – all referred to American engagement with NATO in positive terms.[30] In October/November 2018, the US provided the largest national contingent for Operation Trident Juncture in Norway – NATO's biggest military exercise since 2002. The US-led exercise Defender Europe 2020 had, prior to the COVID-19 pandemic, been scheduled to involve 20,000 American troops – 'the largest deployment of US-based forces to Europe in more than 25 years'.[31]

Reflecting such actions, NATO was also talked up by Trump administration officials. Trump's first Secretary of Defence, Jim Mattis, although taking Trump's hard line on allied defence spending, described NATO as 'a fundamental bedrock for the United States'.[32] A former NATO Supreme Allied Commander Transformation, Mattis persuaded the allies in 2018 to adopt the NATO Readiness Initiative. Mattis's successor, Mark Esper, similarly, urged the allies toward a more 'equitable burden-sharing', and to give NATO 'a broader role in the Middle East'. The core US commitment to NATO ('a willingness to defend one another'), meanwhile, remained 'ironclad'.[33] Secretaries of State Rex Tillerson and Mike Pompeo also delivered to the allies this 'familiar message': scolding them for not spending enough on defence, urging them to support reform of the Alliance but nonetheless emphasizing the special 'bond' they enjoyed with the US through NATO.[34] Even Donald Trump displayed a grudging admiration for the Alliance. One year into his term of office, he suggested 'it was no longer obsolete' (so reversing his earlier well-reported criticism). During 2019, NATO's anniversary year, Trump complimented individual allies for increases in defence spending and the Alliance more broadly for its flexibility, purpose and standing as 'a signal of truth and strength'.[35]

Trump's conversion owed much to vanity – claiming personal credit for the Alliance moving closer to American positions. But there is an underlying and much more resilient dynamic at play. Simply put, NATO delivers clear benefits to the US which are appreciated across the American military and political establishment. The US could, of course, obtain such benefits bilaterally. It has long had significant relations with individual allies (the UK, most obviously), and during the Trump period (in 2019 alone) defence agreements were struck with Poland, Greece, Hungary and the three Baltic States. NATO, however, offers something extra. Its attractiveness – or institutional pull – to the US is based on access to, and leadership of, an 'integrated military command structure' that brings together allies in 'an unrivalled platform' for the conduct of joint military operations.[36] By helping keep the peace in Europe, NATO serves US global priorities. (The US can focus its attention on other hotspots, knowing Europe is reasonably secure.) NATO also reinforces relations with what US Commander Europe Tod Wolters has described as 'some of the most capable and willing Allies and partners on the planet'.[37] It thus gives the US a forward military presence in Europe, so enabling 'quicker air, sea, and land access to other locations of strategic importance, including the Middle East and Africa'.[38]

Because these advantages are so important to the US, NATO has acquired an institutional 'stickiness', exerting a lasting hold on American foreign policy priorities. That very persistence, it is true, has given rise to tension – so the burdens of leading NATO have been felt just as acutely as its benefits. However, that burden has been offset by other institutional effects. The Alliance serves as a mechanism for aligning the preferences of the allies with those of the US. In Chapter 2, we noted the political advantages the US enjoys in NATO decision-making. This does not amount to a simple imposition of America's will. NATO's *modus operandi* – developed over decades – is of consultation and consensus building. Even the most powerful ally will be inclined to play within these multilateral rules of the game. But the 'pecking order' – the hierarchy of political and military influence – in NATO is, nonetheless, stacked in America's favour.[39] In these circumstances, rather than opting for an 'exit' from the Alliance, the US has instead preferred to exercise 'voice': utilizing the collective commitments the allies have themselves made to hold them to account. That voice may have been shrill and loud during the Trump period, but it remained a better option for the pursuit of American interests than withdrawal.[40]

The Institutional Sources of European Followership

In Chapter 3, we suggested that European military capabilities are insufficiently realized to lighten the burden of America's defence commitment to Europe. It is certainly the case that at present, and for the foreseeable future, an integrated European defence actor is not in the offing. But how much of a problem is this for the US? Here we interpret European efforts in a somewhat more positive manner. These may not be a substitute for NATO, but the European contribution to the Alliance is significant, as are other initiatives primarily, though not entirely, centred on the EU. Taken together, such efforts, rather than a hedge against a US withdrawal or a means of balancing American dominance in NATO, indicate that the European allies are pulling their strategic weight in a sustainable transatlantic relationship.

Consider NATO itself first. Discussion of the European role in the Alliance is all too often framed by issues of fiscal and operational burden-sharing. But one should not forget that, in addition, the underlying activities that constitute the regional 'node' of European defence are sustained by key allies.[41] These activities, moreover, benefit the US as much as they do NATO. The UK hosts NATO's Maritime Command (MARCOM), which includes Standing Maritime Group 1 commanded by a US Rear Admiral. The NATO Air Command at Ramstein in Germany is also the command centre of US air forces in Europe. And Naples in Italy, as well as being the location of a NATO Joint Force Command (overseeing NATO's 'regional hub for the south' and the NATO mission in Kosovo), hosts the US Sixth Fleet, US Naval Forces Europe and US Naval Forces Africa. NATO's land-based ballistic missile defence, a system predicated on US equipment and technology, is hosted by Poland and Romania.

Outside of NATO, the European allies have grouped together in a range of formats. These include the JEF, led by the UK and involving the Netherlands alongside Baltic and Scandinavian countries; the French-led European Intervention Initiative ('EI2'); and the Northern Group of countries bordering the Baltic and North Seas, Nordic Defence Cooperation (NORDEFCO). These important 'clusters' we consider further in Chapter 7.

As for the EU, this has been the site since the early 1990s of efforts to obtain a greater 'European autonomy' from the US – defined by two EU experts as 'the political and military capability [. . .] to take decisions and to embark on initiatives involving the projection of military power with limited or no assistance from the United States'.[42] That ambition has not always played well in Washington. Bill Clinton's Secretary of State, Madeleine Albright, warned in 1998 that European collaboration would receive America's support only if it did not decouple the allies from the Alliance, duplicate efforts in NATO or discriminate against non-EU NATO allies such as Turkey.[43] These objections have not gone away. Two Trump administration officials noted in a letter to the EU's High Representative for Foreign Affairs and Security Policy that 'EU capabilities' risked 'developing in a manner that produces duplication, non-interoperable military systems, diversion of scarce resources, and unnecessary competition between NATO and the EU'.[44] Those worries were made worse by the high level of ambition certain European leaders had attached to EU initiatives, with both Emmanuel Macron and Angela Merkel calling for the establishment of a 'European army'.[45]

American concerns are driven, in part, by commercial considerations as many EU initiatives on defence development potentially exclude 'third-party' involvement, so ruling out a place for US defence firms. But the strategic objection, that the EU is driving a wedge between Europe and the US, is misplaced. The idea of the EU developing a credible military arm to rival NATO is, as we pointed out in the previous chapter, overstated. Of the EU member states, France has gone furthest in arguing for European strategic autonomy, but the French vision is not antithetical to NATO. Greater European collaboration is intended not for the traditional NATO task of collective defence but for crisis management operations in the EU's (and NATO's) southern neighbourhood, the aim being to deal with crises when NATO (and, by extension, the US) is not engaged. This, one report has suggested, means 'bring[ing] European armies together as a single set of forces as a complement to, but not a replacement of, other structures such as NATO'.[46] There is, in fact, little evidence to show that the EU's developing security and military remit has harmed NATO or diminished American leadership of the Alliance. All of which suggests that the more constructive approach for Washington would be to promote NATO–EU collaboration.

EU prerogatives in the area of a Common Security and Defence Policy (CSDP) are enshrined in the 2008 Lisbon Treaty. CSDP allows for 'the progressive framing of a common Union defence policy [that] will lead to a common defence'.[47] But this ambition is far from being realized. As the Lisbon Treaty acknowledges, a common defence would need to be compatible with the obligations many EU members have toward NATO. And NATO, a 2017 EU document makes clear, 'continue[s] to be the cornerstone of collective defence for its members'.[48] More credible are 'missions outside the Union for peace-keeping, conflict prevention and strengthening international security'. It is here that the EU has been most active and where it has developed an institutional capacity. Such initiatives, and indeed EU 'defence', are not in practice antithetical to NATO.

The most recent institutional initiative follows on from the adoption in 2016 of the EU Global Strategy (EUGS).

This provided for the creation of a Military Planning and Conduct Capability (MPCC) attached to the EU Military Staff. Considered by some as a possible step toward a permanent EU operational headquarters, the MPCC's remit was actually rather limited: to 'non-executive military missions' (i.e. military training missions) and the planning and conduct of 'one executive military CSDP operation limited to EU Battlegroup size'.[49] The MPCC was also created explicitly 'with the principle of avoiding unnecessary duplication with NATO'.[50] Two years in, the MPCC was appraised positively: it had improved the efficiency of ongoing EU missions and was seen as an 'attractive platform' for future operations. None of this, however, cut across NATO's prerogatives.[51]

A second initiative is Permanent Structured Cooperation (PESCO). Launched in December 2017, PESCO was conceived as a framework for accelerated defence cooperation among self-selecting states within the EU. Forty-seven PESCO projects had been earmarked by November 2019, including unmanned drones, ISR capabilities, radar jamming, space surveillance and upgrades to attack helicopters. PESCO was not designed to draw resources away from NATO. As Thierry Tardy has pointed out, PESCO is designed to 'encourage European states to spend more, develop capacities together and conduct operations in a way [. . .] that will benefit European security and the institutions that support it'. And because armed forces in Europe are national ('PESCO-developed capabilities' are not pre-assigned to the EU), they are as likely to be used in coalitions or in NATO as they are in the EU itself.[52] NATO SACEUR Tod Wolters noted similarly that where PESCO projects filled gaps in European forces (the specific example he gave was mine counter-measures), they were to be welcomed.[53]

The European Defence Fund (EDF), third, was created in 2017 to provide 'financial support for EU Member States [in] the implementation of cooperative defence projects'. In 2018, 13 billion euros was allocated to the EDF for the period 2021–7. The EDF (alongside PESCO and a fourth initiative, the Coordinated Annual Review on Defence [CARD]) was geared toward producing 'a more coherent set of usable, deployable, interoperable and sustainable capabilities and forces available to EU Member States for national and multinational missions and operations'.[54] Some EDF projects have been intended to provide specific EU assets, but in the main, the project outcomes would (as with PESCO) be under national control and so, for those EU members in the Alliance, be available to NATO. EDF-financed weapons systems will be built to the common standards established by the European Defence Standards Reference System (EDSTAR). EDSTAR relies heavily, if not exclusively, on pre-existing NATO standardization agreements. Consequently, it is highly unlikely that EDF projects would degrade NATO interoperability or limit the American ability to establish (indirectly) technological benchmarks for weapons systems. Similarly, the CARD process (an extension of the Capability Development Plans the EU had been running since 2008) was informed by capability assessments already generated in NATO. Because EDF and CARD are actually complementary to NATO, the worry is not that they might succeed but rather that they could fail to deliver. Shifts in EU budgetary priorities imposed by COVID-19 have reined in the level of ambition. The EU's Multiannual Financial Framework for 2021–7 agreed by the European Council in July 2020 saw a 40 per cent reduction in the EDF budget.

To summarize, greater EU autonomy need not be at odds with NATO or American leadership of the Alliance. Undeniably, the development of EU capabilities has progressed because of a desire among some member states to lessen security dependency on the US. This is a trend that pre-dates the divisions generated by the Bush and Trump presidencies, and cannot simply be read as a form of anti-Americanism. In the late 1990s, UK Prime Minister Tony Blair, for instance, saw European autonomy as a way of strengthening the transatlantic relationship by demonstrating the Europeans were a reliable partner. EU statements ever since have emphasized the complementarity of EU and NATO action. NATO and the EU have had a formal working relationship since the early 2000s. That relationship is hardly perfect. Its original focus on conflict management has given rise to just two formal cooperative initiatives: in Macedonia in 2003 and Bosnia in 2004. Joint Declarations signed in 2016 and 2018 have, however, moved it ahead significantly, into areas judged a priority by NATO and US military planners: military mobility in Europe, counter-terrorism, and hybrid and cyber threats. In June 2019, a joint EU–NATO progress report noted seventy-four 'common proposals' for joint action.[55] Practical progress has occurred despite entrenched political problems. Disagreements between Turkey (a member of NATO but not of the EU) and Cyprus (a member of the EU but not of NATO) have for many years meant political deadlock in EU–NATO formats. But workarounds have been found. As noted in Chapter 5, an absence of formally agreed procedures for cooperation has not prevented the EU and NATO coordinating their activities in Kosovo and Afghanistan. The same applies to EU and NATO maritime missions off the Gulf of Aden.

It is noteworthy that within NATO, Turkey, not the US, has been the spoiler of the EU–NATO relationship. Still, the US has not shown much enthusiasm. This is regrettable given that the EU–NATO partnership has the potential to become, according to Thierry Tardy and Gustav Lindstrom, 'a central component of the broad security governance architecture' of Europe. That potential we noted in the previous chapter in the reinforcing roles the EU and NATO can play in region management.

Here, the EU is better placed to cover security-development issues at 'the lower end of the use-of-force spectrum', whereas NATO remains '*the* collective defence organisation' and covers better 'the upper end of the military spectrum'. But, as Tardy and Lindstrom point out, such a division of labour is currently 'ad hoc, under-conceptualised, and [. . .] largely lacking in [. . .] strategic direction'. Consequently, there is no discussion in either the EU or NATO or between the two organizations on 'who does what, when and where'.[56]

There are two ways to tackle this problem. The first is a continuation of technical and operational cooperation as a way of keeping the relationship focused on practical deliverables. The EU's move into military planning and defence budgeting noted above is one area where expert-level cooperation has proven beneficial and largely non-controversial. Other areas might include the sharing of classified information between the two organizations (currently limited owing to the absence of an appropriate security of information agreement), the more active secondment of NATO officials to EU missions and the establishment of thematic working groups (on cyber defence, for instance) to develop joint doctrine.[57] All of these would require American buy-in and the exercise of a greater degree of influence over the EU–NATO relationship than has been evident to date.

A second approach is much more strategic in nature and would entail not simply an extension of EU–NATO relations, but also a deepening of the existing but currently sporadic political and security dialogue between the EU and the US. While this might be seen as adding to the complexity of transatlantic relations, such a dialogue has a clear rationale. As Marianne Riddervold and Akasemi Newsome have suggested, 'no other regions of the world are as closely connected in economics, security and politics as Europe and the US'.[58] Alicia Von Voss and Florence Schimmel have argued similarly that the EU and the US are (along with China and Russia) two of the four 'major players in international relations'.[59] In development, trade, the environment as well as security, the EU has acquired 'actorness' because it can call upon significant financial resources and administrative-legislative capabilities, and because it has a demonstrable impact upon its external environment.[60] NATO has actorness of a sort, but this closely overlaps with the preferences of its leading power. To privilege a US–EU security dialogue, then, is simply to recognize the reality that it is the US that matters when driving forward NATO priorities.

What, then, would such an EU–US dialogue aim to achieve? As Sven Biscop has suggested, it would not be a short cut to some grand strategic bargain. Transatlantic differences render such an outcome improbable. Dialogue, he suggests, 'will not in itself make divergences go away, but it will make them easier to manage'.[61] It would be overly optimistic to imagine such dialogue will close the transatlantic gap on issues such as climate change or Iran (or indeed, substitute for existing international forums should a post-Trump America return to constructive engagement on these issues). But on other issues – China or international responses to COVID-19, for instance – improved EU–US dialogue could pave the way to more practical measures being discussed in NATO and, by extension, between the Alliance and the EU.

American Foreign Policy: A Jacksonian Ascendancy?

The turn toward Jacksonian thinking under Donald Trump (see Chapter 2) was, for some, a 'historical watershed' marking a decisive shift away from the Wilsonian tradition of liberal internationalism in American foreign policy.[62] Jacksonianism, it is true, has solid roots in American culture and its influence under Trump was triggered by a growing disillusionment with what the presumptive President claimed in 2016 was a 'long history of failed policies' carried out by successive US administrations.[63] It is not a given, however, that this break will be so deep and enduring as to render unilateralism, neo-isolationism and 'America First' nationalism the signature features of how the US views the world.

Walter Russell Mead has suggested that Trump's platform was, first and foremost, a political revolt against the American political establishment. It reflected in some ways a lack of trust in those who had for many years conducted foreign policy (in both the Republican and Democratic parties) on America's behalf. But more so, Trump's populist, anti-establishment appeal rested on domestic issues such as immigration, gun control, cultural alienation of working-class white Americans and economic decline.[64] In office, some of Trump's biggest foreign policy departures were on matters that related to this domestic agenda: imposing tariffs to revive certain sectors of the US economy and withdrawing from the Paris Agreement on climate change because it was seen as damaging to American mining and heavy industry. In other regards, one detailed study of the Trump administration found, 'Trump's America First vision [. . .] had much less impact on the nation's strategic course than most imagined it would.' America First was just another way of justifying American primacy, the lodestar that had guided all administrations since World War II.[65] Primacy in the Trump version was premised on transactionalism (giving greater priority to American interests in institutional settings), a desire for status recognition and an emphasis on the special privileges the US should be accorded as the world's 'No 1' power.[66] While such positions connected to a Jacksonian view, they were not dependent on it. The Trump administration eschewed any effort to articulate a coherent intellectual or strategic vision of America's place in the world. Its pursuit of primacy was, rather, structurally determined – a continuation of the default option of American foreign policy.

Two implications follow here. The first is that Jacksonianism as a body of thought has a tenuous hold on American politics. It is likely to recede from view following Trump's defeat in the 2020 presidential election. Biden's victory will not necessarily take the US back to the foreign policy precepts of the Obama period, but it will certainly revive America's engagement with alliances and international organizations, NATO included.[67] That said, the Trump period should not be written off as an irrelevant interlude. The crude rhetoric, political showmanship and disdain for diplomatic niceties might pass but Trump's close questioning of overseas commitments, demand that allies pay their way and recognition that the international realm is a competitive and dangerous place are all likely to persist.[68] '[L]iberal universalism', as two observers of American foreign policy have noted, will 'no longer [be] on the table'.[69]

In such circumstances, what other traditions of thinking in American foreign policy are relevant? We have already noted the waxing and waning influence of Wilsonianism, but another, longer, tradition – what Mead labels the Hamiltonian – is also important. This tradition has always been about the US engaging globally. In its nineteenth- and early twentieth-century elaboration, it mirrored the rise of America's economic status, and a consequent advocacy of open trade and freedom of navigation. 'After World War II,' Mead explains, 'Hamiltonian opinion would support a world-wide web of security treaties, both collective and bilateral, with the object both of containing the Soviet Union and of replacing the British Empire with a global security structure.'[70] Hamiltonian thinking lies behind the US commitment to international order through institutions and law, but this is a commitment shorn of Wilsonian idealism. At its core is an assumption that whatever the nature of America's global engagement, the US is not simply a beneficent hegemon. Like any other state, the US should 'consider its interests, take stock of its strengths and its weaknesses, and develop a policy that [. . .] safeguard[s] those interests within the limits of its resources'.[71] Such limits have not always been a constraint on American action, hence the overstretch we detailed in Chapter 1. A contemporary Hamiltonian approach is more sensitive to US foreign entanglements. It affirms the obligations of America's treaty commitments, provides clear focus as to where those commitments apply and engineers a division of labour between the US and its allies that lightens the burden on America. None of this is new as such: almost every US President in NATO's history has attempted something similar. As far back as 1967, President Richard Nixon warned that 'old institutions' such as the UN and NATO were 'obsolete and inadequate' and a new *modus operandi* had to be engineered with America's allies.[72] While this may sound like the sort of thing Trump would express several decades later, Nixon's purpose was more constructive than Trump's rhetorical brow-beating. It was to obtain a productive *modus operandi* with allies through American leadership. In Henry Kissinger's formulation, the US needed 'to navigate between over-extension and abdication'.[73] That challenge remains. Meeting it requires developing the triangle of NATO–EU–US partnership outlined above and taking advantage of the reservoir of support that still remains for American leadership.

Conclusion: Striking a Viable Transatlantic Bargain

A refreshed Hamiltonian foreign policy provides the greatest opportunity for achieving balance between American leadership and the European quest for greater autonomy; the Jacksonian option is only likely to lead to the marginalization of NATO and a nullification of the Article 5 guarantee contained in the North Atlantic Treaty. Posited in this way, the impression appears to be that American leaders make clear-cut choices between one foreign policy tradition and another. This, of course, is an over-simplification. As Mead suggests, 'American foreign policy is complex at its core. At any given moment it is more likely to be the product of a wide and diffuse coalition [. . .] than of a single unitary vision.'[74] That said, consideration of foreign policy traditions helps us to understand how past practices of American strategy and statecraft shape the options open to US decision-makers. To whatever foreign policy tradition (or mix of traditions) the US steers – the Hamiltonian, Wilsonian or Jacksonian[75] – its leaders would do well to observe the 'Peter Parker principle' that with great power comes great responsibility.[76] Expressed more fully by Winston Churchill, 'Where there is great power there is great responsibility, where there is less power there is less responsibility, and where there is no power there can [. . .] be no responsibility.'[77] The Peter Parker principle requires that US foreign policy assess accurately America's current and future power position in the international system as well as the degree of responsibility the US should assume for global order, the limits of that obligation and the appropriate level of responsibility to be assigned to its allies. The US must assume the greater share of the burden for the security of the transatlantic community owing to its overwhelming power. But the European side of the transatlantic relationship also needs to step up. We have seen in this chapter that the basis for a mutually advantageous partnership still exists, one that continues to be underpinned by broad public support. That relationship has not always been easy and it has run into some particular difficulties in the Trump period. In the next chapter, we consider how it can be repaired by reference to the thorny issues of defence spending and burden-sharing.

CHAPTER SEVEN

Cash, Capabilities and NATO Effectiveness

How much the allies spend on defence has been a central issue in NATO's corrosive burden-sharing debate. The problem here is not just one of resource. Spending more on defence, as we pointed out in Chapter 5, is not necessarily an effective way to tackle the Alliance's shortfalls. Equally, it does not address some of NATO's bigger problems: how to prioritize Alliance tasks and overcome inefficiencies in the organization of national armed forces and, by extension, the duplication of effort between them. Increased resources may also simply be unavailable. In Chapter 3, we pointed out that social and economic trends make any shift from civilian to military budgetary priorities particularly difficult – a situation that has been compounded by the impact of COVID-19.

In this chapter, we address the conjoined problems of fiscal constraint, burden-sharing and capability shortfalls while acknowledging the tight position the NATO allies occupy. Our recommendations follow from a creative rethinking of the underlying nature of these problems. The chapter is divided into three parts. The first revisits the burden-sharing issue, presenting it in a way that goes beyond the divisive caricature of allied 'free-riding'. The second part does something similar with NATO's well-known 2 per cent of GDP defence spending benchmark. The final part considers capability improvements, looking at NATO's own initiatives in this regard and the potential offered by greater collaboration among groups or 'clusters' of allies.

Operational Burden-Sharing: A Fair Share?

The problem of operational burden-sharing is not a simple matter of transatlantic division where the US puts in a disproportionate effort compared to all other allies. As noted in Chapter 3, in out-of-area operations (Afghanistan most notably), many allies have made significant contributions, often over and above their fair share. That said, NATO remains dependent upon US leadership and commitment. Addressing such a state of affairs requires greater allied effort as a way of balancing American input. In Chapter 6, we detailed some ways in which that effort is in train: by way of 'nodal defence', NATO–EU partnership and UK- and French-led initiatives. Here, we pinpoint other areas where the allied contribution is significant and draw out its implications.

NATO 'returned' to Europe operationally after 2014 as a consequence of the Ukraine crisis. That return significantly altered the operational burden-sharing landscape. A snapshot of activities in the autumn of 2020 shows three NATO missions (Baltic Air Policing, missile defence of Turkey and AWACS patrols over Eastern Europe) all absent American participation. Poland, meanwhile, supported by Germany and Denmark, was host to NATO's Multinational Corps Northeast; Romania took a similar role for NATO's Multinational Division Southeast; Poland was the lead nation of the VJTF; and the UK and Germany led two of four battle groups of NATO's eFP located in the Baltic States and Poland. (Canada and the US headed up the remaining two.) In addition, over three-quarters of the personnel involved in KFOR in Kosovo were from NATO European allies or partners, working alongside around 660 American personnel.

Military exercises tell a similar story. From 2014, these increased in scale and number, with a greater emphasis on what the Alliance dubbed 'assurance' and 'readiness'

– signalling to Russia, in other words, an ongoing commitment to collective defence. In the previous chapter, we noted how exercises such as Trident Juncture 2018 and Defender Europe 2020 had seen a massive US commitment. But these exercises also entailed significant allied effort. Prior to 2015, the largest NATO exercise of the preceding decade had been Steadfast Jazz in 2013. That involved a total 4,000 deployed military personnel drawn from seven allies. Trident Juncture 2015 (NATO's largest exercise since 2002) included every ally as well as the integration of seventeen separate national military exercises. Trident Juncture 2018, hosted by Norway, involved 20,000 Americans plus 30,000 personnel from all NATO's twenty-eight other allies as well as partners Sweden and Finland. Defender Europe 2020, originally planned to include 20,000 US and 17,000 allied troops and to span the entire eastern front of the Alliance, was downsized to a joint exercise between American and Polish armed forces because of COVID-19.

Such efforts suggest that any resolution of the burden-sharing problem should begin by differentiating between individual allies. Donald Trump's demand that '*Europe* must do more' is a false reading of the issue.[1] Many European allies, and, indeed, Canada and Turkey also, already contribute significantly to NATO. Further, contributions to NATO operations cannot be captured by a binary classification between those allies carrying an asymmetrically large burden and those dismissed as free-riders. It is rare that a NATO ally makes no contribution to an operation or refuses to participate in a NATO exercise. As Richard Cornes and Todd Sandler once suggested, the problem within the Alliance is more with 'easy riders' than 'free riders'.[2] Hardly anyone in NATO gets a *free* ride (a zero contribution to public provision). An *easy* ride, in which a member is not making the 'right' contribution, is more common. If 'easy riding' were to figure more in policy analyses, it would clarify the state of allied burden-sharing. As a policy matter, the distinction would allow for a more focused marshalling of political effort by identifying states that are unambiguous free-riders and subjecting them to peer pressure from an enlarged coalition of states.

Many analyses have pointed out that the Alliance is already 'multi-tiered'. That characterization is often a source of criticism – again, most often among American policy-makers. The reality, however, is that NATO has hung together rather well despite these differences of effort. It has long tolerated, in effect, a form of 'variable geometry'. Some allies may lack commitment some of the time, but in any given NATO policy, operation or initiative allies who are laggardly are balanced by those who cooperate with greater degrees of enthusiasm and application.[3] In an alliance, one way to better harness such differentiation is through task specialization. As Peter Corterier noted as far back as 1990, specialization minimizes 'wasteful duplication and overlap', and provides an opportunity for smaller allies to contribute to broad alliance goals by taking advantage of either their geographical location or possession of a specific capability.[4] Corterier's point was meant to be an encouragement. As NATO moved into the post-Cold War world, so, he argued, the opportunities for specialization would increase as the Alliance's mission broadened.

In promoting specialization, however, NATO has needed to take account of three important considerations. First, the Alliance sets considerable store by standardization of equipment, weaponry, means of communication and operating procedures. A specialized contribution, therefore, has to fit within, not run counter to, the need for interoperability between national armed forces. Second, for specialization to work it requires an 'alliance-wide division of labour' where a particular capability is developed in the context of NATO's overall force requirements rather than as the by-product of uncoordinated national 'burden-shedding'.[5] Third, specialization carries a certain risk: if an alliance becomes too dependent on the contributions of some allies, then this can cause political and operational problems. As Joshua Foust has noted, '[I]f highly specialized countries disagree with the larger consensus, it might only take one or two countries to hobble any chances of [mission] success by withholding their equipment and personnel.'[6]

NATO has promoted role specialization in the post-Cold War period as part of a search for efficiencies and rationalized defence budgets, and as a way of incorporating new, mainly small and medium-sized members into the Alliance. The 2002 Prague summit referred to specialization as part of the 'continuing Alliance effort to improve and develop new military capabilities'.[7] Similarly, 'Smart Defence', launched in 2011, would, the NATO Secretary General suggested, entail the allies 'focus[ing] on certain capabilities – either alone or working together'.[8] As an official primer for the 2014 NATO summit explained, the aim here was 'specialization by design', concentrating on national strengths and coordinated defence budgets.[9] That injunction came, however, at a watershed. Prior to 2014, specialization was primarily geared to conflict management and expeditionary or out-of-area missions. NATO's reorientation to collective defence after 2014 required a refocus on other capability priorities.

How far, then, has the development of specialized capabilities worked in NATO's case? Jennifer Moroney noted in 2004 that NATO operations in Afghanistan and the Balkans had provided a testing ground for specialized provision. This was to the benefit of some of NATO's smaller new members, who, without a broad spectrum of forces, were still able to provide 'gap-filling capabilities'.[10] In Afghanistan, this included Slovak military engineers, Slovenian special forces, Bulgarian medics and Croatian military police. Hungary, Lithuania and the Czech Republic, meanwhile, all took on lead-nation roles in Provincial Reconstruction Teams. A similar situation has occurred in contingencies focused on Europe. Some small allies – the Baltic States being a good example – have managed to provide 'vital capabilities previously absent from the Alliance's toolbox' (cyber defence in the case of Estonia, counter-propaganda in the case of Latvia).[11]

Such cherry-picking of existing national assets only works up to a point. Coordination remains key. Otherwise, specialization will occur by default rather than by design and some capabilities will be preserved that lack interoperability across the Alliance. Partnering is also important. This has long been recognized even among some of NATO's more able and wealthy members. Using the example of collaboration with Denmark and the Netherlands in air transport and fighter jets, Norwegian Defence Minister Kristin Kohn Devold pointed out as early as 2002 that 'one solution' to capability development was 'to identify strategic partners and to work together with them to maximize capabilities'.[12] We shall return to this point below, looking at the idea of 'clustered' allies.

Measuring the Defence Burden: Shooting at the Right Target

NATO has set great store by its defence spending targets. We have already noted in Chapter 3 that these are a crude way of measuring allied effort. The 2 per cent GDP target is an especially blunt instrument. A 2017 report of the NATO Parliamentary Assembly defended it on the grounds that the measure was 'an important political symbol', one that promoted 'Alliance solidarity and cohesion' as members made collective efforts to meet an agreed metric.[13] But wielding the target can also be a source of political division, as Donald Trump's unsophisticated admonishment of 'delinquent' allies demonstrates. More fundamentally, the GDP spending target is a good example of 'metric dysfunction': judging a well-intentioned objective (in this case, achieving a fairness of spending among allies) against an easily measured but unsatisfactory standard. As Jerry Muller has noted, '[W]hat is most easily measured is rarely what is most important, indeed sometimes not important at all.' Concentrating on the 'easily measurable' is especially tempting in large, multifunctional organizations where the setting of targets seemingly cuts through complexity and provides the organization's leadership with a potent weapon for articulating purpose and berating subordinates.[14] In NATO, that dynamic is not just evident in the comments of American Presidents; NATO Secretaries General have been equally enthusiastic in cajoling allies to spend more on defence. But this political imperative can mask underlying problems.

As Kathleen Hicks and others have suggested, calculating defence spending as a percentage of GDP can give rise to some perverse outcomes. For instance, if defence spending is constant in absolute terms, an economic recession (and an accompanying fall in GDP) will nonetheless increase the percentage GDP figure (a reason why Greece has for many years exceeded the 2 per cent benchmark). The reverse also applies. A country whose GDP increases rapidly may end up with a GDP defence share that appears to be growing only slowly even when the absolute level of defence spending is increasing at pace (a situation that has on occasion pertained to Germany).[15] How defence data are reported can also be an issue. NATO relies on data provided by its members, and its figures are sometimes at odds with those presented by independent sources. The authoritative Stockholm International Peace Research Institute (SIPRI) reported UK defence spending in 2019 at 1.7 per cent of GDP, well short of the 2.13 per cent reported to NATO (so fuelling suspicions that the British government was padding the figures). The figures for Germany were also significantly lower in SIPRI's estimation.[16]

How spending is measured carries political consequences. To be below a target casts allies in a poor light. The UK example is especially telling: meeting the 2 per cent benchmark has become emblematic of the British government's claim to be a leading ally and privileged partner of the US. For Washington, meanwhile, spending guidelines have become a political weapon by which it can cajole the allies. But Washington's argument that it is spending above the NATO average and is being let down by the allies is misleading. The majority of US spending is not dedicated to NATO. The responsibilities of the US are global in scope and only a small proportion (perhaps as little as 5 per cent) of its defence budget is concerned with European security.[17] Canada, Turkey, France and the UK also dedicate significant parts of their defence budgets to non-NATO and non-European tasks (although not on the scale of the US). By contrast, many allies – Poland, Norway, the Baltic States and Germany, for instance – focus almost all of their defence efforts close to NATO's core.

Other problems relate to the narrowness of the GDP measure. It is a metric of *defence* spending only and not of how allies contribute more broadly to international security and stability. The issues here are not merely for the statisticians. NATO in its own Strategic Concept identifies three core tasks: of crisis management, cooperative security as well as collective defence. Judging the performance of allies by defence spending alone thus seems at odds with NATO's own stated purpose and inconsistent with the complexity of contemporary security challenges. Denmark provides a telling example. It has no intention of hitting the share of GDP figure by the 2024 target date, but in NATO missions over the years it has contributed 'without complaint or caveats'.[18]

Further, even with a narrow meaning of defence, the 2 per cent benchmark fails to capture some important ways in which the allies contribute. As two retired US officials have suggested, '[T]he United States gets real fiscal advantages out of the NATO security architecture.' As they noted in 2017, 85,000 US troops were in Europe, with many in Germany, where bases and facilities are offered tax free or with financial waivers, and where road and other communication links to those installations are provided free of charge.[19] Much of this support sits outside calculations of German defence spending.

If NATO's defence GDP measure is flawed, what are the alternatives? First, we should acknowledge that in the Alliance itself the 2 per cent target is by no means the sole measure of commitment. 'Usability targets' for land forces have been around since 2006. The Alliance also uses a relatively sophisticated cost-share formula for funding its common civil and military budgets (used to fund the running costs of NATO HQ and command structures), based on the size of Gross National Income. (And here, in a concession to the Trump administration, it was agreed that from 2021 Germany would match US payments, so making it the joint largest contributor in the Alliance.) These indices are, however, rather narrow in scope. Broader measures focus on what has been dubbed 'security burden sharing'.[20] German Defence Minister Ursula von der Leyen argued in March 2017 in favour of an 'activity index', something that would take into account contributions to overseas military missions (both NATO and non-NATO).[21] Wolfgang Ischinger, the Chair of the annual Munich Security Conference, has suggested bringing together military spending and development aid in a 3 per cent of GDP target. As Garrett Martin and Balazs Martonffy have noted, however, neither of these two German proposals have gained much political traction, in part because they would require measuring through a NATO standard activities that sit outside of the

Alliance. This, in fact, is a problem with many otherwise very laudable suggestions. Once contributions to UN or EU missions are factored in, or account taken of aid (or other inputs such as the costs of imposing sanctions or hosting refugees),[22] then the calculation is not only extraordinarily complex but also far removed from the debate in the Alliance. Martin and Martonffy's answer is to focus on metrics which NATO controls, but to use these in an aggregated manner – what they refer to as an 'Alliance Contribution Rating' that looks at metrics relevant to all three of NATO's core tasks (see Box 7.1).[23] Such an approach incorporates activities across a broad spectrum and so acknowledges the contributions of allies otherwise marginalized by the narrow 2 per cent spending measure. It also pulls together different types of effort we have encountered throughout this volume (and, indeed, in this

Box 7.1 Alliance contribution rating

Collective Defence Grade Rating

- percentage of GDP spent on defence
- proportion of defence budget committed to major equipment and research and development
- passive contributions such as hosting or supporting NATO bases, infrastructure and assets

Crisis Management Grade Rating

- ratio of national forces that are deployable
- proportion of that ratio deployed in NATO missions
- number of missions an ally contributes to
- length of deployment in NATO missions, accounting for years of membership

Cooperative Security Grade Rating

- involvement in NATO exercises
- involvement in future planning activities (e.g. hosting NATO Centres of Excellence)
- contributions to NATO partnership activities

Source: Garrett Martin and Balazs Martonffy, 'Abandon the 2 Percent Obsession: A New Rating for Pulling Your Weight in NATO', *War on the Rocks*, 19 May 2017, *https://warontherocks.com/2017/05/abandon-the-2-percent-obsession-a-new-rating-for-pulling-your-weight-in-nato/*.

chapter). Ultimately, this would involve a weighting of contributions in order to arrive at some sort of grade for each of the three ratings. While there would still be winners and losers in this exercise, the benefit is that it would take the sting out of the blame game that has attended the GDP measure and acknowledge more openly the fine-grained manner in which allies support one another. Such measures aren't necessarily a radical departure from existing practice. For new allies, accession criteria will have already subjected them to something similar. Their relevance also extends to longer-established allies. To take just two examples. Iceland, first, is routinely excluded from NATO defence expenditure calculations as it has no national armed forces. This has proven uncontroversial (Iceland rarely figures in Trump's list of 'delinquent' allies) in part because it makes up for that omission in other important ways. Iceland regularly hosts NATO exercises; is integrated into the NATO air defence system; and US flights from Keflavík air base monitor Russian air and naval activity in the so-called 'Greenland–Iceland–UK' gap. The Iceland Crisis Response Unit has seen action in Afghanistan. Politically more significant is the case of Germany. Although chronically under the GDP target, against most other measures cited in Table 7.1 it performs well. Its much-maligned armed forces are, as noted below, also central to NATO's Framework Nations Concept.

Aggregating Capabilities

As we saw in Chapter 3, the allies have made considerable efforts to modernize their military capabilities. There are some areas, however, where the capability gap with the US is unbridgeable and will persist. Such a state of affairs need not be framed as a problem. Alliances are, after all, about 'capability aggregation': that is, the sharing of resources by allies for mutual benefit.[24] Resources are not always equally provided – allies, after all, differ in their level of ability. It is also inefficient, indeed unnecessary, simply to duplicate assets. If a well-resourced ally is prepared to provide cover in certain areas, there should be less need for others to step in.

The practical consequences of this alliance dynamic have been well laid out by a former UK Permanent Representative to NATO. Noting that in eight of NATO's twenty-one capability shortfalls, the European allies 'are particularly dependent on the United States', Sir Adam Thompson suggested nonetheless that 'if the United States is happy to provide a particular capability, it is not necessarily sensible for European allies to invest heavily in that area as opposed to making up shortfalls in other areas.'[25] There should be no expectation, in other words, that NATO's effectiveness requires both sides of the Atlantic to develop equivalent capabilities. The allies should seek to complement American capabilities not match them. That logic of sharing not matching also applies *within* Europe. Many small and medium-sized allies do not regard it as feasible to field certain capabilities and look to their neighbours for support. Denmark, for instance, decommissioned its submarine fleet in 2004 and now cooperates more closely with the German navy.

Yet even with these qualifications in mind, there remain many areas in which greater allied effort is expected. NATO itself has, in recent years, developed interesting ways to aggregate resources more effectively. These we outline below.

The NATO Defence Planning Process

NATO lacks any enforcement powers over allies. What military capabilities a nation develops or how much it spends on defence is ultimately a sovereign national decision. However, throughout its history, NATO has sought to influence those decisions through allied defence planning (and a parallel force generation process). The point, as a 2001 edition of the *NATO Handbook* explained, is that 'in reaching their individual decisions, member countries take into account the overall needs of the Alliance'. In 2001, NATO had just introduced a 'single, coherent and streamlined process' to 'ensure that [it] continue[d] to develop the forces and capabilities needed to conduct the full range of Alliance missions'. Questionnaires, reports, reviews and so on were generated with a view to steering allies toward the requirements of an overall NATO Force Plan and Defence Review backed by Ministerial Guidance agreed among NATO Defence Ministers.[26]

In 2009, a new NATO Defence Planning Process (NDPP) was introduced with a tighter focus on capability requirements. Overall, capabilities were geared toward meeting NATO's 'level of ambition' – defined at the time as 'two major joint operations and six small joint operations, if required'. With a view toward fairer burden-sharing, it was also expected that no single ally would furnish more than half of any given capability.[27] In 2019, it was reported that 'seventeen critical capability shortfalls' had been identified by the NDPP.[28] The NATO Secretary General noted around the same time that the NDPP was still crucial to 'ensure [that] Allies are investing in new technologies'.[29] It was also, he pointed out, the most effective way for aggregating capabilities. '[M]any small- or medium-sized Allies, [. . .] cannot provide all the different capabilities you need to provide a credible deterrence and defence.' The aim of the NDPP was to 'fit' their capabilities 'together' alongside those of the larger allies.[30] The NDPP process still lacks enforcement powers, and allies can ignore even agreed benchmarks. However, it has become a sophisticated and precise guide to identifying exactly what is required in NATO. (Allies, consequently, cannot use the excuse of imperfect knowledge or an absence of political consultation for shirking their responsibilities.) The influence of peer pressure and the continuous scrutiny of allied commitments also means the NDPP works as a 'disciplining tool' influencing how some allies (small and medium members of NATO being the most susceptible) develop their capabilities.[31]

Shared capabilities

Assets assigned to NATO are, by and large, national: that is, they are owned and ultimately controlled by sovereign nations. Loyalty and trust in alliance, however, mean that national capabilities are pooled for particular missions, and national militaries are structured so that working with allies in NATO takes priority. There are some in-built inefficiencies to this way of doing things. Retaining national militaries can result in duplication and an over-supply of particular capabilities. Across Europe in 2012, there were 154 separate major weapons systems compared to twenty-seven in the US. (The European allies, for instance, produced fourteen different main battle tanks compared to just one in the US, the M1 Abrams.) By 2017, that number had risen to 178.[32] Sovereign prerogatives thus have a powerful hold. However, NATO has developed some significant common assets, 'acquired by NATO and [. . .] collectively paid for by Allies'.[33] Some of these are at the level of command and control (NATO's integrated air defence system, missile defence, the Cyberspace Operations Centre and the Euro-Atlantic Disaster Response Coordination Centre); others involve knowledge exchange and research (NATO's Science and Technology Organization and bodies such as the Joint Warfare Centre, the NATO Defence College and the Joint Analysis Lessons Learned Centre). Further, NATO has long deployed a fleet of AWACS aircraft. That fleet has been modernized with an expected service life through to 2035. It has seen service in missions in Turkey, Afghanistan and Libya, patrolled US airspace after 9/11 and been NATO's main contribution to the International Coalition to Defeat ISIS. Since 2017, NATO has also possessed an Alliance Ground Surveillance (AGS) capability comprising five Global Hawk drones backed by the development since 2010 of a JISR 'architecture' of NATO agencies, command elements and protocols. These integrated systems are highly sophisticated and are complemented by national ISR assets (American, German, British, French, Italian, Polish, Danish) which can be provided to NATO operations.[34]

'Smart' capabilities

The Smart Defence initiative alluded to above was designed to align the development of national capabilities with NATO-wide defence needs. The NATO Secretary General in 2012 referred to an 'initial package' of twenty multinational projects geared toward 'critical capability' shortfalls plus a parallel focus on longer-term and 'strategic projects for 2020 and beyond'.[35] Many of these early projects were modest in ambition, focused, for instance, on maintenance, small arms, logistics, training and mine-clearance. Others were a repackaging of existing projects. These included the Strategic Airlift International Solution (SALIS), involving a grouping of NATO allies with agreed access to commercial providers of heavy airlift, and the Strategic Airlift Capability (SAC), a consortium of ten allies and two NATO partners (Finland and Sweden) who manage a small fleet of Boeing C-17 transport aircraft. Dissatisfaction at the progress of Smart Defence has increased intra-alliance solutions among self-selecting allies. Examples include improvements to the Baltic air surveillance network involving the three Baltic States, neighbouring allies Poland and Germany and partners Finland and Sweden; and the European Amphibious Initiative, a NATO construct which dates back to 2000 but which attracted renewed attention in 2018 with the formulation of the Allied Maritime Posture Initiative.

Working with the EU

We have already pointed to the potential (and, in some cases, actual) benefits of NATO–EU cooperation. In Chapter 6, we noted that this has meant EU and NATO capability goals have developed in parallel and largely complementary directions. A NATO–EU Capability Group has, in fact, existed since 2003. The 2019 progress report on NATO–EU cooperation, meanwhile, noted that expert exchanges had raised mutual awareness of the two organizations' capability and defence planning processes. Despite this progress, much more could be done. Political reporting and technical consultations between EU and NATO experts has meant a passive, rather than active, interaction between the two sides' capability development processes. What the 2019 progress report politely referred to as a process based on shared understanding (or a 'tak[ing] into consideration') between the two organizations, one expert report dismissed as 'heavy on rhetoric and light on substance'.[36] What was missing, an analysis that year pointed out, was a 'formal agreement between NATO and the EU on the standards that should be implemented when delivering future military capabilities'.[37] There was no 'European joint force planning construct' – no guide, in other words, to how members of both the EU and NATO should develop capabilities appropriate to both sets of organizational missions, or how the small but important group of non-EU NATO allies (which included the US, the UK, Turkey and Norway) might develop capabilities through the Alliance to partner up with the EU.[38]

The need to get this right is compelling. NATO used to be well ahead of the EU in its defence planning competence, but the balance shifted with the launch in 2017 of the EU's EDF and CARD (see Chapter 6). A 2017 report of the NATO Parliamentary Assembly argued the case, in consequence, for a 'joint NATO–EU Capability Framework' that would bring together capability planning across the two organizations.[39] This would minimize the bureaucratic duplication inherent in having two largely uncoordinated planning processes side by side. The key part of the label here is 'joint' (not single). A unified process is currently unimaginable given sensitivities on both sides. Many EU states not in NATO (neutrals such as Austria, Ireland, Finland and Sweden) would not be willing to tolerate a process that would inevitably bring overbearing American influence; some in NATO – Turkey, for instance – would be unhappy with an EU state (Cyprus, most obviously) involving itself in defence discussions.

'Clustered' allies[40]

NATO's efforts at capability improvement are not insignificant. The Alliance has undertaken a range of initiatives, many of which reflect its unique institutional character. Sophisticated defence planning, 'smart' initiatives and multinational ventures have been made possible because of decades of experience of national armed forces and defence ministries working side by side. This does not solve the capability problem. The disparity between American and allied defence spending (and the size of their respective defence industries) is simply too great to be closed. Further, the unstoppable march of technological innovation also ensures that defence planners, military leaders and expert commentators will always want to integrate the latest weapons, communication systems, transportation, uniforms and personal equipment – and do so in an ambitious way, across all six 'domains of modern conflict (Air, Land, Maritime, Space, Cyberspace and Information)'.[41] The acquisition of better capabilities is, therefore, a never-ending preoccupation – all in a fiscal context of tight budgets and a political environment where (as the COVID-19 pandemic has shown) urgent civil priorities loom large and are often viewed as more important. Aware of the Sisyphean nature of the task of capability improvement, we outline here an approach which supplements the account of NATO's own efforts above. We cannot claim that it will deliver all that the Alliance requires (such requirements are, ultimately, unrealizable), but it is a reasonable way to think about capability delivery and development.

That NATO is in danger of losing its military credibility is an assumption of many commentaries on the Alliance's future. These concerns reflect the broadened range of military and civil contingencies which the Alliance must prepare for and act upon. Task discretion, as outlined in Chapter 5, helps, but it doesn't relieve NATO of making difficult choices. Pressures upon defence spending have divided NATO allies into three categories: those with broad spectrum military capabilities (the US, France and the UK); those with 'bonsai' armed forces that are too small in size, too limited in the range of capabilities or too invested in prestige or niche military capabilities;[42] and those with 'Potemkin' force structures that possess a broad spectrum of military capabilities, but are at such a low level of operational readiness that the ally either is unable to contribute to an operation or can do so only in limited circumstances.

Proposals for dealing with these challenges converge on some ostensibly unobjectionable goals: aggregating allied capabilities; aligning NATO's policy competency and toolkit with present and future security threats; and reducing the number of competing European weapons platforms to facilitate interoperability and the substitutability of national forces.[43] Yet, whatever the logic of efficiency that informs such proposals, politics can still get in the way. France, for instance, is expressly opposed to any increase in the scope of NATO common funding or greater capability development. 'Allies', the website of the French delegation to NATO asserts, 'remain the key players [. . .] within the Alliance, since NATO cannot be a substitute for states' responsibility in defending themselves'.[44] Such a view reflects France's particular circumstances as one of NATO's leading military powers. For smaller allies, by contrast, defence self-sufficiency is out of the question and their preferred role instead is to partner with other allies and develop specialization.

These differences do matter. Any proposals, therefore, should seek to reconcile collective with national interests when addressing the capability issues we have highlighted. That is best achieved by cultivating the strategic affinity which already exists between 'clusters' of allies complemented, in turn, by a practical consideration of the comparative strengths of individual NATO allies and partners. Such an approach allows for a differentiation of roles and a specialization of tasks, so minimizing the risk of non-participation in NATO activities, enhancing the operational interoperability of states clustered together and optimizing allied capabilities and defence budgets.

Cooperation among clusters of countries working in sub-regional, bilateral and minilateral formats is already a discernible tendency in Europe aimed at 'address[ing] the challenges posed by limited European defence capabilities'.[45] Examples outside NATO include the European Air Transport Command, the Anglo-French Combined Joint Expeditionary Force, the UK-led Northern Group, the French-led European Intervention Initiative and regional arrangements embracing the Benelux, Nordic and Central European countries. Within NATO, we have already referred to allies working together on Baltic air defences and amphibious forces. The most innovative development, however, is the so-called 'Framework Nations Concept' (FNC). Stemming from a German proposal, this was adopted at the 2014 NATO summit with the aim of bringing together 'groups of Allies

[. . .] to work multinationally for the joint development of forces and capabilities'.[46] The idea had a long pedigree with roots in multinational commands and military formations going back to the Cold War. NATO also has considerable experience of utilizing 'frameworks' routinely in operations and deployments, as in ISAF, for instance. What made the German initiative different and a potential 'game changer' was its emphasis on capability development.[47] The FNC recognized implicitly what Dick Zandee referred to as NATO's 'diverse capabilities landscape'. Despite the best intentions of coordination at the NATO (or EU) level, force planning and defence acquisition, he pointed out, was still subject to powerful national preferences. Equally important, most allies simply lacked the wherewithal to address NATO's main capability shortfalls. Closing those gaps, Zandee concluded, thus rested on 'the shoulders of the larger [NATO] countries and of those smaller member countries willing and able to join them'.[48]

Three initiatives are usually seen as falling under the FNC ambit. The first, the British-led JEF, is principally concerned with generating forces for coalition and NATO operations. (In February 2020, the UK committed the force to NATO's Readiness Initiative.) Primarily through exercises among its members, the JEF also aims to 'enhance the interoperability of national armed forces'. The initiative is not, however, 'capability oriented' nor 'closely tied to alliance processes' of capability planning and development.[49] The second initiative is an Italian-led group (ITA-FNC) involving Albania, Hungary, Montenegro and Slovenia (plus NATO partner Austria) concerned with 'the development of capabilities for stabilization operations', 'support for local security forces' in NATO's south and the establishment of 'rapidly deployable multinational command structures'.[50] This initiative is generally seen as underdeveloped but, in light of NATO's Projecting Stability agenda to the south, still of some potential importance (see Chapter 5).

The third, German-led, initiative has been viewed as best typifying the FNC approach and carrying its greatest promise. It was conceived with two important considerations to the fore. First, it was closely tied to the NATO NDPP process with a view to making good certain capability gaps. And, second, participating allies would obtain a share of influence alongside the framework nation; they would retain command over their contributing units and would have a say in proposing projects. Germany itself was keen to avoid the idea that this was a project intended to cement its dominance, citing it, rather, as a form of constructive multilateralism or, in the words of Defence Minister Ursula von der Leyen, an example of Berlin 'leading from the centre'.[51] The idea met with broad support. The US, the UK and France did not participate but welcomed the FNC as a way of harnessing Germany's influence in NATO. As of 2019, sixteen NATO allies plus partners Austria, Finland, Sweden and Switzerland had signed up, with involvement spread across twenty-four 'capability clusters' as well as military formations in land, maritime, air, logistics and medical support. The FNC format has been particularly important in reinforcing cooperation between Germany and the Netherlands, Poland and Norway. Some Dutch, Czech, Lithuanian and Romanian brigades, meanwhile, have, in effect, been integrated into the Bundeswehr.[52]

FNC initiatives are to be commended as a creative approach to the capability problem. They take advantage of the credentials of NATO's more capable allies, are informed by capability requirements identified in both NATO and EU planning processes and avoid cumbersome decision-making at the NATO level, by investing principal responsibility for development among those states involved in a particular initiative. The British, German and Italian FNCs also conform to NATO's regionalization – the '360 degree' approach that looks to the north, east and south of Europe.[53] But there are also limitations. FNCs' biggest achievement may well be in force generation as much as capability development. The German and British initiatives are expressly geared toward helping NATO deploy multinational forces in response to a crisis involving Russia. This brings benefits of preparedness and greater interoperability as the FNCs engage in exercises and training, but the capability gains at present are mainly through a 'pooling' of existing resources rather than the development of new ones. The Italian FNC, meanwhile, is too small to have had any meaningful impact on capability development. Further, the most advanced FNC led by Germany is centred on a country (as noted in Chapter 3) with a lacklustre military reputation. If Germany is an example of 'Potemkin' forces, then it is essential the FNC acts as an incentive to continued efforts at reform and the more effective utilization of Germany's own defence budget.[54] In the longer term, it is hoped that groups or pairs of allies involved in FNCs will develop joint procurement initiatives, coordinate national defence plans and so achieve greater efficiencies in their defence spending.[55] But for the FNC initiative to have an Alliance-wide effect, it needs to be scaled up and spread among a greater number of allies. That France, Turkey and the US are currently not involved as framework nations is a weakness that needs to be corrected.

Conclusion: Quality or Quantity?

An alliance as sophisticated and long-lived as NATO need not stake its future on recreating capabilities the US possesses. However, balance, if not parity, is important. There is a significant political imperative at work in this regard. For many years, the US has made clear it would not take NATO seriously if the allies continued to shun their burden-sharing obligations. Equally, if the European allies are serious about strategic autonomy – either within NATO or (for some) via the EU – then capability development is essential. It is unfortunate that (at least since 2014) the test of equity and fairness in this regard has become the rigid 2 per cent GDP benchmark. Nonetheless, a series of initiatives have been undertaken, considered in this chapter, that focus on qualitative, not simply quantitative, capability improvements. These should continue.

NATO's predicaments are as old as the Alliance itself: how to incentivize burden-sharing while curtailing practices of burden-shifting; how to aggregate capabilities in the face of sovereign national priorities; and how to design benchmarks of effort that allies can agree to and that are fair and credible. Our analysis has steered toward options that are in tune with NATO practice or policy debate. There are other options we could have considered: for instance, a single NATO defence budget rather than many national ones; the end of voluntarism in defence planning and its replacement by a supranational NATO authority. One might imagine some of NATO's smaller and even medium-sized allies welcoming such moves. But they would fall foul of the larger powers: the US, France, Turkey and the UK would simply not sign up. Equally, just as countries such as Greece, Hungary, Poland, Italy (and, of course, the UK) have found EU supranationalism hard to stomach, so too would these same countries resent a parallel NATO process that touched upon the most significant expression of sovereignty: the right to determine one's own national defence. For these reasons, the sorts of pragmatic and incremental steps we have outlined in this chapter are a better way forward.

CHAPTER EIGHT

Mending NATO–Russia Relations

The fall-out of the 2014 Ukraine crisis notwithstanding, both NATO and Russia have remained committed, nominally at least, to a return to partnership. But a partnership of what sort? It should be clear from the discussion in Chapter 4 that a relationship based on an underlying normative or strategic convergence was never really on the cards. Even during the relatively benign period of the 1990s and early 2000s, partnership was limited to an on–off institutional set-up centred on narrowly delineated spheres of cooperation. Even that came unstuck and 'business as usual' was abandoned on both sides after 2014.

This chapter focuses on five potential options for how the NATO–Russia relationship might be repaired. Some of these could be readily dismissed as 'foreign policy unicorns': fantastical creations that do not, and indeed cannot, exist in the real world.[1] Even these unicorns are, however, contextually interesting, revealing of the attitudes of those who have proposed them. All five options are thus worth considering. In doing so, we concentrate on the NATO–Russia relationship as such. Important bilateral relations exist between individual NATO allies (not least the US) and Moscow, but for analytical convenience, these are largely set aside. While an improvement in, say, US–Russia relations is clearly consequential, without a neater and more workable NATO–Russia relationship, there will always be limits to how far the US (or, for that matter, Germany, France, Poland, the UK or any other

NATO member) can forge ahead in its dealings with Moscow on European security matters. Our subject is the Alliance, but improving the NATO–Russia relationship is not simply about shifting the NATO position; Russia has also exhibited some distinctly unhelpful policies. Our conclusion, that a 'tacit security regime' is a helpful way forward, requires flexibility on both sides.

Option 1: Enhancing Pan-European Security Structures

Suggestions that the division of Europe into competitive spheres or blocs could be overcome by the creation of inclusive and institutionalized pan-European security frameworks have a long historical pedigree. They can be traced back to ideas sporadically floated by Moscow in the early to mid-1950s on German unification and Soviet membership of NATO. Such ideas were received with great scepticism among the allies in the US and Western Europe, who regarded them as ploys to divide the West.[2] Somewhat different were the ideas that circulated at the time of *détente* in the late 1960s and early 1970s and which reached their high point with the Helsinki Final Act and the meeting of the CSCE in 1975. These had greater promise insofar as they were premised on an agreement between both sides of the Cold War. But the NATO members, at least, never imagined the CSCE would be a replacement for their alliance. The CSCE option, as Chapter 1 made clear, was effectively nullified in preference to NATO at the Cold War's end.

Debates on possible pan-European security solutions nonetheless persisted, mainly as a result of ongoing Russian support. Yet the *rhetorical* interest was not backed up by meaningful, *practical* proposals. The most high-profile suggestion was that floated by then Russian President Dmitry Medvedev in November 2008. Medvedev's outline of a 'draft European Security Treaty' was vague and sketchy even on vital issues such as security guarantees or the basis on which participating states would make decisions.[3] Further, the Russian government did not subsequently flesh out these skeletal proposals, nor was any effort made to convene a grand diplomatic conference (akin to the CSCE in 1975) to begin formal negotiations on it. Russian officials were quoted as saying that Medvedev was content to merely 'toss out the idea and see how they [Western governments] reacted to it'.[4]

It is also worth noting that Russian governments since 1991 have been ambiguous in their support for beefing up the CSCE and its successor organization. When the Cold War was winding down, there had been a flurry of interest in broadening the remit of the CSCE. Some Soviet officials and analysts envisaged the organization as the foundation for the construction of a 'Common European Home' – an idea publicly advanced by the last Soviet President, Mikhail Gorbachev. The CSCE's roles were later enhanced, chiefly in the areas of conflict management and election monitoring. Reflecting these new functions as well as the creation of a settled institutional structure, the CSCE was renamed the *Organization* for Security and Cooperation in Europe (OSCE) in 1994. Russia at that point sought to enhance the OSCE's position still further – giving it, in the words of Russian Foreign Minister Andrei Kozyrev, 'overriding responsibility for the maintenance of peace and the strengthening of democracy and stability in the Euro-Atlantic area'. According to a Russian Charter of European Security drafted in 1994, such a construct would oversee the operations of European security bodies, NATO included.[5]

The sincerity of Russia's commitment to the OSCE, however, was tested in the two wars it waged in the separatist region of Chechnya in 1995 and 1999. Russia permitted the establishment and operation of an OSCE mission on the territory but did little to act upon that body's findings that Russian forces had been guilty of human rights violations. Elsewhere, too, the OSCE departed from Russian preferences. Missions in the Baltic States, which Russia hoped would promote the cause of Russian speakers, were closed in the early 2000s. The OSCE mission to Moldova pursued a settlement to the vexed issue of the Trans-Dniester region which, Russia claimed, deliberately undermined its interests.[6] During the 2004 Orange Revolution, the OSCE was criticized both by Moscow and by the defeated pro-Russian presidential candidate Alexander Yanukovych for its alleged bias.[7] The upshot was that Russia developed 'into an increasingly open and sharp critic' of the OSCE and, in parallel, lost any serious interest in promoting its pan-European role.[8] Tellingly, the OSCE was accorded no function in Medvedev's European Security Treaty proposal.

Putin's return to the Russian presidency in 2012 consolidated this trend. Russia, on occasion, continued to extol the OSCE as an alternative to 'NATO centrism' in Europe, but its practical engagement with the organization was characterized by a mixture of pragmatism, opportunism and obstructionism.[9] This was plain to see in Ukraine. Following the 2014 crisis, two monitoring missions were deployed to the east of the country with Russia's blessing. (The OSCE works by consensus and Moscow could have withheld its endorsement.) The OSCE also provided the negotiating framework (involving Russia, Ukraine and rebel forces in eastern Ukraine) which led to the Minsk agreements aimed at a ceasefire. These agreements, however, did little to shift the battlefield stalemate toward a political solution. (The same was also true of the efforts of the Normandy Format, a group involving Russia, Ukraine, France and Germany.) In Crimea itself, Russia would tolerate no OSCE presence, including inspections under the auspices of the OSCE Vienna Document on

Confidence and Security Building Measures (CSBMs), and used its veto to block OSCE ministerial discussion of Ukraine. Russia's behaviour seemed driven by a desire to project its status as a European power and defend its self-declared prerogatives in neighbouring states.[10]

The OSCE is the only extant pan-European security framework, with, in 2020, fifty-seven members stretching 'from Vancouver to Vladivostok'. The allies, however, do not view it as a substitute for NATO. Russia's ambivalent support, meanwhile, has done little to strengthen the case in its favour.

Option 2: Russian Membership of NATO

Building on the 'security dilemma' concept briefly discussed in Chapter 4, Samuel Charap and Mikhail Troitskiy have argued that at the heart of the unresolved tensions between NATO and Russia is an 'integration dilemma'. Such a phenomenon, they suggest, develops when 'one state perceives as a threat to its own security or prosperity its neighbours' integration into military alliances or economic groupings that are closed to it'. Simply put, 'exclusivity is the source of the dilemma'.[11] The perception that underpins the problem has certainly been evident in some of the statements made by Russian leaders: for example, Vladimir Putin's warning to NATO at the Bucharest summit in 2008 and later when justifying the annexation of Crimea (see Chapter 4). With this in mind, it could be argued that one way to proceed is to open NATO to Russia itself. Such thinking was for a while accepted in the West. One Clinton official, US Deputy Secretary of State Strobe Talbott, reflected in his memoirs that enlargement 'always included [. . .] the idea of Russia's eventual membership'.[12] Similar views were held by figures in Gerhard Schröder's government in Germany at the turn of the millennium. But this was a minority position. No consensus existed in the Alliance on Russian entry and the Clinton administration did not pursue the idea with any enthusiasm. (It fell out of favour completely once George W. Bush came to power in 2001.) Such lack of support has been criticized by some Russian analysts. '[H]ad Russia been included into NATO's enlargement strategy,' Nadia Arbatova has suggested, 'the [August 2008 Georgia] crisis would never have happened.'[13] Sergei Karaganov has argued, similarly, that the Ukrainian crisis could have been avoided had NATO (and EU) members entertained 'repeated' Russian pleas 'to join Western organizations and to reformat institutions into pan-European ones'.[14]

Karaganov's claim draws upon the diplomatic record. According to then US Secretary of State James Baker, Mikhail Gorbachev raised the possibility of Soviet membership on three separate occasions during discussions on the unification of Germany in 1990.[15] Both Yeltsin and Putin ruminated publicly, if briefly, on NATO membership for Russia at the start of their respective presidential terms.[16] Further consideration was given to the matter during Medvedev's presidency in 2010–11.[17] Vincent Pouliot claims there were several instances during the 1990s and early 2000s when working-level Russian officials broached the subject with their NATO interlocutors, only to receive a firm rebuff on each occasion.[18]

Rejection by NATO governments is only part of the problem. What is striking about all approaches from Moscow is how fleeting and how vaguely couched they have been. What, then, has been Russia's purpose? President Putin gave a revealing insight at a press conference in November 2002 with NATO Secretary General Lord Robertson:

> Never before have we raised the question of our full-fledged participation in NATO. [. . .] [I]f NATO [. . .] continues to transform, to implement its internal reforms, something that we have heard many times the desire to do, and if [. . .] cooperation would [. . .] correspond to the national security

> interests of the Russian Federation, and if we see that the organisation can serve as a tool that could resolve our common problems and help to promote our cooperation, then of course our forms of participation could change and we could consider a broader involvement, a broader participation in that work.[19]

A generous interpretation of this position is that Moscow has a real interest in NATO adaptation, wanting to see it open up to mutually advantageous cooperation and issues of shared concern. Less constructively, Russian leaders may also have had tactical objectives in mind: painting NATO members and officials as resistant to bold new ideas whilst also perhaps unnerving them by forcing consideration of the potential impact, however remote, of an eventual Russian application to join. As an editorial in the Russian newspaper *Izvestia* instructively pointed out at the time Yeltsin aired the possibility of Russian membership in December 1991, '[T]o admit Russia into the alliance would mean either [. . .] completely re-examin[ing] the alliance's aims or [. . .] essentially end[ing] it in its current form.'[20]

The potential disruption caused by Russian accession has also, no doubt, affected thinking among key allies. As German Defence Minister Volker Rühe tellingly put it in 1994, '[I]f Russia were to become a member of NATO it would blow NATO apart.'[21] As NATO enlarged from the late 1990s, such views gained ground. It was fantastical to assume that Poland, for instance, a country with deep distrust of Russia, would welcome enlargement to include its large eastern neighbour. The debates that have taken place on the Russian side have also indicated a scepticism regarding the benefits of membership. One problem here is the requirement that Russia, as an Alliance member, would have to submit sensitive military information to the detailed scrutiny of allies as part of NATO's defence planning process. It is by no means clear that the transparency required would fit with the secretive culture and mindset of Russian political and military leaders. In addition, analysts have noted the constraining influence of NATO's consensus-based decision-making on Russia's freedom of action in the international arena – the potential limits it would erect to Russia's position as a self-styled 'sovereign democracy' and 'reviving great power'.[22]

All told, therefore, Russian membership of NATO presents itself as a foreign policy unicorn. Despite sporadic speculation by some Russian leaders and officials, there is no evidence to suggest that it has ever been *seriously* considered on either side as a viable or desirable option. In the end, it is hard to disagree with Michael Rühle, a senior NATO official, who has written that speculation on the possibility of eventual Russian membership amounts to little more than 'an expression of helplessness' at times when NATO–Russia relations are stalled or seem uncertain, rather than 'a serious strategic option'.[23]

Option 3: 'Concert'-Type Management of Regional Security in Eastern Europe

Since the Russian military interventions in Georgia and Ukraine, there has been growing debate about the possibility of moving toward some kind of European security system based on a nineteenth-century 'concert'-type model. Henry Kissinger, former US Secretary of State (and himself a historian of the nineteenth-century Concert of Europe), suggested in 2015 that in defusing tensions surrounding Georgia, Ukraine and other 'borderland' states, Western leaders should 'explore the possibilities of a [. . .] non-military grouping on the territory between Russia and the existing frontiers of NATO'. Here, a 'militarily nonaligned' Ukrainian state would be the subject 'of some cooperation between the West and Russia'.[24]

Similar ideas have been put forward by some Russian scholars and a growing number of Western analysts. The bottom line here is to establish 'Ukraine as a neutral buffer zone' and to forgo any further enlargement into the former Soviet area.[25] This view at least possesses the virtue of capturing present-day reality: that NATO has effectively ruled out membership for Georgia and Ukraine, no matter what it continues to claim about an 'open door' in official statements. The mixed signals here we discussed in Chapter 1. They are a consequence of a lack of consensus among NATO's own membership and the worry of some allies that the Alliance might be unable (or unwilling) to defend new members in the face of Russian destabilization. Integrating Ukraine and Georgia in such circumstances thus risks deterrence failure and a broader unravelling of NATO's credibility.[26] But the downside of such inaction is that it cedes the initiative to Russia, creating the impression that Moscow's objections have effectively blocked enlargement. Here, the strategic 'grey zone' that NATO enlargement had sought to remove in Eastern Europe has been pushed further to the east, leaving Ukraine and Georgia in a limbo of contestation between NATO and Russia. In such circumstances, one option is simply to abandon the two countries to their fate. In the words of the British journalist and former Conservative Member of Parliament Matthew Parris, '[T]he world's best approach is to throw an invisible cordon around the angry, stumbling quasi-empire [i.e. Russia], defend what's outside that cordon and leave what's within to rot.'[27] Few others have been as blunt as this, and an alternative suggestion draws on the manufactured neutrality of Austria and Finland during the Cold War, proposing a similar model for Ukraine and Georgia.[28] The Austrian and Finnish model was based on an understanding between the Soviet Union and NATO (and with leaders in Vienna and Helsinki) that the two countries would maintain foreign and security policy nonalignment and thus not be considered part of either Cold War bloc. At the same time, they would develop normal economic, commercial and diplomatic relations with both East and West.

There are significant, indeed decisive, practical obstacles to the adoption of any such approach resting on cooperative power and security management between Russia and the major NATO allies. Previous cooperative agreements proved to have no bearing once Russia decided to intervene in Ukraine during 2014. The main text overridden by the Putin regime was the Budapest Memorandum, negotiated and signed on the fringes of the CSCE summit in 1994. This agreement offered Russian security assurances to Kiev in return for Ukraine's abandonment of its Soviet-era nuclear arsenal. The US and the UK also signed on, effectively underwriting the deal. At the time, the agreement could be seen as a prototype of great power management. Two decades later, however, the ease with which its non-aggression elements were disregarded – by Russia in an act of commission and the US and UK in an act of omission – indicated, in the words of Vladimir Zocor, that the Memorandum had 'prove[n] to be useless'.[29]

Indeed, the Russian move undermined a whole network of political and legal assurances previously given to Ukraine. Both Russia and the US had signed individual security agreements with the Ukrainian government during the 1990s. Additionally, NATO had in 1997 concluded a 'Distinctive Partnership' with Kiev. Coming as it did just after the signing of the NATO–Russia Founding Act, there was always a sense that this agreement was some sort of consolation prize rather than the foundation for a significant cooperative relationship. And to be fair, the agreement was not designed to be a security pact as such, although it did include the usual statements about respecting sovereignty and territorial integrity, and the right of states to choose their own alliance arrangements.[30]

In 2014, however, this 'partnership' with NATO would prove to be as irrelevant to Ukraine's sovereignty and territorial integrity as the Budapest Memorandum. The Alliance 'condemn[ed] in the strongest terms Russia's escalating and illegal military intervention in Ukraine'[31] but struck a cautious position on practical assistance to the beleaguered authorities in Kiev. This did not mean that support was negligible. Considerable financial and training support to the Ukrainian security sector was provided, mainly via national 'trust funds' loosely coordinated in a 'Comprehensive Assistance Package' under NATO auspices. Nonetheless, self-imposed restrictions were levied by NATO members – chiefly on the provision of so-called 'lethal aid' – justified by the argument that a decisive tilt in fortunes on the battlefield in eastern Ukraine could actually *worsen* the relatively low-level conflict there by provoking further Russian military intervention. The most significant aid to Ukraine was provided by the US, in part, outside of NATO channels. Between 2014 and 2019, the US delivered an estimated $1.6 bn of military assistance to the country, including lethal equipment such as Javelin anti-tank missiles, night-vision rifles and grenade launchers. But according to one analysis, while stabilizing the battlefield situation, this aid did not provide the Ukrainian side with any decisive advantage.[32] American aid also demonstrated the fragility of great power support. Despite condemning the Russian intervention, President Obama was clear that any escalation of military involvement would only spur Russia to greater effort, which ultimately the US and its allies would not be able to match. 'The fact is,' he stated in a 2016 interview, 'Ukraine, which is a non-NATO country, is going to be vulnerable to military domination by Russia no matter what we do.' He did not see membership of NATO as a solution to the problem.[33] The Trump administration increased military assistance, but with conditions attached (Javelin missiles were to be kept in storage rather than deployed) and with a distinct lack of empathy for Ukraine's predicament. Secretary of State Rex Tillerson reportedly questioned why American taxpayers should care about Ukraine; and President Trump triggered an impeachment inquiry, in part, because of his unilateral termination of military aid to the country.[34]

Option 4: Reviving the NATO–Russia Council (NRC)

In 2014, NATO members decided not to completely suspend all their institutional channels of communication with Russia. The NRC met periodically thereafter at ambassadorial level and statements from both sides continued to reaffirm an interest in maintaining dialogue. At their Warsaw summit in 2016, NATO members declared that:

> We remain open to a periodic, focused and meaningful dialogue with a Russia willing to engage on the basis of reciprocity in the NRC, with a view to avoiding misunderstanding, miscalculation, and unintended escalation, and to increase transparency and predictability. We also have military lines of communication. We have agreed to continue to use all these channels to address the critical issues we face, and call on Russia to make good use of all lines of communication.[35]

In London three years later, the allies reiterated that 'we remain open for dialogue, and to a constructive relationship with Russia when Russia's actions make that possible'.[36] Russian leaders have periodically made comparable statements. Referencing the partial suspension of the NRC in January 2015, Foreign Minister Sergei Lavrov asserted that:

> Russia did not initiate this situation. We believe that with all the global twists and turns and disasters, leading nations that have a decisive influence on the global stability and security

> cannot afford to stop talking to each other. Therefore, if our partners come to their senses and confirm their readiness to talk with us with respect and on an equal footing, we are always willing to do so.[37]

The NRC meetings that have taken place since 2014 have occasionally yielded useful results. In July 2016, NATO Secretary General Jens Stoltenberg reported on a Russian proposal to increase air safety in the Baltic region. Given heightened tensions there since the Ukraine crisis erupted, with reports of Russian military aircraft 'buzzing' the Baltic States' airspace, prospective agreement in this area could be seen as a valuable crisis-management tool in its own right. But overall, little of enduring substance has been achieved. Jens Ringsmose and Sten Rynning described the functioning of the NRC in 2017 as 'a mere barometer of political tensions' between NATO and Russia.[38] Accounts of NRC meetings since highlight deep and enduring divisions over Ukraine and other substantive issues, such as alleged violations of the INF Treaty.[39]

Against this unpromising backdrop, it is difficult to see how the NRC could be revitalized in any meaningful way. Its structure, purpose and working methods remain no different from the body which was by-passed in the 2008 and 2014 Georgian and Ukrainian crises. The main argument in its favour is that there is an existing institutional mechanism to fall back on, but reverting to the NRC as is would indicate a lack of ambition and acceptance of a self-limiting relationship bound down by the inconsequential working practices of the past. In Chapter 4, we suggested that the vitality of NATO–Russia relations was to be judged by how far agreement could be reached when both sides took a different view of the same problem. Against this 'Goltz test', the NRC has consistently failed. The cooperation which has occurred in the NRC format (on Russian support for the NATO missions in Afghanistan, for example) has been premised on *a priori* agreement between NATO and Russia (on preventing Islamist militants in Afghanistan from using the country as a staging post for international terrorist attacks). But even that has proven fragile; evidence of a Russian operation to provide the Taliban with bounties for killing British and American troops does not augur well for a revived NRC agenda.[40] How much more exacting, then, for the NRC would be issues previously regarded as off limits, not least enlargement. Given that problem, the working of the NRC needs to be situated in a more propitious context – hence our next option.

Option 5: Tacit Understandings on Future NATO Enlargement

As the discussions in Chapter 4 made clear, enlargement has proven the most controversial issue in the NATO–Russia relationship. Many observers have assumed that the Russian leadership is implacably opposed to this core NATO initiative and that the issue will forever doom any rapprochement between Moscow and the Alliance. It may seem excessively optimistic, therefore, to suggest that pursuing an accommodation on future enlargement offers a viable means of resuscitating the overall relationship. There are, however, some grounds for flexibility.

Upon closer examination, it appears that Russian opposition to NATO enlargement has, at times, been motivated by specific instrumental concerns, rather than any truly existential objection. The strongest evidence for this has been the circumscribed official reaction to the actual enlargement rounds that have taken place since the late 1990s. This becomes especially apparent when contrasted to the crises – vividly described by Richard Sakwa as the 'wars to stop NATO enlargement'[41] – over the status of two states, Georgia and

Ukraine, which have *not* joined the Alliance. With regard to the enlargement rounds completed between 1997 and 2020, the Russian government has effectively accommodated itself to *all* of them once presented with opportunities for negotiating explicit or tacit *quid pro quos*. Thus in 1997, as NATO was preparing to announce the candidate states for the first round of post-Cold War enlargement, it simultaneously initiated the negotiations with Russia that would lead to the creation of the PJC. As Anatoly Chubais, President Yeltsin's then Chief of Staff, observed at the time, 'Russia has never said it was against any kind of enlargement.' A satisfactory NATO–Russia agreement would, he suggested, 'open doors for future NATO enlargement'. This is essentially what then happened, paving the way to Czech, Polish and Hungarian accession in 1999.[42]

Moscow's reaction to the next enlargement round in 2004 was remarkably relaxed, considering it embraced no fewer than seven states, including Estonia, Latvia and Lithuania (so extending for the first time NATO's area of responsibility into the territory of the former Soviet Union). President Putin noted that Russia's relations with NATO were 'developing positively' and that he had 'no concerns about [. . .] expansion'.[43] Defence Minister Sergei Ivanov noted similarly that 'Russians have been remarkably calm about the latest stage of NATO's eastward enlargement.'[44] In the post-9/11 context, the Russian leadership was evidently anticipating both strategic and political rewards for its willingness to stand shoulder-to-shoulder with the US in the unfolding 'war on terror'. Specifically, Putin's government was invested at the time in getting the new and more inclusive NRC forum up and running. The terms of the tacit bargain by which Russia accepted NATO enlargement in exchange for enhanced institutionalized consultative rights with its members and officials were similar to those that Boris Yeltsin had agreed to in 1997.

Despite the failure of the earlier PJC to live up to expectations, the new strategic and political environment ushered in by the events of 9/11 evidently helped persuade the Russian government to try again.

Equally striking was Moscow's lack of response to the enlargement round completed in 2009. This embraced Albania and Croatia and was confirmed by NATO Foreign Ministers in December 2008, less than six months after the Russo-Georgia conflict. Despite what might have been considered some provocatively forward-leaning language adopted by the Foreign Ministers in their final communiqué,[45] the Russian government offered no significant protests. It was similarly passive in December 2015 when NATO Foreign Ministers invited Montenegro to begin negotiations to join the Alliance,[46] and again in July 2018 when the same invitation was extended to North Macedonia. (The two countries would go on to join NATO in 2017 and 2020, respectively.)

The absence of serious objections to these later rounds, all of which were confined to the Balkan region, indicated Russian leaders' *de facto* toleration of an enlargement process that did not encroach upon their defined 'privileged sphere' of influence in the former Soviet area. Russian statements going back to the early 1990s have made clear that such an area does exist. Foreign Minister Kozyrev noted in 1994 that the territory of the former Soviet Union, including the Baltic States, constituted 'a region where the vital interests of Russia are concentrated'.[47] In the aftermath of the Russo-Georgia war in August 2008, then President Medvedev asserted that 'Russia, just like other countries in the world, has regions where it has its privileged interests. In these regions, there are countries with which we have traditionally had friendly cordial relations, historically special relations.'[48]

What is interesting here is that Russia appears to have made an exception for the Baltic States. Why did the accession of

Estonia, Latvia and Lithuania not prompt the sort of response that occurred later over Georgia and Ukraine? Part of the answer was timing.[49] The three Baltic States had pursued a joint diplomatic campaign since the mid-1990s to be admitted to NATO. They had made a good fist of domestic reform and the restructuring of their armed forces. And after 9/11, when Russia's relations with the US and the Alliance improved, Moscow, as we have already noted, looked upon enlargement in a reasonably sanguine fashion. The Baltic States joining NATO, Putin suggested in June 2002, would be 'no tragedy' as long as the terms of the NATO–Russia Founding Act were upheld (meaning the Alliance would have to refrain from stationing permanent military infrastructure in these three countries).[50] Further, Putin did not bargain on Baltic accession setting a precedent. At that point, there was no talk in NATO of the Alliance moving toward any other of the former Soviet republics. The Georgia crisis in 2008 changed that perception and, ever since, Russia has been strident in opposing NATO membership in the former Soviet space that embraces Belarus, Moldova and Ukraine, as well as the Transcaucasian states of Armenia, Azerbaijan and Georgia. It has also shown a degree of seller's remorse over its earlier stance on Estonia, Latvia and Lithuania. Russia has since pursued a significant strengthening of its Baltic fleet and a military build-up in the Western Military District bordering the Baltic States (a district that also borders Ukraine and Russian ally Belarus).[51]

Russian leaders saw their military actions in Georgia in 2008 and in Ukraine six years later as sending the clearest possible warning that NATO should not countenance admitting those two states as future members. By the same token, the absence of comparable Russian responses to NATO enlargement into the Balkans indicates a tacit acceptance of that region as sitting within an alliance (and EU) sphere. Russia continues to perform a spoiler role in the Balkans given its close ties to Serbia and its opposition to Kosovan independence, but the evidence appears to suggest an acceptance of what might be called demarcated enlargement.

This opens up the thorny question of whether Russia has been handed, in effect, a power of veto over Georgia and Ukraine. This is the wrong way to frame the issue. NATO is itself divided on the issue of membership for both countries. No consensus exists on their accession. There is an influential strand of expert opinion in the US and Eastern Europe that continues to support future membership,[52] but most serious analysis concedes that NATO will not enlarge to incorporate these countries any time soon, if at all.[53] Recognizing and working with this reality is a far more practicable option than continuing to alienate Russia by keeping to the pretence that both Georgia and Ukraine are poised to join NATO's ranks.

Some have objected to this position on the grounds of legality and ethics. Timothy Garton Ash has asked, with reference to Ukraine and Georgia, 'What right have we to instruct other independent, sovereign countries to be neutral buffer states?'[54] Such objections should not be casually dismissed. The post-Cold War security order was supposed to have been founded, amongst other things, 'on the freedom of states to choose their own security arrangements', along with a reaffirmation of the UN Charter commitment that states 'refrain from the threat or use of force against the territorial integrity or political independence of any [other] state'.[55] Yet while a noble end, the realization of this bright future for Europe might, too, now stand as a foreign policy unicorn. Pessimism descended with the vicious and bloody conflicts in the former Yugoslavia. These prompted some of the earliest NATO–Russia division. For many Russians, the Alliance's Kosovo intervention in 1999 constituted an egregious violation of international law, whilst many on the NATO side said the same thing about

Russia's annexation of Crimea and military interference in eastern Ukraine from 2014. What is apparent here is that the option of the two sides pursuing the development of an agreed, rules-based approach to managing European security does not currently exist. Thus, the least unsatisfactory *practical* option for the foreseeable future would be for NATO members and Russia to build on their existing tacit understandings over respecting the other's core interests and spheres of interest. Over time, such tacit understandings on enlargement (and the tangible sense of predictability this builds up in the relationship) could be extended to embrace other long-standing issues such as how to revive the CFE Treaty, tackle Russian objections to NATO missile defence and engage in meaningful demilitarization. This would not necessarily entail, at least initially, disarmament or the withdrawal of forces, but it might be possible to agree in the first instance to a return to the CSBMs developed during the 1980s and 1990s and currently embodied in the 2011 Vienna Document. The extent to which the CSBM regime has broken down was illustrated by the disputes over the nature and scale of Zapad-2017 – and a reluctance on the part of Russia to give prior notice of other large-scale military exercises.[56] CSBMs, which might be seen on the face of it as being of limited utility given the depth of NATO–Russia disagreements, could play an important role in helping to mitigate the impact and potential consequences of the security dilemma into which relations between the two parties have fallen, owing to mutual distrust, limited channels of communication and an increased tendency to view the approaches and actions of the others in worst-case zero-sum terms.[57]

Above we noted the limitations of a revived NRC, but with an agenda concerned with such substantive issues, that body would be granted a significant boost in its status. The approach suggested here would not in itself amount to a full-blown joint understanding on managing security threats and challenges in hitherto contested regions of Europe. Yet there is at least the possibility that a more institutionalized and proactive system of this type might emerge over time if NATO members and Russia could develop or revive diplomatic mechanisms and modalities that progressively drew the sting from future enlargement, whilst at the same time giving Russian leaders confidence that institutionalized relations with the Alliance were now qualitatively better than those that had prevailed up to the time of the NRC's partial suspension in 2014.

Conclusion: A Tacit NATO–Russia Security Regime

The NRC and its predecessor the PJC were envisaged as means to formalize an essentially cooperative relationship on key security matters. Both failed because they were premised, on the NATO side at least, on the implicit belief that it was possible to develop some kind of normative partnership with Russia. The actual relationship since the end of the Cold War offers little evidence to suggest that any such hope can be realized. A better approach is to develop tacit and practical understandings, principally on the future of NATO enlargement. This might in time generate momentum to allow for negotiations on other contested issues and to revive CSBMs in the military domain.

Success is not, of course, guaranteed, and NATO will continue to face the central dilemma of what to do about Georgia and Ukraine short of membership. The approach effectively in place since 2008 – to maintain a rhetorical commitment to the 'open door' but to avoid practical moves toward accession – is, as we pointed out in Chapter 4, unsatisfactory. Its core problem of keeping both countries in a strategic limbo we have explored in this chapter. Granting membership to Georgia and Ukraine is politically unacceptable to many NATO members and would, even if that hurdle was overcome, prompt yet further episodes of Russian destabilization. The main powers in NATO – France, Germany, the UK and, since Obama, the US – recognize this reality but find it difficult to concede the point in order not to give the impression that Russia has exercised a veto over the enlargement process. The way out has been through a tacit agreement within NATO not to push enlargement too hard (hence, both Georgia and Ukraine have not been elevated to MAP status). Equally, and perhaps more subtly, NATO has projected a similar message to Russia. The commitment to enlargement remains as a matter of principle, but the NATO allies have not sought to effect in Ukraine a shift in the balance of forces that would pave the way to the country entering the Alliance. For its part, Russia has stridently opposed enlargement but has *de facto* accepted it, with the important exceptions of Georgia and Ukraine, where it has taken active measures to prevent any moves toward accession.

What we have seen emerge, in other words, is a tacit NATO–Russia security regime. Formal regimes are usually understood as forms of regulation, often involving treaties, agreements and organizational structures, in 'issue areas' (such as trade, finance, human rights, the environment) where common problems give rise to a need for mutual cooperation. A *tacit* regime is somewhat different. It involves parties that are adversaries not allies, with a limited interest in cooperation, no shared normative foundation that might stabilize their relationship and a lack of institutional connection. Their disagreements, however, are recognized as destabilizing and so they reach an informal understanding on a 'clearly defined security issue'. The aim here is not to resolve the issue at hand (divergent positions may make that impossible) but rather to 'deconflict' it through a shared understanding of the interests of the other side and consequent modifications of behaviour to accommodate those interests.[58]

The sceptic here might suggest that in a chapter on how to fix NATO–Russia relations all we have done is pointed to the actuality of the relationship rather than prescribed a way forward. We would suggest, however, that a tacit regime, while it may describe an important feature of NATO–Russia interaction, has not yet been acknowledged as such. The existence of that regime might be apparent to the close observer, but it would be beneficial if NATO and Russia took more active steps to advance it. This, of course, would prove controversial if it were too overt – NATO cannot publicly admit to a cooling of its commitment to enlargement without a loss of face. It might entail, therefore, a far more active diplomacy behind the scenes (indeed, tacit regimes, are often secretive in their operation in order to allow the 'maximum maneuverability' of their participants[59]) – a revival, for instance, of the channels of diplomacy NATO and the US exploited with Russia in the 1990s and after 9/11. Such a proposal aims to rescue the embattled NATO–Russia relationship. NATO was, in large part, founded in 1949 to deal with Russia's predecessor the Soviet Union. Over the ensuing decades, the Alliance has demonstrated an ability to balance military and political approaches toward Moscow. The former is currently in the ascendant, but militarizing the relationship only perpetuates mistrust and fuels antagonism. NATO needs to work with Moscow to revive the political dimension and so, step by step, restore trust and engender reciprocity.

Conclusion: Improvement, Repair and NATO's Future

NATO has experienced a series of crises over its long history. These often appear as passing episodes of deep internal division (the Iraq crisis in 2003, for instance) or arise from compelling external events (as in the Balkans, Afghanistan and Libya). As we argued in an earlier book, crisis is normal for the Alliance and it has done a good job over the years of weathering the storms.[1] Yet one should not be complacent. Despite its longevity (perhaps, even, because of it), NATO has incubated a series of problems that have impeded its effectiveness. In this book, we have set out four entrenched problems that go beyond the episodic occurrences noted above.

First, NATO has overextended itself. Second, the US has grown weary of leadership yet NATO remains dependent on American commitment. Third, divisive assumptions about burden-sharing have created a narrative that has misinformed US statecraft and misdirected debates about the capabilities necessary for the Alliance to discharge its essential security functions. And, fourth, the relationship with Russia has failed to move much beyond the old Cold War animosities that once characterized NATO's interactions with the Soviet Union.

Our approach to addressing these problems has not been to identify an optimum solution and then make the case for its implementation. In some cases, there is no obvious remedy to be had. NATO has experienced its own version of the 'wicked problem' syndrome: having to deal with issues that are too complex, too interconnected and too open-ended to allow a resolution. The best that can be hoped for in such circumstances is to ameliorate the problem, not solve it.[2] Fixing NATO, in other words, is about repair and improvement, not a fruitless search for a perfect answer. Further, we have tried to give a fair hearing to NATO's own efforts at managing its difficulties and, in some cases, to point out how a certain problem might have been exaggerated or poorly defined. And in that spirit we have steered toward a standard of feasibility: identifying the overlap between those policy recommendations and outcomes that are desirable and those that are possible. To paraphrase some of the analyses in the previous chapter, we have sought to avoid policy 'unicorns': remedies that might be attractive but which for various reasons are unrealizable.

With these caveats in mind, in this chapter we bring together our analyses of NATO's problems and the potential palliatives (or 'fixes') as we see them. We then follow up with a more forward-looking set of considerations, examining some major contemporary issues – Brexit, the influence of China and the COVID-19 pandemic – which have emerged with force or suddenness as the book was being written and which are likely to have a shaping effect on the Alliance in the years to come.

How to Fix NATO

Task discretion

Our most important recommendation is that NATO must do less. The NATO policy portfolio can no longer expand indefinitely in step with the securitization of issues far outside the competencies identified in the North Atlantic Treaty. The Alliance has acquired tasks for which it is unsuitable (nation-building in Afghanistan, for instance) and it has claimed others (Projecting Stability) which are too ill defined to have meaningful application. Task discretion suggests a rebalancing of responsibilities within the Alliance, but also a more systematic division of responsibility with other bodies, most obviously the EU, which have the political and material resources to act in overlapping areas of interest.

The necessary alignment of allied capabilities and NATO missions would reverse the 'policy thinning' that has occurred since 1990, a process whereby the Alliance's capabilities and institutional mechanisms have failed to keep pace with the demands of an expanded policy portfolio. Such an alignment requires clarity, however, on those security issues that are beyond NATO's reach and those that are essential to its existence. The past twenty years have demonstrated that the further afield NATO engages, the greater is the potential for intra-alliance conflict, selective participation and recrimination. But the Alliance cannot simply return to European defence and, with it, a concentration on Russia. It needs to marry that traditional focus with a realistic out-of-area mission, one defined by 'region management' with an emphasis on limited missions to NATO's south.

American leadership

US leadership and, with it, America's capabilities, credibility and commitment are essential for the Alliance's viability. Without US leadership, there is simply no NATO; the EU or some other coalition of European states does not represent a viable alternative. The allies, despite recurrent grousing about American high-handedness, understand that only the US can ensure their security in the event of an Article 5 contingency. A viable transatlantic bargain, the pivot around which NATO has turned throughout its history, remains within reach. The anxieties occasioned by American disillusionment with NATO in general, and with some allies in particular, do not indicate a structural erosion of American commitment. As we saw in Chapter 6, political and public opinion in the US has remained well disposed to the Alliance despite President Trump's voluble disparagements. Europe's willingness to latch itself to American leadership and to sustain transatlantic partnership is also reasonably sound. This may not always be obvious given the headlines of European governments at odds with the Trump administration, but a deeper look shows how the allies have pursued initiatives aimed at consolidating NATO and demonstrating their credentials as security providers. These initiatives might be also construed as a 'hedge' against American abandonment, but their practical effects have been to demonstrate the viability of a reshaped transatlanticism, not to widen the divide. They take two important forms (described across Chapters 5–7): first, the existence and strengthening of what Angela Merkel has referred to as 'the European section of NATO',[3] or what we have conceptualized as 'nodal defence' and 'clustered' allies; and, second, a set of arrangements housed within the EU which complement NATO's efforts in conflict management, regional stability, capability development and military mobility.

Resourcing, capabilities and operational credibility

Operational credibility has a number of interrelated components: burden-sharing; sustainable defence budgets and national capabilities; and force structures. Many of the problems here are a matter of interpretation and political spin. We made a strong case in Chapter 7 that NATO's capstone metric of shared effort – the target 2 per cent of GDP spent on defence – distorts judgement on what is fair and what is appropriate. Other measures are available which would provide a more comprehensive and, arguably, more accurate benchmark to judge how the allies promote *security* and not merely defence. Moving in this direction is desirable for two reasons: first, because simply spending more on defence is not always the best solution if it adds to waste, duplication and misdirected priorities; and, second, because real limits exist to how much more the NATO allies can find to boost defence budgets. Within this constrained context, it is vital that creative approaches are taken to capability development. For all the American complaints about burden-sharing, it should not be forgotten that a certain element of competition exists between the US and its allies, resulting in an unwillingness on America's part to share the necessary technologies that promote interoperability. That said, the sophistication and expense of some capabilities held by the US render them out of reach for others in NATO. This reality may simply be the price of alliance, a manifestation of the technological division of labour that arises when capabilities are brought together.

However, the non-American allies could do more collectively, not least because maintaining discrete national armed forces in an alliance of thirty is inherently inefficient. In Chapter 7, we argued that considerable promise resides in the FNC, even if the current initiatives are too few in number. FNC clusters, if they are to be credible contributors to NATO's level of ambition, should have compatible security outlooks (particularly with respect to the use of force), similar force structures and operate in the same sub-regions of interest. The existing UK-, Italian- and German-led FNCs meet these criteria (albeit at differing levels of development), as do the eFP in Poland and the Baltic States and the tFP in the Black Sea region. But other clusters might involve Italy, Greece and Turkey for the Balkans and eastern Mediterranean; France, Spain and Portugal for the western Mediterranean; and Canada, Denmark and Norway for the High North.

Relations with the Russia

It was anticipated at the end of the Cold War that the Soviet Union, and then Russia, would become a productive partner in a NATO-centred European security order. The Alliance did not abandon its caution with respect to Russian intentions after 1992, but there was an expectation throughout much of the 1990s that Russia would become a *status quo* partner firmly embedded in a NATO-centred system of security governance. That assumption has been proven incorrect.

NATO Deputy Secretary General Alexander Vershbow suggested in April 2014 that Russia was 'now less of a partner and more of an adversary'.[4] Russia had already reached a similar conclusion. Its statement of Military Doctrine adopted in 2010 described NATO as one of the 'main external military dangers' facing Russia owing to enlargement and a desire to 'endow [the Alliance] with global functions'.[5]

Some analysts lay the blame for this deterioration squarely on NATO's shoulders. The Alliance's misguided commitment to embracing Georgia and Ukraine gave rise to illegal but entirely predictable preventive interventions on Russia's part.[6] Others are much less forgiving of Russia. Its actions are regarded as expansionist, aggressive and designed to destabilize NATO by creating a 'strong sense of insecurity and vulnerability among Russia's neighbors', particularly the Baltic States.[7] A middle position sees the Ukraine crisis as the culmination of a cycle of mistrust going back many years – 'a dramatic exclamation point' that 'eliminated the prospect that any time soon' the two sides would restore some form of normality to their relationship.[8] As Andrew Monaghan has suggested, the deeper problem here is a 'strategic dissonance' whereby Russia and NATO have failed to achieve any sort of common ground on the fundamentals of partnership or to appreciate the differing interpretations each side has placed on its own actions.[9] The Ukraine crisis drew these issues out starkly, and, in the period since, NATO has returned to what Robert Levgold has dubbed an 'ersatz containment of Russia'.[10] This intransigent set of circumstances brooks no easy resolution, although it might be said that some elements of the new dispensation appear to have worked, at least on NATO's side. The Alliance has restored deterrence and shown every sign it is prepared to defend its eastern members. Trump's prevarications on Article 5 notwithstanding, the material commitment of the US and the other allies to the defence of the Baltic States, Poland, Romania and Bulgaria, among others, has been plain to see.

But over and above policies of deterrence and reassurance, we see considerable merit in trying to restore some element of common understanding between NATO and Russia. Grand schemes of great power concert or even integrating Russia in NATO are not the answer here. Instead, the Alliance needs to seriously rethink the scope of enlargement, ruling out for the foreseeable future membership for both Georgia and Ukraine. In parallel, more should be made of the tacit understandings which already exist between the two sides. Packaged in an admittedly loose and unbinding 'tacit security regime' complemented by a revived NRC, this would help neutralize the toxic issue of Ukrainian and Georgian accession. The Alliance and Russia would then be able to turn their attention to other blocked issues of disagreement.

What's Next? Through a Glass, Darkly

According to the well-known saying, usually attributed to the American baseball legend 'Yogi' Berra, 'It's tough to make predictions, especially about the future.' The seemingly paradoxical point here is that however perceptive we are of present conditions, the future remains unknowable and difficult to chart. But at least the effort at prediction should be made. To cite another of Berra's aphorisms, 'If you don't know where you are going, you will wind up somewhere else.' NATO's direction of travel will depend on whether problems deepen, how far those problems are addressed and to what extent the Alliance's most influential member, the US, continues to shoulder its transatlantic responsibilities. The problems just considered are those which have structured the book's approach. But there are others. These have been touched upon in our analysis. They are worth further consideration here. How NATO deals with them will also impact on its likely future.

Brexit

In June 2016, the UK voted narrowly (by 51.89 to 48.11 per cent) to leave the EU. The formal exit occurred at the end of January 2020. A further twelve-month transition period was intended to allow time for an agreement on a long-term UK–EU relationship. The impact of this process has been profound. No other member state has ever left the EU, and the UK is abandoning arguably its most important institutional relationship. As Michael Clarke and Helen Ramscar have noted, Brexit amounts to 'the greatest strategic and economic change in the status of the country for well over half a century'.[11]

Much has been made of the deleterious consequences of Brexit, both for the UK and for the EU. The issue paralysed British domestic politics for years before the referendum and continues to do so. The prospect of the UK abandoning the Union generated warnings that the country's stock as an international leader and partner would be forever damaged.[12] Brexit was also seen by some as a first step in the EU's unravelling, with other members following the UK out of the exit or refusing to uphold the obligations of membership.[13] By contrast, the UK Prime Minister Boris Johnson rejected the idea of British decline as the misguided view of 'doomsters and gloomsters'.[14] The EU also issued a series of pronouncements arguing that Brexit would not deflect the Union from its business.[15] As we write, it is too early to pronounce on the validity of these claims, but what has been clear almost from the outset of Brexit is that its effect on NATO will be negligible and maybe even positive.

The UK was always a reluctant participant in EU missions which fell under the ambit of the CSDP. And while it was not opposed to EU measures aimed at capability development and defence efficiencies, its principal concern in the defence field was always NATO and, in consequence, ensuring that EU initiatives did not undermine alliance prerogatives. Brexit means the UK bridge between the EU and NATO has been lost, although it has been assumed it can be compensated, at least in part, by a more active German role. The EU's loss is arguably NATO's gain. The UK is a founding member of the Alliance and possibly its greatest enthusiast. As Brexit gathered steam, the British government made clear it would enhance its relationship with the Alliance. The UK upped its participation in the eFP, took on the (elected) role of Chair of the NATO Military Committee in June 2018, hosted the NATO Leaders' Meeting in December 2019 and (as noted in Chapter 7) in February 2020 committed the UK-led JEF to the NATO Readiness Initiative. The UK is also, of course, one of Europe's principal military powers. A 2018 analysis by the European Parliament found that the UK possessed 50 per cent of attack submarines held by the twenty-seven EU member states, as well as 49 per cent of heavy transport aircraft, 38 per cent of electronic surveillance aircraft and 53 per cent of intelligence and surveillance drones. None of this will be lost to NATO but, as the European Parliament study pointed out, Brexit has 'greatly compromised' any ambition the EU might have (through CSDP) to develop a fighting capability.[16] The case, outlined in Chapter 6, for a greater European contribution *within* NATO is only likely to be strengthened by such a refocusing of British capabilities.[17] A bigger question concerns the capabilities themselves. The UK government postponed an integrated defence and foreign policy review in early 2020 in response to COVID-19. Relaunched in the summer, it was widely assumed that painful economic adjustment – 'the double whammy of COVID-19 and Brexit' – would likely turn the review into a cost-cutting exercise.[18]

China

At their London meeting in December 2019, leaders of the Alliance took the historic decision to make China a subject of NATO policy. 'We recognise', the London Declaration noted, 'that China's growing influence and international policies present both opportunities and challenges that we need to address as an Alliance.'[19] This move reflected, first and foremost, the elevated significance the US had given to China as a military and commercial competitor. Successive US administrations had worried about China's rise, but none prior to Trump had wanted to make China a policy issue for NATO. The approach instead was to prod the NATO allies 'to do more of the heavy lifting in Europe in order to facilitate US policy in the Pacific'.[20] The US and its local allies (Japan, South Korea, the Philippines) would, in other words, balance China, while NATO would do the same in regard to Russia and, where necessary, take the lead in regional intervention (as was America's preference in Libya in 2011). This understanding didn't quite work out. The US through NATO has remained firmly engaged in Europe (even under Trump), and China has, so to speak, come to NATO by its encroachments on and near the continent.

China, the German Foreign Minister Heiko Maas suggested in April 2019, presents 'security implications on almost every topic'.[21] NATO Secretary General Jens Stoltenberg has been even blunter. China, he noted in remarks to the European Parliament, had the world's second largest military budget and in the five years up to 2019 had deployed new naval forces equivalent to the size of the Royal Navy. China, he continued, 'is coming closer to us: in cyberspace [and] in investing heavily in our critical infrastructure'. It was also, he warned, 'developing weapon systems, which more and more are able to reach all [. . .] Allied countries, including [in] Europe'.[22]

Stoltenberg and others would be hard pressed to provide evidence of any malign Chinese intent against NATO itself. Their concerns instead were fuelled by the potential consequences of vulnerability as China's global influence increased. A first issue here related to the implications of China's behaviour in its own neighbourhood. Territorial disputes in the South China Sea arguably threaten the integrity of the United Nations Convention for the Law of the Sea (UNCLOS). China has argued it possesses rights over a 24-nautical-mile contiguous zone rather than the 12 nautical miles specified by UNCLOS. It has also laid territorial claim to reefs and island chains contiguous to Vietnam, Malaysia and the Philippines. Far from Europe, the worry here is that others, Russia for instance, might follow China's lead, and so degrade NATO maritime security in the waters of the Black and Baltic Seas and the Arctic Ocean. Such concerns have only been compounded by growing evidence of Chinese and Russian maritime cooperation in the Baltic and Mediterranean Seas.[23]

China's Belt and Road Initiative as well as the derivative Polar Silk Road present other challenges. Under these initiatives, China has signalled its intent to become a major economic player across Eurasia. In Europe, it has made significant investments in transport and infrastructure. 'Chinese state-owned or state-controlled firms', a May 2019 article noted, 'now control 10 percent of European port volume, raising long-term concerns about maritime security and control of key waterways.'[24] A 2018 Bloomberg survey of acquisitions noted that in Europe 'China has bought or invested in assets amounting to at least $318 billion over the past ten years.' This figure, more than double American investment, meant

Chinese entities wholly or partially owned four airports, six seaports (including the main Greek port of Piraeus) and wind farms in 'in at least nine countries'.[25]

A similar situation has emerged in technology. The US and its NATO allies had long assumed that America and Europe would remain the source of major technological innovations, particularly those with military applications. That confidence has been shaken. Stoltenberg has suggested that 'emerging technologies' such as 'artificial intelligence, autonomous weapon platforms [and] big data [. . .] will change the nature of warfare as much as the industrial revolution'. And that, he continued, was 'linked to the rise of China', which, through its own investments, now rivalled NATO's 'technological edge'.[26] Related to this, China's presence in space has long been a worry. China, which possesses an operational anti-satellite missile capability, has for many years been capable of disabling US and NATO space assets.[27] Such worries may seem exaggerated. However, Stoltenberg's comments were made at a point when Chinese actions were already impinging upon government action. A major issue here concerned the roll-out of 5G communication networks. The Chinese company Huawei's leading role in developing the necessary hardware meant adopting countries needed to look at 5G, a NATO-commissioned study recommended, 'as a strategic rather than merely a technological choice'. 'The fear remains', it suggested, 'that adopting 5G technology from Huawei would introduce a reliance on equipment which can be controlled by the Chinese intelligence services and the military in both peacetime and crisis.'[28] Similar fears had been raised in the US for many years (a 2012 House Intelligence Committee report suggested Huawei 'pose[d] a security threat to the United States'[29]) and the Trump administration went on to effectively ban the company from operating in the country.

China, then, has clearly emerged as an object of NATO's attention. But the response following the 2019 Leaders' Meeting was low key: the only practical decision made was to launch a series of internal studies on what two observers referred to as 'the scope and nature of NATO vulnerabilities'.[30] The plan, Stoltenberg made clear, was 'not to move NATO into the South China Sea'.[31] NATO has had to move slowly for several reasons. First, as we pointed out in Chapter 2, there is no alliance-wide view on how to deal with China. Several European allies, including France, Germany and the UK, have followed the American lead and placed restrictions on the operation of Huawei. But more broadly NATO is divided between those such as Italy, Greece, Hungary and Portugal who have courted Chinese investment and others such as Germany, France, the UK, Poland and, of course, the US, who are sceptical of China's growing global influence. Tellingly, none of the allies have followed America's lead in banning Huawei (although some, such as the UK, have imposed restrictions on its operation). Second, there is very little that NATO can or, indeed, should offer militarily. Only a small number of allies – Canada, France and the UK – possess naval assets of relevance to an American-led operation in the Asia-Pacific, and even if these were to be utilized it would be in a coalition not NATO format (where a consensus decision on deployment would be difficult, if not impossible, to achieve). Further, many allies are sensitive to the problem of provoking Beijing. Designating China as a rival and taking measures in response would likely lead the Alliance to the poor position it has found itself in with Russia. A NATO presence in Asia would simply confirm the view in Beijing that NATO seeks security at China's expense.[32]

Where this leaves NATO is not clear. As of 2020 it had neither a policy nor a strategy toward China. A narrative had emerged that China was a 'challenge' for the Alliance, but as the 2019 London Declaration pointed out, the country also presented an 'opportunity'. Formal dialogue and institutional connections between the Alliance and China were, however, at that point virtually non-existent. These, as much as countermeasures that would entrench rivalry, seemed a good place to start in developing the relationship.[33]

The COVID-19 pandemic

In March 2020, the World Health Organization (WHO) declared the COVID-19 outbreak to be a global pandemic as the illness caused by the novel coronavirus SARS-CoV-2 spread across the globe. A disease that had originated in China at the end of 2019 had by the beginning of October 2020 led to 35.8 million reported infections and just over a million deaths. Unlike previous twenty-first-century pandemics (such as Ebola and SARS), COVID-19 hit hard in Europe and North America. During its first few months, the five countries worst affected by the disease (measured by death count) were all NATO members: the US, the UK, Italy, Spain and France. Rising fatalities in Central and South America, Iran, India and Russia shifted this balance, but the US was in the autumn of 2020 still recording the world's highest numbers of infections and fatalities (with 211,000 deaths). Just over 42,000 COVID-19 deaths had occurred in the UK, with 36,000 in Italy, just over 32,000 in both France and Spain. Belgium was the site of the world's second highest figure (after Peru) for deaths relative to size of population.[34]

Glimmers of hope were hard to find. UN Secretary General António Guterres said the scale of the calamity made it 'the biggest test the world has faced since World War II'.[35] Colin Kahl and Arian Berengaut suggested that COVID-19 was a 'once-in-a-century occurrence' likely to leave profound 'geopolitical wreckage' in its wake.[36] Analysing an event of such magnitude while it is still unfolding is an uncertain business. It is simply too early to judge whether COVID-19 will, as some have suggested, come to define the trajectory of the 2020s,[37] even less so whether it is the 'beginning of a new epoch'.[38] It could well turn out that the disease is curtailed, vaccines are rolled out and the colossal economic stimulus packages announced in 2020 will help keep the global economy afloat, primed to rebound once the pandemic subsides – a process, according to some projections, likely to unfold during 2021.[39] If for now one has to reserve judgement on its lasting consequences, some signs of COVID-19's impact are already clear. Even in its 'first wave', it had accelerated trends already underway in both domestic and international politics.[40]

What specifically does this mean for NATO? Stefanie Babst, former Head of NATO's Strategic Foresight Team, noted in April 2020 that there were at least five 'potential implications'.[41] The first of these, constraints on the deployment of NATO forces, was obvious immediately. Military exercises planned for 2020 were curtailed or cancelled as military personnel succumbed to infection. NATO troop rotations in Kosovo, Afghanistan, Iraq and the eFP were also rethought as disease took hold in some units. Senior officers in the US army planning Defender Europe 2021 conceded that the exercise would need to be scaled back.[42] Not all was bad news, however. The militaries in a number of countries (the UK being a prime example) enhanced their standing by becoming involved in civil emergency planning and the execution of mass testing programmes. Throughout 2020, NATO itself mounted a series of airlifts of medical equipment coordinated by the Euro-Atlantic Disaster Response Coordination Centre to NATO allies and partners (as far afield as Mongolia, Columbia, Tunisia, Iraq, Georgia and Ukraine).

COVID-19 also impacted upon defence budgets. The economic and social lockdowns imposed by governments to curtail the spread of the coronavirus had an unparalleled effect on growth. Under even the most optimistic scenario for economic performance, the US and European economies were expected to shrink in 2020 at a rate not seen since the end of World War II and much worse than during the financial crash of 2008. Government stimulus packages to keep economies afloat were, on average across the G20, three times the size of those implemented in 2008. The UK government as of July 2020 had committed the equivalent of 14.5 per cent of its GDP to such measures. The figures in France were 13.9 per cent and in the US 12.1 per cent. Germany, meanwhile, committed a staggering 33 per cent.[43] The resulting accumulation of huge national debts alongside a shift in spending priorities to health care and social provision was hardly propitious for military expenditure. Among the bigger spenders, the immediate effect was not clear as defence budgets in most NATO countries had already been set for 2020 and, in the US case, for 2021. Further, some countries sought to protect defence spending despite the pandemic. The draft 2021 French defence budget (unveiled in October 2020), for instance, envisaged year-on-year spending increases through to 2023.

Even so, the circumstances looked challenging. Some allies (the UK, for instance) reaffirmed their commitment to NATO's 2 per cent of GDP target in the midst of the pandemic, but even meeting that benchmark could result in significant overall spending reductions as GDP shrinks in a COVID recession.[44] The parallel here with 2008 is instructive. That global economic crisis led to defence spending reductions across several years. The 'pandemic depression' is likely to be deeper and more prolonged.[45] Military budgets may well go into a long-term decline in consequence, so wiping out the gains registered since 2014. Allies may also abandon the 2 per cent target or argue for its postponement beyond 2024 (as Germany had done even before the arrival of COVID-19).

Strains on budgets will feed a third implication of the pandemic: allied unity and cohesion. The burden-sharing agenda,

Thierry Tardy has suggested, 'is likely to feature as collateral damage of the COVID-19 crisis' as allies seek to justify defence spending cuts.[46] The political direction of the debate here will depend on the generosity of the US. If it, too, ends up curtailing military expenditure, then a readiness to tolerate similar moves in Europe and Canada might follow. This could well be part of President Biden's signature approach to the Alliance. If so, one could imagine a NATO summit in 2021 agreeing a post-pandemic budget realignment – so modifying NATO's 2014 defence spending pledge. Allied unity is also likely to be strained by other COVID-related issues. The pandemic, Tardy has pointed out, has fed the debate on NATO's adaptation. Should the Alliance now give greater attention to pandemic response and biosecurity and so develop a more forward-looking and prominent civilian role? But if so, what does this mean for NATO's recent turn toward deterring Russia and the future of its 'cutting-edge military capacity'?[47] Would any such turn meet with alliance-wide consensus? And what of existing and emerging priorities? The pandemic has not lessened the significance of Russia or, indeed, China for NATO. (In the midst of the pandemic, Beijing announced an increase in its military budget for 2021; Russia, meanwhile, was accused by the US, British and Canadian authorities of attempting to hack into sensitive vaccine research.) Such a juggling of priorities in an environment of constrained resources returns us to the pressing matter of task discretion. COVID-19 only reinforces the argument we have made in this book for a more discretionary NATO. If expeditionary missions such as Afghanistan were already on the way out, then the pandemic has probably put paid to them for the foreseeable future. This, at least, is one thing upon which there will be little disagreement among allies.

Related to this, COVID-19 has cast doubt on America's international leadership. The US, one former NATO official noted, was 'missing in action' as the pandemic accelerated, 'preoccupied only with itself'.[48] The actions the US did take were positively damaging. President Trump threatened to cut funds to the WHO as the disease took off, charging the body was too sympathetic to China. The administration went on to serve formal notice that the US would leave the organization in July 2021. The G20, too, was hampered by American antipathy. (A meeting of G20 Health Ministers in late April ended without agreement when the US withheld its support on a final statement.) Further, the high fatality numbers in the US led many to question the Trump administration's competence, so denting America's soft power.[49] This was hardly conducive to transatlantic amity. That said, Trump's domestic handling of the pandemic significantly lengthened the odds on his re-election. Joe Biden, the candidate generally viewed as more conducive to a repair of relations with NATO allies and a restoration of American leadership, emerged victorious in November.

Babst, finally, points to the potential for COVID-19 to further disrupt NATO's south. Countries already under severe strain because of civil war – Syria, Libya, Yemen – proved unable to mount effective public health responses to the disease. The same was also true further afield in Afghanistan. (In July 2020, the Afghan Health Minister estimated that nearly a third of the country's population had already been infected.) The social and economic consequences of the disease (stagnation, curtailed income and lowered living standards) were all likely to exacerbate existing conflicts and render political accommodation more difficult.[50] A repeat of the 2015 migration crisis was more probable as a consequence. NATO's willingness or ability to intervene would not, however, increase in parallel as COVID-19 truncated foreign policy ambition and military capability.

All these developments speak directly to the themes covered in this book. But their sudden emergence does not make our earlier analysis redundant. We have already argued for a more efficient and effective approach to burden-sharing and capability development, for a wiser way of looking at transatlantic leadership and for a more strategic approach to NATO's south. Further, the pressure of circumstances occasioned by the pandemic could well generate creative responses in NATO to new problems (creating allied stockpiles of medical equipment for swift delivery) as well as old ones (practical cooperation with Russia on an issue untarnished by past disputes). Whatever the trajectory of the pandemic, it will end up as more than simply a public health episode. COVID-19 has compounded existing crises and seeded new ones. Security bodies like NATO become more not less necessary in such circumstances. Exactly how will require the Alliance to revisit its 'added-value' in a world where threats and risks continue to multiply.[51]

Conclusion: Fixing NATO

The old adage 'If it ain't broke, don't fix it' does not apply to NATO. As should be clear, the Alliance requires repair and ongoing maintenance. There is a common tendency in commentary on NATO to regard its troubles as terminal. As we pointed out in the introductory chapter, however, such declinist views have proven wrong time and time again. The evidence of this book is that for all its travails, the Alliance has proven remarkably adept at adapting to changing circumstances. NATO, in other words, has done more than merely survive. It is neither a 'paper alliance' nor a 'zombie organization': repulsive, lifeless and devoid of direction. But NATO's animation has required constant attention. This should not be regarded as a source of weakness. Successful organizations are those with an ability to adapt and an awareness among their members of what is needed to effect change. Of course, this is a process that is always, by definition, incomplete – and in a large and politicized body, one that may be controversial and contested.

This is a perspective somewhat removed from the more dewy-eyed encomiums that NATO has sometimes attracted. It is increasingly difficult to see the Alliance as some principled embodiment of the values of 'democracy, individual liberty and the rule of law', where these values propel its 'engagement with the rest of the world' and serve as a 'magnet' attracting other countries to membership and partnership.[52] This is not simply because populism and quasi-authoritarianism have found their way into the politics of NATO's own members. Rather, it is because the Alliance's own *modus operandi* has tended to be reactive rather than driven by some grand vision of political community. This is not fatalism or cynicism on our part. When called into action, NATO can still uphold values, and, as we argued in Chapter 5, prudence in decision-making is a noble end in its own right. But these higher calculations are made in messy circumstances. NATO's benefit to its members has been to deliver, however imperfectly, a range of security goods which the allies (even, arguably, the US) are incapable of delivering alone. It is also a format which, in the execution of that common purpose, no other body can rival. The EU, the UN and the OSCE perform similar and sometimes vital functions, but NATO is still unrivalled when it comes to shared security and defence, in its functional competences and institutional depth, and in its political bridging of the Atlantic. For these reasons, it is worth preserving, adapting and, where possible, fixing.

Notes

Preface and Acknowledgements

1 Tom Clark, 'The Contagion Effect', *Prospect*, May 2020, p. 1.
2 Joseph S. Nye Jr, 'COVID-19 Might Not Change the World', *Foreign Policy*, 9 October 2020, *https://foreignpolicy.com/2020/10/09/covid-19-might-not-change-the-world/*.

Introduction: What *Is* Wrong with NATO?

1 Christian Whiton, 'NATO Is Obsolete', *The National Interest*, 6 July 2018, *https://nationalinterest.org/feature/nato-obsolete-25167*.
2 Mary Dejevsky, 'Donald Trump Is Right about One Thing: NATO Is Obsolete', *The Independent*, 7 April 2016, *https://www.independent.co.uk/voices/donald-trump-right-about-one-thing-nato-obsolete-a6973231.html*.
3 Interviewed in *The Economist*, 7 November 2019, *https://www.economist.com/europe/2019/11/07/emmanuel-macron-warns-europe-nato-is-becoming-brain-dead*.
4 Jochen Bittner, 'Does NATO Still Exist?', *New York Times*, 7 July 2016, *https://www.nytimes.com/2016/07/08/opinion/does-nato-still-exist.html*.
5 Jonathan Clarke, 'Replacing NATO', *Foreign Policy*, No. 93, 1993–4, pp. 22–40.
6 'The Future of NATO: NATO Flexes Its Muscle Memory', *The Economist*, 30 August 2014, *https://www.economist.com/international/2014/08/30/nato-flexes-its-muscle-memory*.
7 Ian Bremmer, 'The Hollow Alliance', *Time*, 27 June 2016, *https://time.com/4371195/nato-transatlantic-alliance-us-europe/*.
8 Elizabeth Pond, *Friendly Fire: The Near-Death of the Transatlantic Alliance* (Washington, DC: Brookings Institution Press, 2004).

9 Cited in Thom Shanker and Steven Erlanger, 'Blunt US Warning Reveals Deep Strains in NATO', *New York Times*, 10 June 2011, *http://www.nytimes.com/2011/06/11/world/europe/11nato.html*.
10 Jens Ringsmose and Mark Webber, 'No Time to Hedge? Articulating a European Pillar within the Alliance', NATO Defence College, *Policy Brief*, No. 5, 2020, *http://www.ndc.nato.int/news/news.php?icode=1423*.
11 'Çavuşoğlu: Turkey Will Consider Exit from NATO', *Katehon*, 10 August 2016, *https://katehon.com/news/cavusoglu-turkey-will-consider-exit-nato*.
12 BBC News, 7 May 2019, *https://www.bbc.co.uk/news/av/world-europe-48189096/iceland-s-green-pm-jakobsdttir-on-nato-membership*.
13 Roger Cohen, 'Anti-Semitic Anti-Zionism', *New York Times*, 18 October 2016, *https://www.nytimes.com/2016/10/19/opinion/anti-semitic-anti-zionism.html*.
14 Ted Galen Carpenter, 'NATO Is an Institutional Dinosaur', *War on the Rocks*, 25 August 2016, *https://warontherocks.com/2016/08/nato-is-an-institutional-dinosaur/*.
15 Wallace J. Thies, *Why NATO Endures* (Cambridge etc.: Cambridge University Press, 2009), p. 296.
16 Kori Schake, 'NATO after the Cold War, 1991–1995: Institutional Competition and the Collapse of the French Alternative', *Contemporary European History*, 7(3), 1998, p. 381.
17 Carl Cavanagh Hodge, 'Full Circle: Two Decades of NATO Intervention', *Journal of Transatlantic Studies*, 11(4), 2013, pp. 350–67.
18 James Sperling, 'Introduction: A Stable Crisis? NATO into the Twenty-First Century', in James Sperling and S. Victor Papacosma (eds), *NATO after Sixty Years: A Stable Crisis* (Kent, OH: The Kent State University Press, 2012), p. 1.
19 Celeste A. Wallander, 'Institutional Assets and Adaptability: NATO after the Cold War', *International Organization*, 54(4), 2000, pp. 705–35.
20 Seth A. Johnston, *How NATO Adapts: Strategy and Organization in the Atlantic Alliance since 1950* (Baltimore: Johns Hopkins University Press, 2017), pp. 118–75.
21 Brian C. Rathbun, *Trust in International Cooperation: International Security Institutions, Domestic Politics and American Multilateralism*

(Cambridge etc.: Cambridge University Press, 2011), pp. 1–23, 163–208.

22 This idea was conceived originally by Karl Deutsch and colleagues in *Political Community in the North Atlantic Area* (Princeton: Princeton University Press, 1957), which is the source of the quotation (p. 5).

23 Patricia A. Weitsman, *Waging War: Alliances, Coalitions, and Institutions of Interstate Violence* (Stanford: Stanford University Press, 2014), p. 190.

24 We borrow here from Kenneth W. Abbott, Jessica F. Green and Robert O. Keohane, 'Organizational Ecology and Institutional Change in Global Governance', *International Organization*, 70(2), 2016, pp. 247–77.

25 *Munich Security Conference Report 2020: Westlessness*, *https://securityconference.org/assets/user_upload/MunichSecurityReport2020.pdf.*

26 Vincent Pouliot, *International Pecking Orders: The Politics and Practice of Multilateral Diplomacy* (Cambridge etc.: Cambridge University Press, 2016), pp. 86–116.

27 Jamie Shea, 'NATO at Full Stretch', *International Politics Reviews*, 4, 2016, pp. 36–42.

28 John J. Mearsheimer, 'The False Promise of International Institutions', *International Security*, 19(3), 1994/1995, p. 7.

29 Michael N. Barnett and Martha Finnemore, 'The Politics, Power, and Pathologies of International Organizations', *International Organization*, 53(4), 1999, pp. 699–700.

30 Robert O. Keohane and Lisa L. Martin, 'The Promise of Institutionalist Theory', *International Security*, 20(1), 1995, pp. 39–51.

31 Ivan Krastev and Stephen Holmes, *The Light that Failed: A Reckoning* (London: Allen Lane, 2019); Stephen Walt, 'The Global Order after COVID-19', Institute for Security Policy, Vienna, Working Paper, 2020.

32 Robert O. Keohane, 'International Organization and the Crisis of International Interdependence', *International Organization*, 25(2), 1975, pp. 357, 359.

33 Hugh Miall (ed.), *Redefining Europe: New Patterns of Conflict and Cooperation* (London and New York: Pinter Publishers, 1994).

34 Edward Newman, *A Crisis of Global Institutions? Multilateralism*

and International Security (London and New York: Routledge, 2007), p. 21.

35 See, for instance, Julian Lindley-French, *NATO: The Enduring Alliance 2016* (Warsaw: Foundation for Polish–German Cooperation, 2016); R.N. Burns and J.L. Jones, Jr, *Restoring the Power and Purpose of the NATO Alliance* (Washington, DC: Atlantic Council 2016); J.R. Deni, *NATO and Article 5: The Transatlantic Alliance and the Twenty-First-Century Challenges of Collective Defence* (Lanham, MD: Rowman and Littlefield, 2017); John Andreas Olsen (ed.), *Future NATO: Adapting to New Realities (Whitehall Paper 95)* (London: Royal United Services Institute, 2020).

Chapter 1 Doing Too Much: The Problem of Task Proliferation

1 'North Atlantic Council, Declaration on Atlantic Relations', 19 June 1974, paras 3–4, *http://www.nato.int/cps/en/natohq/official_texts_26901.htm.*

2 Timothy Andrew Sayle, *Enduring Alliance: A History of NATO and the Postwar Global Order* (Ithaca, NY, and London: Cornell University Press, 2019), pp. 33, 35–6, 47, 50–5, 64.

3 'Operations and Missions: Past and Present', *https://www.nato.int/cps/en/natohq/topics_52060.htm.*

4 NATO, 'The Alliance's New Strategic Concept', November 1991, *https://www.nato.int/cps/en/natohq/official_texts_23847.htm?.*

5 NATO, 'London Declaration Issued by the Heads of State and Government Participating in the Meeting of the North Atlantic Council', 4 December 2019, *https://www.nato.int/cps/en/natohq/official_texts_171584.htm.*

6 Joanna Spear, 'Organizational Survival: NATO's Pragmatic Functionalism', in Ian Shapiro and Adam Tooze (eds), *Charter of the North Atlantic Treaty Organization* (New Haven and London: Yale University Press, 2018), p. 283.

7 NATO Secretary General, Jens Stoltenberg, address to the United States Congress, 3 April 2019, *https://www.nato.int/cps/en/natohq/opinions_165210.htm.*

8 Anthony King, 'Overload: Problems of Governing in the 1970s', *Political Studies*, 23(2–3), 1975, pp. 162–74.

9 Michael E. Brown, 'Minimalist NATO: A Wise Alliance Knows When to Retrench', *Foreign Affairs*, 78(3), 1999, p. 210.

10 Beatrice Heuser, oral evidence to the House of Commons Defence Committee, Hearings on 'The Future of NATO', Question 83, 12 June 2002, *https://publications.parliament.uk/pa/cm200102/cmselect/cmdfence/914/2061207.htm.*

11 House of Commons Defence Committee, *The Future of NATO and European Defence* (Ninth Report of Session 2007–8) (London: The Stationery Office, 2008), p. 17.

12 'Global NATO: Overdue or Overstretch?', speech at the SDA conference, Brussels, 6 November 2006, *https://www.nato.int/docu/speech/2006/s061106a.htm.*

13 Reynell Andreychuk (rapporteur), 'Alliance Cohesion', NATO Parliamentary Assembly, Political Committee, November 2010, p. 5, *https://www.nato-pa.int/document/2010-219-pc-10-e-bis-alliance-cohesion-andreychuk-report.*

14 Jamie Shea, 'NATO at 70: An Opportunity to Recalibrate', *NATO Review*, April 2019, *https://www.nato.int/docu/review/articles/2019/04/05/nato-at-70-an-opportunity-to-recalibrate/index.html.*

15 Sacha Garben, 'Competence Creep Revisited', *Journal of Common Market Studies*, 57(2), 2019, pp. 205–22.

16 Michael Barnett and Martha Finnemore, *Rules for the World: International Organizations in Global Politics* (Ithaca, NY, and London: Cornell University Press, 2004).

17 James G. March and Johan P. Olsen, 'Institutional Perspectives on Political Institutions', in Michael Hill (ed.), *The Policy Process: A Reader* (second edition, New York and London: Routledge, 2017), p. 150.

18 Ashok Swain, *Understanding Emerging Security Challenges: Threats and Opportunities* (London and New York: Routledge, 2013), p. 2.

19 Michael J. Williams, *NATO, Security and Risk Management: From Kosovo to Kandahar* (Abingdon: Routledge, 2009).

20 James Goldgeier, 'NATO's Charter: Adaptable but Limited', in Shapiro and Tooze (eds.), *Charter of the North Atlantic Treaty Organization*, pp. 288–301.

21 'The NATO Command Structure' (February 2018), *https://www.nato.int/nato_static_fl2014/assets/pdf/pdf_2018_02/1802-Factsheet-NATO-Command-Structure_en.pdf.*

22 Christian Tuschhoff, 'The Impact of NATO's Defence Planning

and Force Generation on Member States', in Sebastian Mayer (ed.), *NATO's Post-Cold War Politics: The Changing Provision of Security* (Houndmills, Basingstoke, and New York: Palgrave Macmillan, 2014), p. 207.

23 On this sort of problem see Michael D. Cohen, James G. March and Johan P. Olsen, 'A Garbage Can Model of Organizational Choice', *Administrative Science Quarterly*, 17(1), 1972, pp. 1–25.

24 A phrase borrowed from Asle Toje, 'The First Casualty in the War against Terror: The Fall of NATO and Europe's Reluctant Coming of Age', *European Security*, 12(2), 2003, p. 64.

25 Cited in Eckhard Lübkemeier, 'NATO's Identity Crisis', *Bulletin of the Atomic Scientists*, 46(8), 1990, pp. 30–3.

26 Cited in Kristina Spohr, *Post Wall, Post Square: How Bush, Gorbachev, Kohl, and Deng Shaped the World after 1989* (New Haven and London: Yale University Press, 2019), p. 286.

27 Adrian G.V. Hyde-Price, *European Security beyond the Cold War: Four Scenarios for the Year 2010* (London etc.: The Royal Institute of International Affairs and SAGE Publications, 1991), p. 201.

28 Cited in Jennifer Medcalf, *Going Global or Going Nowhere? NATO's Role in Contemporary International Security* (Oxford etc.: Peter Lang, 2008), p. 67.

29 Zbigniew Brzezinski, 'NATO – Expand or Die?', *New York Times*, 28 December 1994, *https://www.nytimes.com/1994/12/28/opinion/nato-expand-or-die.html*.

30 Robert E. Hunter, 'Maximizing NATO: A Relevant Alliance Knows How to Reach', *Foreign Affairs*, 78(3), 1999, pp. 190–1.

31 Lord George Robertson, 'Reflections on 9/11', NATO YouTube channel, 7 September 2011, *https://www.youtube.com/watch?v=EkaBVwnod7g*.

32 Andrew Cottey, 'NATO: Globalization or Redundancy?', *Contemporary Security Policy*, 25(3), 2004, p. 394.

33 'Forward', *Prague Summit 2002: Selected Speeches and Documents* (Brussels: NATO Public Diplomacy Division, 2003), p. 4.

34 Anne Deighton, 'The Eleventh of September and Beyond: NATO', *Political Quarterly*, 73(1), 2002, pp. 131–2.

35 Commenting in February 2008 and cited in Mark Webber, Ellen Hallams and Martin A. Smith, 'Repairing NATO's Motors', *International Affairs*, 90(4), 2014, p. 981.

36 House of Commons Defence Committee, *Towards the Next Defence and Security Review: Part Two – NATO* (third report of

session, 2014–15), para. 65, *https://publications.parliament.uk/pa/cm201415/cmselect/cmdfence/358/35802.htm.*

37 Cited in James Sperling and Mark Webber, 'NATO and the Ukraine Crisis: Collective Securitization', *European Journal of International Security*, 2(1), 2017, p. 41.

38 Ian Hope, 'Introduction. Projecting Stability: Elixir or Snake Oil?', in Ian Hope (ed.), *Projecting Stability: Elixir or Snake Oil?* (Rome: NATO Defence College, 2019), pp. 1–5.

39 'Brussels Summit Declaration', 11 July 2018, para. 29, *https://www.nato.int/cps/en/natohq/official_texts_156624.htm.*

40 Stephen Sestanovich, *Maximalist: America in the World from Truman to Obama* (New York: Alfred A. Knopf, 2010), pp. 259–72.

41 Sestanovich, *Maximalist*, p. 261. (Sestanovich was an ambassador-at-large in the Clinton administration.)

42 George W. Bush, *Decision Points* (London and New York: Virgin Books, 2010), pp. 396–7.

43 Derek Chollet, *The Long Game: How Obama Defied Washington and Redefined America's Role in the World* (New York: Public Affairs, 2016), pp. 203–31.

44 Cited in Andreas Krieg, 'Externalizing the Burden of War: The Obama Doctrine and US Foreign Policy in the Middle East', *International Affairs*, 92(1), 2016, p. 104.

45 Elbridge A. Colby and A. Wess Mitchell, 'The Age of Great-Power Competition: How the Trump Administration Refashioned American Strategy', *Foreign Affairs*, 99(1), 2020, *https://www.foreignaffairs.com/articles/2019-12-10/age-great-power-competition.*

46 Caitlin Oprysko, '"NATO Plus ME": Trump Proposes NATO Expansion into Middle East', *Politico*, 9 January 2020, *https://www.politico.com/news/2020/01/09/trump-nato-expansion-proposal-096772.*

47 Judith Goldstein and Robert O. Keohane, 'Ideas and Foreign Policy: An Analytical Framework', in Judith Goldstein and Robert O. Keohane (eds), *Ideas and Foreign Policy: Beliefs, Institutions and Political Change* (Ithaca, NY, and London: Cornell University Press, 1993), pp. 3–30.

48 NATO 'Rome Declaration on Peace and Cooperation', November 1991, paras 1 and 2, *https://www.nato.int/docu/comm/49-95/c911108a.htm.*

49 See the Clinton administration sources cited in Frank Schimmelfennig, 'NATO Enlargement: A Constructivist Explanation', *Security Studies*, 8(2–3), 1998, pp. 198–234.
50 Fatjona Mejdini, 'Albanian PM Talks Balkans and Security with Obama', *Balkan Insight*, 15 April 2016, *https://balkaninsight.com/2016/04/15/albanian-primer-meets-obama-to-talk-balkans-and-security-04-15-2016/*.
51 Press Statement of US Secretary of State Michael R. Pompeo, 23 October 2019, *https://www.state.gov/welcoming-u-s-senate-approval-of-nato-accession-protocol-for-north-macedonia/*.
52 Speech before the Chicago Economic Club, 22 April 1999, *https://www.globalpolicy.org/component/content/article/154/26026.html*.
53 Hélène Mulholland, 'Libya: Military Action Necessary, Legal and Right, Says David Cameron', *The Guardian*, 21 March 2011, *https://www.theguardian.com/politics/2011/mar/21/libya-military-action-necessary-david-cameron*; Paul Harris, 'Barack Obama Defends US Military Intervention in Libya', *The Guardian*, 29 March 2011, *https://www.theguardian.com/world/2011/mar/29/barack-obama-us-speech-libya*.
54 NATO, 'Chicago Summit Declaration on Afghanistan', 21 May 2012, para. 2, *https://www.nato.int/cps/en/natolive/official_texts_87595.htm*
55 Sten Rynning, *NATO in Afghanistan: The Liberal Disconnect* (Stanford: Stanford University Press, 2012), p. 3.
56 Patrick Porter, 'Why Britain Doesn't Do Grand Strategy', *RUSI Journal*, 155(4), 2010, pp. 8–9.
57 NATO, 'London Declaration', para.1.
58 Dominic Tierney, 'The Ethics of Unwinnable Wars', in Andrew R. Hom, Cian O'Driscoll and Kurt Mills (eds), *Moral Victories: The Ethics of Winning Wars* (Oxford etc.: Oxford University Press, 2017), p. 127.
59 'Afghanistan; Worth the Cost', speech by NATO Secretary General Anders Fogh Rasmussen to the NATO Parliamentary Assembly, 17 May 2013, *https://www.nato.int/cps/en/natolive/opinions_100598.htm?selectedLocale=en*.
60 Peter Beaumont, 'Afghanistan Papers Reveal US Public Was Misled about Unwinnable War', *The Guardian*, 9 December 2019, *https://www.theguardian.com/world/2019/dec/09/afghan-papers-reveal-us-public-were-misled-about-unwinnable-war*.

61 Joseph Votel, 'Ending America's Endless War in Afghanistan', *New York Times*, 11 December 2019, *https://www.nytimes.com/2019/12/11/opinion/war-afghanistan-talks.html*; Anthony H. Cordesman, 'Afghanistan: A War in Crisis' (Washington, DC: Centre for Strategic and International Studies, September 2019), p. 2, *https://www.csis.org/analysis/afghanistan-war-crisis*.
62 'Afghanistan: Background and US Policy in Brief', Congressional Research Service, 5 December 2019, pp. ii, 6, *https://fas.org/sgp/crs/row/R45122.pdf*.
63 Max Fisher, 'In Afghanistan's Unwinnable War, What's the Best Loss to Hope For?', *New York Times*, 1 February 2018, *https://www.nytimes.com/2018/02/01/world/asia/afghanistan-war.html*.
64 George Packer, *Our Man: Richard Holbrooke and the End of the American Century* (London: Jonathan Cape, 2019), pp. 488–540.
65 George Kennan, 'A Fateful Error', *New York Times*, 5 February 1997, *https://www.nytimes.com/1997/02/05/opinion/a-fateful-error.html?searchResultPosition=1*.
66 John J. Mearsheimer, *The Great Delusion: Liberal Dreams and International Realities* (New Haven and London: Yale University Press, 2018), p. 176.
67 First Deputy Foreign Minister Igor Frolov cited in Jeremy Black, 'Russia and NATO Expansion Eastward: Red-lining the Baltic States', *International Journal*, 54(2), 1999, p. 257.
68 Joseph A. Day, 'Reinforcing NATO's Deterrence in the East', NATO Parliamentary Assembly, Defence and Security Committee, 168 DSC 18E fin, 17 November 2018, *https://www.nato-pa.int/document/2018-deterrence-east-day-report-168-dsc-18-e-fin*.
69 Karl-Heinz Kamp, 'NATO Entrapped: Debating the Next Enlargement Round', *Survival*, 40(3), 1998, pp. 170–86.
70 Lieutenant General (rtd) Ben Hodges, interview with Voice of America, 13 February 2019, *https://civil.ge/archives/276491*.
71 Charles A. Kupchan, 'Is NATO Getting too Big to Succeed?', *New York Times*, 25 May 2017, *https://www.nytimes.com/2017/05/25/opinion/nato-russia-donald-trump.html*.
72 Markus Kaim, 'Reforming NATO's Partnerships', *SWP Research Paper* (Berlin: Stiftung Wissenschaft und Politik), no. 1, 2017.
73 Wolfgang Rudischhauser, 'Adaptations Needed: NATO Partnership Programmes in the 21st Century', *Security Policy*

Working Paper (Berlin: Federal Academy for Security Policy), no. 11, 2019.

74 Kris Quanten, 'What [is] NATO's Counter-Terrorism Strategy?', *NDC Policy Brief*, no. 12, May 2019, *http://www.ndc.nato.int/news/news.php?icode=1323*.

75 NATO, 'Brussels Summit Declaration', 11 July 2018, para. 50, *https://www.nato.int/cps/en/natohq/official_texts_156624.htm*.

76 Benedetta Berti and Ruben-Erik Diaz-Plaja, 'Two Ages of NATO Efforts to Project Stability – Change and Continuity', in Hope (ed.), *Projecting Stability*, p.24.

77 Julio Miranda Calha (general rapporteur), 'Instability in the South', NATO Parliamentary Assembly, Political Committee, General Report, 177 PC 18 E rev.1 fin, 18 November 2018, p. 4, *https://www.nato-pa.int/document/2018-instability-south-miranda-calha-report-177-pc-18-e-rev1-fin*.

78 Arab Reform Initiative, 'Dossier. COVID-19: Impact on MENA Countries', *https://www.arab-reform.net/dossier/covid-19-impact-on-mena-countries/*.

79 Calha (general rapporteur), 'Instability in the South', p. 11.

80 Jeffrey A. Larsen, 'Projecting Stability in a New Cold War: A NATO Mission?', in Hope (ed.), *Projecting Stability*, p. 24.

81 For this type of problem, see Larry D. Terry, 'The Thinning of Administrative Institutions in the Hollow State', *Administration and Society*, 37(4), 2005, pp. 433–4.

82 Patricia A. Weitsman, *Waging War: Alliances, Coalitions and Institutions of Interstate Violence* (Stanford: Stanford University Press, 2014), p. 32.

83 Alexander Mattelaer, 'How Afghanistan Has Strengthened NATO', *Survival*, 53(6), 2011, p. 127.

84 Aaron Bazin and Dominika Kunertova, 'An Alliance Divided? Five Factors that Could Fracture NATO', *Military Review*, January–February 2017, pp. 82–8.

85 Celeste Wallander, 'NATO's Enemies Within: How Democratic Decline Could Destroy the Alliance', *Foreign Affairs*, 97(4), 2018, p. 72.

86 Sinan Ulgen, 'Don't Blame Turkey for NATO's Woes', *Foreign Policy*, 3 December 2019, *https://foreignpolicy.com/2019/12/03/dont-blame-turkey-for-natos-woes*.

87 Remarks by NATO Deputy Secretary General Alexander Vershbow at the NATO Future Leaders Summit, Cardiff,

5 September 2014, *https://www.nato.int/cps/en/natohq/opinions_112977.htm?selectedLocale=en.*

Chapter 2 Weary or Wary? The Problem of American Leadership in NATO

1 Stanley Sloan, *Defence of the West: NATO, the European Union and the Transatlantic Bargain* (Manchester: Manchester University Press, 2016), p. 6.
2 'The North Atlantic Treaty' (signed in Washington, DC, 4 April 1949), *https://www.nato.int/cps/en/natolive/official_texts_17120.htm.*
3 Sloan, *Defence of the West*, pp. 10–11.
4 Robert Endicott Osgood et al., *Retreat from Empire: The First Nixon Administration* (Baltimore, MD: Johns Hopkins University Press, 1973).
5 Sean Kay, *NATO and the Future of European Security* (Lanham etc.: Rowman & Littlefield, 1998), p. 124.
6 Cited in Elaine Sciolino, 'Bosnia Policy: Shaped by US Military Role', *New York Times*, 29 July 1996, *https://archive.nytimes.com/www.nytimes.com/library/politics/0729clinton-bosnia.html.*
7 General Wesley Clarke (NATO Supreme Allied Commander Europe), cited in Dag Henriksen, *NATO's Gamble: Combining Diplomacy and Airpower in the Kosovo Crisis 1998–1999* (Annapolis, MD: Naval Institute Press, 2007), p. 198.
8 NATO, 'Comprehensive Political Guidance', 29 November 2006, para. 5, *http://www.nato.int/cps/on/natohq/official_texts_56425.htm.*
9 House of Commons Defence Committee, *The Future of NATO and European Defence, Ninth Report of Session 2007–08* (London: House of Commons, 2008), para. 41, *https://publications.parliament.uk/pa/cm200708/cmselect/cmdfence/111/11107.htm.*
10 Cited in Thomas S. Mowle and David H. Sacko, 'Global NATO: Bandwagoning in a Unipolar World', *Contemporary Security Policy*, 28(3), 2007, p. 599.
11 Angela Merkel, 'Regierungserklärung von Bundeskanzlerin Dr Angela Merkel zum Nato-Gipfel vor dem Deutschen Bundestag am 26. März 2009 in Berlin', *Bulletin*, 39(1), *https://www.bundesregierung.de/Content/DE/Bulletin/2009/03/39-1-bk-bt.html.*

12 Hillary Clinton, 'America's Pacific Century', *Foreign Policy*, 11 October 2011, *http://foreignpolicy.com/2011/10/11/americas-pacific-century/*.
13 Ryan Lizza, 'Leading from Behind', *New Yorker*, 26 April 2011, *https://www.newyorker.com/news/news-desk/leading-from-behind*.
14 Cited in Reuters, World News, 30 January 2020, *https://www.reuters.com/article/us-britain-usa-pompeo-china/us-sees-chinese-communist-party-as-central-threat-of-our-times-pompeo-says-idUSKBN1ZT1FL*.
15 Emily Tamkin, 'In Poland Trump Paints His Vision of Civilization and Commits to Article V', *Foreign Policy*, 6 July 2017, *https://foreignpolicy.com/2017/07/06/in-poland-trump-paints-his-vision-of-civilization-and-commits-to-article-v/*.
16 Anne Gearan, 'Trump Confirms Plans to Slash US Troop Presence in Germany', *Washington Post*, 24 June 2020, *https://www.washingtonpost.com/politics/trump-confirms-plan-to-slash-us-troop-presence-in-germany-some-probably-will-relocate-to-poland/2020/06/24/5233ad54-b662-11ea-aca5-ebb63d27e1ff_story.html?utm_campaign=wp_todays_worldview*.
17 Cited in David Smith, 'Trump "Treasonous" after Siding with Putin on Election Meddling', *The Guardian*, 16 July 2018, *https://www.theguardian.com/us-news/2018/jul/16/trump-finds-putin-denial-of-election-meddling-powerful*.
18 Jon Henley, 'Angela Merkel: EU Cannot Completely Rely on US and Britain Any More', *The Guardian*, 28 May 2018, *https://www.theguardian.com/world/2017/may/28/merkel-says-eu-cannot-completely-rely-on-us-and-britain-any-more-g7-talks*; Zachary Young, 'Macron: Europe Can't Depend on US for Security: French President Sets Out His Diplomatic Vision for the Year Ahead', *Politico*, 27 August 2018, *https://www.politico.eu/article/europe-defense-macron-cant-depend-on-us-for-security/*.
19 Impeachment hearings centred on evidence that Trump had threatened to withhold military aid to the government in Kiev until it had undertaken an investigation into the affairs of Trump's Democrat rival, Joe Biden.
20 Steven Erlanger, 'What If Trump Wins? Europeans Fear a More Permanent Shift Against Them?', *New York Times*, 18 February 2020, *https://www.nytimes.com/2020/02/18/world/europe/trump-europe-nato.html*.
21 Hans von der Burchard, 'EU Slams China as "Systemic Rival"

as Trade Tension Rises', *Politico*, 3 December 2019, *https://www.politico.eu/article/eu-slams-china-as-systemic-rival-as-trade-tension-rises/*.

22 Joseph Lepgold, 'NATO's Post-Cold War Collective Action Problem', *International Security*, 23(1), 1998, pp. 86–91.

23 Wallace J. Thies, *Friendly Rivals: Bargaining and Burden-Shifting in NATO* (Armonk, New York and London: M.E. Sharpe, 2003).

24 Ellen Hallams and Benjamin Schreer, 'Towards a "Post-American Alliance"? NATO Burden-Sharing after Libya', *International Affairs*, 88(2), 2012, p. 322.

25 Cited in Jim Garamone, 'NATO Has Become a Two-Tiered Alliance', Department of Defence News, 10 June 2011, *https://archive.defense.gov/news/newsarticle.aspx?id=64268*.

26 David M. Herszenhorn, 'Trump Makes Forceful NATO Debut', *Politico*, 25 May 2017, *https://www.politico.eu/article/trump-nato-demands-allies-make-up-for-many-years-lost-on-military-spending/*.

27 OECD, 'International Migration Database', *Stats.OECD, 2019, https://stats.oecd.org/Index.aspx?DataSetCode=MIG*; International Migration Organization, *World Migration Report* (Geneva: IMO, 2018), pp. 34, 50 and 65.

28 Anna Wieslander, 'NATO Must Engage in the Arctic', *Defense One*, 16 September 2019, *https://www.defenseone.com/ideas/2019/09/its-time-nato-arctic/159887/?oref=d-river*.

29 MCDC Countering Hybrid Warfare Project, *Understanding Hybrid Warfare* (MCDC, January 2017), pp. 3–4, *https://assets.publishing.service.gov.uk/government/uploads/system/uploads/attachment_data/file/647776/dar_mcdc_hybrid_warfare.pdf*.

30 NATO, 'NATO's Response to Hybrid Threats', 17 July 2018, paras 20–1, *https://www.nato.int/cps/en/natohq/topics_156338.htm*.

31 These categories are derived from Toshihiro Ihori and Martin C. McGuire, 'National Self-Insurance and Self-Protection against Adversity: Bureaucratic Management of Security and Moral Hazard', *Economics of Governance*, 11(2), 2010, p. 104.

32 James E. King, Jr, 'Collective Defence: The Military Commitment', in Arnold Wolfers (ed.), *Alliance Policy in the Cold War* (Baltimore, MD: Johns Hopkins University Press, 1959), p. 109.

33 A.W. DePorte, 'The First Forty Years', in Stanley R. Sloan (ed.), *NATO in the 1990s* (Washington, DC, etc.: Pergamon-Brasseys, 1989), pp. 43–4.

34 Christopher Layne, *The Peace of Illusions: American Grand Strategy from 1945 to the Present* (Ithaca, NY, and London: Cornell University Press, 2006), p. 96.
35 Guillaume Parmentier, 'Redressing NATO's Imbalances', *Survival*, 42(2), 2000, p. 99.
36 Lawrence S. Kaplan, *NATO 1948: The Birth of the Transatlantic Alliance* (Lanham, MD, etc.: Rowman & Littlefield, 2007), p. 232.
37 Bradley S. Klein, 'How the West Was One: Representational Politics of NATO', *International Studies Quarterly*, 34(3), 1990, pp. 311–25.
38 Michael Brenner, 'The US, NATO and East-West Relations', in Gustav Schmidt (ed.), *A History of NATO – the First Fifty Years, Volume 2* (Houndmills, Basingstoke: Palgrave, 2001), p. 98.
39 Douglas Brinkley, 'Democratic Enlargement: The Clinton Doctrine', *Foreign Policy*, 106, 1997, p. 127.
40 G. John Ikenberry, Thomas J. Knock, Anne-Marie Slaughter and Tony Smith, *The Crisis of American Foreign Policy: Wilsonianism in the Twenty-First Century* (Princeton: Princeton University Press, 2009), pp. 5–10.
41 John Glaser, Christopher A. Preble and Trevor Thrall, *Fuel to the Fire: How Trump Made America's Broken Foreign Policy Even Worse and How We Can Recover* (Washington, DC: The Cato Institute, 2019).
42 Robert D. Blackwill, 'Trump's Foreign Policies Are Better Than They Seem' (Washington, DC: Council on Foreign Relations), *Council Special Report*, no. 84, April 2019, pp. 65–8.
43 Walter Russell Mead, 'The Jacksonian Tradition and American Foreign Policy', *The National Interest*, 58, Winter 1999/2000, pp. 5–29.
44 Walter Russell Mead, 'The Jacksonian Revolt: American Populism and the Liberal Order', *Foreign Affairs*, 96(2), 2017, pp. 2–7; Matthew Kroenig, 'The Case for Trump's Foreign Policy: The Right People, the Right Policies', *Foreign Affairs*, 96(3), 2017, pp. 30–4; Barry R. Posen, 'The Rise of Illiberal Hegemony: Trump's Surprising Grand Strategy', *Foreign Affairs*, 97(2), 2018, pp. 20–7.
45 Michael Clarke and Anthony Ricketts, 'Donald Trump and American Foreign Policy: The Return of the Jacksonian Tradition', *Comparative Strategy*, 36(4), 2017, p. 374.
46 Ivo H. Daalder and James M. Lindsay, *America Unbound: The*

Bush Revolution in Foreign Policy (Washington, DC: Brookings Institution Press, 2003), p. 13.

47 Magnus Petersson, 'The United States as the Reluctant Ally', *Parameters*, 46(1), 2016, p. 44.

48 The Federal Government, *White Paper on German Security Policy and the Future of the Bundeswehr* (2016), p. 49, *https://issat.dcaf.ch/Learn/Resource-Library/Other-Documents/The-2016-German-White-Paper-Strategic-Review-and-Way-Ahead*.

49 Elliot Cohen, 'America's Long Goodbye: The Real Crisis of the Trump Era', *Foreign Affairs*, 98(1), 2019, pp. 138–46.

Chapter 3 Fiscal Constraints, Military Capabilities and Burden-Sharing

1 Robert M. Gates, 'The Security and Defence Agenda (Future of NATO)', Brussels, 10 June 2011, *https://archive.defense.gov/speeches/speech.aspx?speechid=1581*.

2 Stephanie Gaskell, 'Hagel Wants Finance Ministers to Attend NATO Meeting on Defense Spending', *Defense One*, 2 May 2014, *http://www.defenseone.com/threats/2014/05/hagel-wants-finance-ministers-attend-nato-meeting-defensespending/83659/?oref=search_Hagel%20AND%20NATO*.

3 Jeffrey Goldberg, 'The Obama Doctrine', *The Atlantic*, April 2016, *http://www.theatlantic.com/magazine/archive/2016/04/the-obama-doctrine/471525/*.

4 Remarks in press conference with NATO Secretary General Jens Stoltenberg, 18 June 2018, *https://www.atlanticcouncil.org/blogs/natosource/trump-believes-us-paying-a-lot-of-money-to-protect-nato-allies/*.

5 NATO, 'Wales Summit Declaration', 5 September 2014, para. 14, *https://www.nato.int/cps/en/natohq/official_texts_112964.htm*.

6 The three were Greece, the UK and the US. The nine were Bulgaria, Estonia, Greece, Latvia, Lithuania, Poland, Romania, the UK and the US. See NATO Public Diplomacy Division, 'Defence Expenditure of NATO Countries (2013–2019)', 29 November 2019, Table 3, *https://www.nato.int/nato_static_fl2014/assets/pdf/pdf_2019_11/20191129_pr-2019-123-en.pdf*.

7 'Defence Expenditure of NATO Countries (2013–2019)', Tables 2, 3 and 4.

8 Stoltenberg press conference, 29 November 2019, *https://www.nato.int/cps/en/natohq/news_171458.htm.*
9 'Comparative Defence Statistics', *The Military Balance*, 120, 2020, p. 21.
10 'Defence Expenditure of NATO Countries (2013–2019)', Table 2.
11 Credit Suisse, 'European Demographics & Fiscal Sustainability', *Global Demographics and Pensions Research*, 17 January 2013, p. 1, *https://plus.credit-suisse.com/rpc4/ravDocView?docid=VUrElj.*
12 Economic and Financial Affairs Committee, *The 2015 Ageing Report: Economic and Budgetary Projections for the 28 EU Member States (2013–2060)* (Brussels: European Commission, 2015), p. 11.
13 Jordan Becker, 'Accidental Rivals? EU Fiscal Rules, NATO, and Transatlantic Burden-Sharing', *Journal of Peace Research*, 56(5), 2019, pp. 697–713.
14 'COVID-19 Impact', *Janes Defence*, 8 June 2020, *https://news.cision.com/jane-s-group-uk/r/covid-19-impact--defence-spending-down-among-nato-s-top-european-spenders--predicts-janes,c3128889.*
15 David Yost, 'The US–European Capabilities Gap and the Prospects for ESDP', in Jolyon Howorth and John T. Keeler (eds), *Defending Europe: The EU, NATO and the Quest for European Autonomy* (New York: Palgrave Macmillan, 2003), p. 83.
16 Douglas Barrie et al., *Protecting Europe: Meeting the EU's Military Level of Ambition in the Context of Brexit* (International Institute for Strategic Studies and the German Council on Foreign Relations, November 2018), p. 2, *https://dgap.org/en/research/publications/protecting-europe.*
17 Douglas Barrie et al., *Defending Europe: Scenario-Based Capability Requirements for NATO's European Members* (International Institute for Strategic Studies and the German Council on Foreign Relations, April 2019), *https://www.iiss.org/blogs/research-paper/2019/05/defending-europe.*
18 Yost, 'The US–European Capabilities Gap', p. 86.
19 *NATO Handbook* (Brussels: NATO Office of Information and Press, 2001), p. 51.
20 NATO, *Comprehensive Political Guidance*, 29 November, 2006, paras 16 and 18, *https://www.nato.int/cps/en/natohq/official_texts_56425.htm?.*
21 'Wales Summit Declaration', paras 9, 14, 54 and 64.
22 NATO, 'Warsaw Summit Communiqué', 9 July 2016, paras 47 and 100, *https://www.nato.int/cps/en/natohq/official_texts_133169.*

htm#; NATO, 'Brussels Summit Declaration', 12 July 2018, paras 31–41, *https://www.nato.int/cps/en/natohq/official_texts_156624.htm#*.

23 House of Lords Media Notices, 5 November 2019, *https://www.parliament.uk/business/lords/media-centre/house-of-lords-media-notices/2019/november-2019/nato-meeting-in-london-must-address-capability-shortfalls-russian-aggression-and-turkey-russia/*.

24 Benoit Pelopidas, 'The Nuclear Straitjacket: American Extended Deterrence and Nonproliferation', in Stéfanie Von Hlatky and Andreas Wenger (eds), *The Future of Extended Deterrence: The United States and Beyond* (Washington, DC: Georgetown University Press, 2015), p. 77.

25 'NATO's Nuclear Deterrence Policy and Forces' (as updated 16 April 2020), *https://www.nato.int/cps/en/natohq/topics_50068.htm*.

26 'NATO Nuclear Deterrence' Factsheet, February 2020, *https://www.nato.int/nato_static_fl2014/assets/pdf/2020/2/pdf/200224-factsheet-nuclear-en.pdf*.

27 Alexander Lanoszka, 'Do Allies Really Free Ride?', *Survival*, 57(3), 2015, p. 138.

28 Madeleine Moon (rapporteur), 'The Space Domain and Allied Defence', NATO Parliamentary Assembly, Defence and Security Committee, 8 October 2017, p. 9, *https://www.nato-pa.int/document/2017-space-domain-and-allied-defence-moon-report-162-dscfc-17-e-rev1-fin*.

29 Tim Vasen, 'Is NATO Ready for Galileo?', *JAPCC Journal*, June 2019, *https://www.japcc.org/is-nato-ready-for-galileo/*.

30 Figures derived from Flight Global, *World Air Forces 2020*, *https://www.flightglobal.com/reports/world-air-forces-2020/135665.article?adredir=1*.

31 Gene Germanovich et al., *NATO's Amphibious Forces: Command and Control of a Multibrigade Alliance Task Force* (Santa Monica, CA: RAND Corporation, 2019), p. xiii, *https://www.rand.org/content/dam/rand/pubs/research_reports/RR2900/RR2928/RAND_RR2928.pdf*.

32 Cited in Rajnish Singh, 'EDA and NATO Look at Ways to Work Together on Air to Air Refueling', *The Parliament Magazine*, 10 October 2018, *https://www.theparliamentmagazine.eu/articles/opinion/eda-and-nato-look-ways-work-together-air-air-refueling*.

33 Yvonni-Stefanie Efstathiou, 'European Strategic Airlift: A Work

in Progress', IISS *Military Balance Blog*, 10 January 2019, *https://www.iiss.org/blogs/military-balance/2019/01/european-strategic-airlift*; Erik Brattberg and Tomáš Valašek, 'EU Defence Cooperation: Progress Amid Transatlantic Concerns', Carnegie Endowment for International Peace, November 2019, p.11, *https://carnegieendowment.org/files/WP_Brattberg_Valasek_EU_Def_Coop_v3.pdf*.

34 'Oral Evidence: The Indispensable Ally? US, NATO and UK Defence Relations', House of Commons Defence Committee, 31 October 2017, *http://data.parliament.uk/writtenevidence/committeeevidence.svc/evidencedocument/defence-committee/the-indispensable-ally-us-nato-and-uk-defence-relations/oral/72419.html*.

35 Cited in Rick Noack, 'Afraid of a Military Conflict: The German Military Is Currently Unavailable', *Washington Post*, 24 January 2018, *https://www.washingtonpost.com/news/worldviews/wp/2018/01/24/afraid-of-a-major-conflict-the-german-military-is-currently-unavailable/*.

36 'Interoperability: Connecting NATO Forces', *https://www.nato.int/cps/en/natolive/topics_84112.htm*.

37 Hans Binnendijk and Richard L. Kugler, 'Transforming European Forces', *Survival*, 44(3), 2002, pp. 122, 126.

38 Pierre Nolin (general rapporteur), 'Interoperability: The Need for Transatlantic Harmonisation', NATO Parliamentary Assembly, November 2008, para. 66. *https://www.europarl.europa.eu/meetdocs/2004_2009/documents/dv/261/261006/261006transatlanticharmonisationen.pdf*.

39 Stew Magnuson, 'NATO Nations Strive to Standardize Training Systems', *National Defense*, 1 July 2019, *https://www.nationaldefensemagazine.org/articles/2019/7/1/nato-nations-strive-to-standardize-training-systems*.

40 Press conference after a meeting of NATO Defence Ministers, 14 February 2018, *https://www.nato.int/cps/en/natohq/opinions_151504.htm*.

41 Ben Zyla, 'Who is Free-Riding in NATO's Peace Operations in the 1990s?', *International Peacekeeping*, 23(6), 2016, pp. 416–41.

42 Peter K. Forster and Stephen J. Cimbala, *The US, NATO and Military Burden-Sharing* (Abingdon: Frank Cass, 2005), p. 135.

43 Ivo H. Daalder (US Permanent Representative to NATO) and James G. Stavridis (Supreme Allied Commander Europe),

'NATO's Victory in Libya: The Right Way to Run in an Intervention', *Foreign Affairs*, 91(2), 2012, p. 2.

44 Daalder and Stavridis, 'NATO's Victory in Libya', p. 2.

45 William J. Burns, *The Back Channel: American Diplomacy in a Disordered World* (London: Hurst and Company, 2019), pp. 317–18. (Burns was US Undersecretary for Political Affairs and then Deputy Secretary of State at the time of the Libyan intervention.)

46 Derek Chollet, *The Long Game: How Obama Defied Washington and Redefined America's Role in the World* (New York: Public Affairs, 2016), pp. 99–100.

47 Lee Willett, 'The Maritime Contribution', in *Accidental Heroes: Britain, France and the Libya Operation* (London: Royal United Services Institute, September 2011), p. 9.

48 Willett, 'The Maritime Contribution', p. 9.

49 Cited in Tim Haesebrouck, 'NATO Burden Sharing in Libya: A Fuzzy Set Qualitative Comparison', *Journal of Conflict Resolution*, 61(10), 2017, p. 2251.

50 Michael Clarke, 'Curious Victory for NATO in Libya', RUSI *Commentary*, August 2011, *https://rusi.org/commentary/curious-victory-nato-libya*.

51 'A Troubling Victory', *The Economist*, 3 September 2011, *https://www.economist.com/international/2011/09/03/a-troubling-victory*.

52 Samantha Power, *The Education of an Idealist* (London: William Collins, 2019), p. 310.

53 Christopher Chivvis, 'Libya and the Future of Liberal Intervention', *Survival*, 54(6), 2013, p. 81.

54 Aidan Hehir, 'The Permanence of Inconsistency: Libya, the Security Council and the Responsibility to Protect', *International Security*, 38(1), 2013, pp. 137–59.

55 Recounted in Robert M. Gates, *Duty: Memoirs of a Secretary at War* (London: W.H. Allen, 2014), pp. 214–15.

56 Cited in Elisabeth Bumiller, 'Gates Faults US Allies on Afghan War', *New York Times*, 11 March 2011, *https://www.nytimes.com/2011/03/12/world/europe/12gates.html*.

57 James Sperling and Mark Webber, 'NATO's Intervention in the Afghan Civil War', *Civil* Wars, 14(3), 2012, p. 348; Anthony Zannella, 'An Analysis of Burden Sharing in NATO and the Problem of Free Riding', *Political Analysis*, 21(5), 2020, p. 8.

58 Jo Jakobsen, 'Is European NATO *Really* Free-Riding? Patterns of

Material and Non-Material Burden-Sharing after the Cold War', *European Security* 27(4), 2018, p. 5.

59 Hew Strachan, 'Learning Lessons from Afghanistan: Two Imperatives', *Parameters*, 49(3), 2019, p. 9.

60 Stephen M. Saideman and David P. Auerswald, 'Comparing Caveats: Understanding the Sources of National Restrictions on NATO's Mission in Afghanistan', *International Studies Quarterly*, 56(1), 2012, pp. 67, 76–8.

61 Kathleen J. McInnes, *How and Why States Defect from Contemporary Military Coalitions* (Cham, Switzerland: Palgrave Macmillan, 2020), p. 12.

62 Olivier Schmitt, 'International Organization at War: NATO Practices in the Afghan Campaign', *Cooperation and Conflict*, 52(4), 2017, pp. 6–9.

63 Seth A. Johnston, 'NATO's Lessons', *Parameters*, 49(3), 2019, pp. 13–20.

64 The text of the agreement is available at: *https://www.washingtonpost.com/context/u-s-taliban-peace-deal/7aab0f58-dd5c-430d-9557-1b6672d889c3/?itid=lk_inline_manual_3*.

65 John Allen (former Commander of ISAF, 2011–13), 'The US–Taliban Peace Deal: A Road to Nowhere', Brookings Institution, 5 March 2020, *https://www.brookings.edu/blog/order-from-chaos/2020/03/05/the-us-taliban-peace-deal-a-road-to-nowhere/*.

66 *https://www.defenseone.com/policy/2020/10/all-us-troops-afghanistan-withdraw-christmas-trump-tweets/169105/*.

67 Johnston, 'NATO's Lessons', p. 25.

Chapter 4 NATO and Russia: Cold War Redux

1 On 'othering', see Iver B. Neumann, *Uses of the Other: The 'East' in European Identity Formation* (Manchester: Manchester University Press, 1999).

2 'NATO–Russia Council Joint Statement', 20 November 2010, *https://www.nato.int/cps/en/natohq/news_68871.htm*.

3 Mark Kramer, 'The Myth of a No-NATO-Enlargement Pledge to Russia', *Washington Quarterly*, 32(2), 2009, pp. 39–61; Mary Elise Sarotte, 'A Broken Promise?', *Foreign Affairs*, 93(5), 2014, *https://www.foreignaffairs.com/articles/russia-fsu/2014-08-11/*

broken-promise; and Joshua Itzkowitz Shifrinson, 'Deal or No Deal? The End of the Cold War and the US Offer to Limit NATO Expansion', *International Security*, 40(4), 2016, pp. 7–44.

4 Cited in Shifrinson, 'Deal or No Deal?', p. 12.

5 Quoted in *Rossiiskiye Vesti*, 18 November 1993. Translated in *The Current Digest of the Post-Soviet Press* (hereafter *CDPSP*), XLV(46), 1993, pp. 11–12.

6 See Martin A. Smith, *Russia and NATO since 1991: From Cold War through Cold Peace to Partnership?* (Abingdon: Routledge, 2006).

7 On 'co-binding', see Daniel Deudney and G. John Ikenberry, 'The Nature and Sources of Liberal International Order', *Review of International Studies*, 25(2), 1999, pp. 182–4. For its relevance in the NATO–Russia case, see Andrej Krickovic, 'When Ties Do Not Bind: The Failure of Institutional Binding in NATO–Russia Relations', *Contemporary Security Policy*, 37(2), 2016, pp. 175–99.

8 'Founding Act on Mutual Relations, Cooperation and Security between NATO and the Russian Federation', 27 May 1991, *http://www.nato.int/cps/en/natohq/official_texts_25468.htm*.

9 *Izvestia*, 28 May 1997 in *CDPSP*, XLIX(21), 1997, p. 5.

10 Cited in 'Russia and European Security', Document A/1722 (Paris: Assembly of the Western European Union, 2000).

11 'Ambassador Pickering Response to Question from Senator Hagel', *The Debate on NATO Enlargement*, Senate Foreign Relations Committee, 105th Congress, First Session, 1997 (Washington, DC: US Government Printing Office, 1998), *https://www.gpo.gov/fdsys/pkg/CHRG-105shrg46832/html/CHRG-105shrg46832.htm*.

12 Col. Gen. Leonid Ivashov, 'Russia–NATO: Matters of Cooperation', *International Affairs* (Moscow), 44(6), 1998, p. 113.

13 Quoted in *Segodnya*, 10 December 1998, in *CDPSP*, L(49), 1998, p. 19.

14 Klaus-Peter Klaiber, 'The NATO–Russia Relationship a Year after Paris', *NATO Review*, 46(3), 1998, pp. 16–19.

15 One expert report concluded that Russia's 'rigid commitment to veto any enforcement action' at the UN had been 'the major factor forcing NATO into an unmandated action'. See Independent International Commission on Kosovo, *Kosovo Report* (Oxford: Oxford University Press, 2000), p. 161.

16 Oleg Levitin, 'Inside Moscow's Kosovo Muddle', *Survival*, 42(1), 2000, pp. 130–40.

17 The incident involved Russian troops assigned to a joint NATO–Russia peacekeeping force in Bosnia occupying Pristina airport in what appeared to be a pre-emptive move to carve out a sector of operations independent of NATO. See Paul Latawski and Martin A. Smith, *The Kosovo Crisis and the Evolution of Post-Cold War European Security* (Manchester: Manchester University Press, 2003), pp. 103–5.
18 Peter Trenin-Straussov, *The NATO–Russia Permanent Joint Council in 1997–1999: Anatomy of a Failure* (Berlin: Berlin Information Center for Transatlantic Security, 1999), *http://www.bits.de/public/researchnote/rn99-1.htm.*
19 See 'Russia and European Security'.
20 Quoted in *Nezavisimaya Gazeta*, 12 October 1999, in *CDPSP*, LI(41), 1999, p. 3.
21 'Joint Statement on the Occasion of the Visit of the Secretary General of NATO, Lord Robertson, in Moscow on 16 February 2000', *http://www.nato.int/cps/en/natohq/news_17913.htm?selectedLocale=en.*
22 Quoted in Ewen MacAskill, 'NATO and Russia Re-establish Ties as Tensions Ease', *The Guardian*, 17 February 2000, *https://www.theguardian.com/world/2000/feb/17/ewenmacaskill.*
23 'Press Conference with NATO Secretary General, Lord Robertson, 22 November 2001', *http://nato.int/docu/speech/2001/s011122b.htm.*
24 See *Noviye Izvestia*, 16 May 2002, in *CDPSP*, 54(20), 2002, p. 5; and *Trud*, 30 May 2002, in *CDPSP*, LIV(22), 2002, p. 4.
25 Michael Evans, 'Russia to Move into NATO HQ', *The Times*, 15 May 2002.
26 Quoted in Kathleen Moore, 'NATO: Alliance Mulls Details of Larger Role for Russia', *Radio Free Europe/Radio Liberty*, 27 February 2002, *http://www.rferl.org/a/1098934.html.*
27 See Robertson's speech, 'A New Russian Revolution: Partnership with NATO', *http://www.nato.int/docu/speech/2002/s021213a.htm.*
28 'Press Conference by NATO Secretary General, Lord Robertson Following the Meeting of the NATO–Russia Council', 13 May 2003, *http://www.nato.int/docu/speech/2003/s030513a.htm.*
29 Maj. Gen. Peter Williams, 'NATO–Russia Military Co-operation: From Dialogue to Interoperability?', *RUSI Journal*, 150(5), 2005, pp. 44–7.

30 Dmitri Trenin, 'Russia Leaves the West', *Foreign Affairs*, 85(4), 2006, p. 90.
31 'Meeting of the NATO–Russia Council at the Level of Heads of State and Government Held in Bucharest', 4 April 2008, *http://www.nato.int/docu/pr/2008/p08-050e.html*.
32 Oksana Antonenko, 'A War with No Winners', *Survival*, 50(5), 2008, pp. 23–36.
33 NATO, 'Bucharest Summit Declaration', 3 April 2008, para. 23, *http://www.nato.int/docu/pr/2008/p08-049e.html*.
34 William J. Burns, *The Back Channel: American Diplomacy in a Disordered World* (London: Hurst and Company, 2019), p. 239.
35 Condoleezza Rice, *No Higher Honour* (New York: Simon & Schuster, 2011), p. 673.
36 William H. Hill, *No Place for Russia: European Security Institutions since 1989* (New York: Columbia University Press, 2018), pp. 252–3.
37 Johanna Popjanevski, 'From Sukhumi to Tskhinvali: The Path to War in Georgia', in Svante Cornell and Frederick Starr (eds), *The Guns of August 2008: Russia's War in Georgia* (London: M.E. Sharpe, 2009), p. 160.
38 James Sherr, 'Culpabilities and Consequences', Chatham House Report, BN 08/01, p. 2, *https://www.chathamhouse.org/sites/default/files/public/Research/Russia%20and%20Eurasia/0908rep_sherr.pdf*.
39 See 'Final Communiqué (Press Release (2008) 153)', para. 25, *http://www.nato.int/docu/pr/2008/p08-153e.html*.
40 Julie Ray and Neli Esipova, 'Before Crisis, Ukrainians More Likely to See NATO as a Threat', Gallup, 14 March 2014, *http://www.gallup.com/poll/167927/crisis-ukrainians-likely-nato-threat.aspx*.
41 James Marson, 'Putin to the West: Hands off Ukraine', *Time*, 25 May 2009, *http://content.time.com/time/world/article/0,8599,1900838,00.html*.
42 'Press Statement and Answers to Journalists: Questions Following a Meeting of the Russia–NATO Council', 4 April 2008, Bucharest, *http://en.kremlin.ru/events/president/transcripts/24903*.
43 'Address by President of the Russian Federation', 18 March 2014, Moscow, *http://en.kremlin.ru/events/president/news/20603*.
44 Eugene Rumer, *Russia and the Security of Europe*, Carnegie Endowment for International Peace, 30 June 2016, p. 32,

http://carnegieendowment.org/2016/06/30/russia-and-security-of-europe-pub-63990.

45 Quoted in Timothy Snyder, 'Ukraine: Putin's Denial', *NYR Daily*, 13 December 2013, *https://www.nybooks.com/daily/2013/12/13/ukraine-putins-denial/.*

46 Anatol Lieven, 'Russian Opposition to NATO Expansion', *The World Today*, October 1995, p. 198.

47 'Joint Statement at the Meeting of the NATO–Russia Council held in Lisbon on 20 November 2010', *http://www.nato.int/cps/en/natohq/news_68871.htm.*

48 Heidi Reisinger, 'Does Russia Matter? Purely Political Relations Are Not Enough in Operational Times', NATO Defence College, Conference Report, January 2014, p. 2, *https://www.jstor.org/stable/pdf/resrep10322.pdf.*

49 Quoted in Roger McDermott, 'NATO–Russia Relations Post-Crimea', *Eurasia Daily Monitor*, 11(56), 2014, *https://jamestown.org/program/nato-russia-relations-post-crimea/.*

50 'North Atlantic Council Statement on the Situation in Ukraine', 2 March 2014, *http://www.nato.int/cps/en/natohq/official_texts_107681.htm?selectedLocale=en.*

51 'Statement by NATO Foreign Ministers', 1 April 2014, *http://www.nato.int/cps/en/natolive/news_108501.htm.*

52 NATO, 'Warsaw Summit Communiqué', 9 July 2016, para. 15, *http://www.nato.int/cps/en/natohq/official_texts_133169.htm.*

53 NATO, 'Brussels Summit Declaration', 12 July 2018, para. 6, *https://www.nato.int/cps/en/natohq/official_texts_156624.htm.*

54 NATO, 'London Declaration', 4 December 2019, para. 3, *https://www.nato.int/cps/en/natohq/official_texts_171584.htm.*

55 Busra Nur Bilgic Cakmak, 'NATO Concerned by Russia's Increasing Presence in E. Med', Anadolu Agency, 16 June 2020, *https://www.aa.com.tr/en/middle-east/nato-concerned-by-russia-s-growing-presence-in-emed/1879045.*

56 'Presidential Address to the Federal Assembly', 1 March 2018, *http://en.kremlin.ru/events/president/news/56957.*

57 Tom O'Connor, 'Russia Warns NATO Is "Approaching Our Borders"', *Newsweek*, 22 November 2019, *https://www.newsweek.com/russia-nato-borders-strategy-new-decade-1473617.*

58 NATO, 'Wales Summit Declaration', 5 September 2014, paras 5–12, *https://www.nato.int/cps/en/natohq/official_texts_112964.htm.*

59 Joseph A. Day (general rapporteur), 'Reinforcing NATO's Deterrence in the East', NATO Parliamentary Assembly, Defence and Security Committee, 17 November 2018, *https://www.nato-pa.int/document/2018-deterrence-east-day-report-168-dsc-18-e-fin*.
60 'NATO–Russia Relations: The Facts', updated 9 August 2019, *https://www.nato.int/cps/en/natohq/topics_111767.htm#cl803*.
61 Day (general rapporteur), 'Reinforcing NATO's Deterrence in the East', p. 8.
62 Miro Kovac (rapporteur), 'NATO–Russia Relations – a Snapshot', NATO Parliamentary Assembly, Political Committee, October 2019, p.3, *https://www.nato-pa.int/document/2019-pcnp-report-nato-russia-relations-snapshot-kovac-145-pcnp-19-e*.
63 *Reducing the Risks of Conventional Deterrence in Europe: Arms Control in the NATO–Russia Contact Zones* (Vienna: OSCE Network, 2018), p. 7, *https://osce-network.net/file-OSCE-Network/Publications/RISK_SP.pdf*.

Chapter 5 Task Discretion: Doing Less but Better

1 Anthony King, 'Overload: Problems of Governing in the 1970s', *Political Studies*, 23(2–3), 1975, pp. 173–4.
2 Adam Taylor, 'Germany Finally Pledges to Increase Defence Spending to NATO Levels, But Trump Still Won't be Happy', *Washington Post*, 8 November 2019, *https://www.washingtonpost.com/world/2019/11/08/germany-finally-pledges-increase-military-spending-nato-levels-trump-still-wont-be-happy/*.
3 NATO Public Diplomacy Division, 'Defence Expenditure of NATO Countries (2013–2019)', 29 November 2019, Tables 3 and 4, *https://www.nato.int/nato_static_fl2014/assets/pdf/pdf_2019_11/20191129_pr-2019-123-en.pdf*.
4 Tobias Buck, 'German Armed Forces in "Dramatically Bad" Shape, Report Finds', *Financial Times*, 20 February 2018, *https://www.ft.com/content/23c524f6-1642-11e8-9376-4a6390addb44*.
5 Mathew Karnitschnig, 'Germany's Soldiers of Misfortune', *Politico*, 19 April 2019, *https://www.politico.eu/article/germany-biggest-enemy-threadbare-army-bundeswehr/*.
6 Robert Hariman, 'Prudence/Performance', *Rhetoric Society Quarterly*, 21(2), 1991, p. 26.

7 John A. Vasquez, 'Ethics, Foreign Policy, and Liberal Wars: The Role of Restraint in Moral Decision Making', *International Studies Perspectives*, 6(3), 2005, pp. 312–13.
8 As suggested by Stephen Walt, for instance, in *The Hell of Good Intentions: America's Foreign Policy Elite and the Decline of US Primacy* (New York: Farrar, Straus and Giroux, 2018), pp. 269–70.
9 *National Security Strategy of the United States of America* (Washington, DC, 2017), p. 48, *https://www.whitehouse.gov/wp-content/uploads/2017/12/NSS-Final-12-18-2017-0905.pdf.*
10 Dominic Tierney, 'Obama and Trump: Foreign Policy Opposites or Twins?', e-notes, Foreign Policy Research Institute, 13 December 2019, *https://www.fpri.org/article/2019/12/obama-and-trump-foreign-policy-opposites-or-twins/.*
11 Brad Stapleton, 'Out of Area Ops are Out: Reassessing the NATO Mission', *War on the Rocks*, 7 July 2016, *https://warontherocks.com/2016/07/out-of-area-ops-are-out-reassessing-the-nato-mission/.*
12 Speech of German Defence Minister Annegret Kramp-Karrenbauer, London School of Economics and Political Science, 16 January 2020, *https://www.bmvg.de/en/the-minister-of-defence/akk-kramp-karrenbauer-london-speech-minister-of-defence-175342.*
13 Alice Pannier and Olivier Schmitt, 'To Fight Another Day: France between the Fight against Terrorism and Future Warfare', *International Affairs*, 95(4), 2019, p. 911.
14 Patrick Porter, *Blunder: Britain's War in Iraq* (Oxford etc.: Oxford University Press, 2018), p.157.
15 Matthew Uttley, Benedict Wilkinson and Armida Van Rij, 'A Power for the Future? Global Britain and the Future Character of Conflict', *International Affairs*, 95(4), 2019, p. 805.
16 See the comments of ministers and officials reported in House of Commons Defence Committee, *Beyond 2 Per Cent: A Preliminary Report on the Modernising Defence Programme* (Seventh Report of Session 2017–19, June 2019), pp. 9–10, *https://publications.parliament.uk/pa/cm201719/cmselect/cmdfence/818/818.pdf.*
17 Peter Roberts, 'The UK and the Northern Group: A Necessary Partnership', *Whitehall Papers*, 93(1), 2018, p. 59.
18 Hew Strachan, 'The Lost Meaning of Strategy', *Survival*, 47(3), 2005, p. 34.
19 Richard K. Betts, 'Is Strategy an Illusion?', *International Security*, 25(2), 2000, pp. 5–50.

20 Villiam Krüger-Klausen and Liselotte Odgaard, 'Introduction', in Liselotte Odgaard (ed.), *Strategy in NATO: Preparing for an Imperfect World* (Houndmills, Basingstoke, and New York: Palgrave Macmillan, 2014), pp. 2–3.
21 Betts, 'Is Strategy an Illusion?', pp. 16, 49–50.
22 Lawrence Freedman, 'The Future of Strategic Studies', in John Baylis, James J. Wirtz, Colin S. Grey and Eliot Cohen (eds), *Strategy in the Contemporary World: An Introduction to Strategic Studies* (Oxford etc.: Oxford University Press, 2007), p. 363.
23 Lawrence Freedman, *Strategy: A History* (Oxford etc.: Oxford University Press, 2013), p. 611.
24 'Why a Strategy Is Not a Plan', *The Economist*, 2 November 2013, *https://www.economist.com/books-and-arts/2013/11/02/why-a-strategy-is-not-a-plan*.
25 Patrick Porter, 'Why America's Grand Strategy Has Not Changed: Power, Habit and the US Foreign Policy Establishment', *International Security*, 42(4), 2018, p. 13.
26 Cited in Freedman, *Strategy*, pp. 609–10.
27 'Comprehensive Political Guidance', adopted 29 November 2006, *https://www.nato.int/cps/en/natohq/official_texts_56425.htm?*
28 Jens Ringsmose and Sten Rynning, 'Introduction. Taking Stock of NATO's New Strategic Concept', in Jens Ringsmose and Sten Rynning (eds), *NATO's New Strategic Concept: A Comprehensive Assessment* (Copenhagen: Danish Institute of International Studies, 2011), p. 15.
29 Jens Ringsmose and Sten Rynning, 'Come Home, NATO? The Atlantic Alliance's New Strategic Concept', *DIIS Report*, No. 4, 2009, p. 27.
30 Diego A. Ruiz Palmer, 'A Strategic Odyssey: Constancy of Purpose and Strategy-Making in NATO, 1949–2019', NATO Defence College, *Research Paper*, No. 3, June 2019, p. 93.
31 General Tod Wolters, Press Briefing on USEUCOM Priorities, 3 October 2019, *https://www.defense.gov/Newsroom/Transcripts/Transcript/Article/1979994/gen-tod-wolters-supreme-allied-commander-europe-and-commander-us-european-comma/*.
32 'London Declaration Issued by NATO Heads of State and Government', 4 December 2019, *https://www.nato.int/cps/en/natohq/official_texts_171584.htm*.
33 Daniel Fiott, 'What If ... the United States Pulls Out of Europe?',

in Florence Gaub (ed.), 'What If ...? Scanning the Horizon: 12 Scenarios for 2021', *Chaillot Paper*, 150, February 2019, pp. 55–8.

34 Richard Barrons, 'NATO – Time to Wake Up or Shut Down', *Standpoint*, 118, March 2020, p. 17.

35 House of Commons Defence Committee, *Indispensable Allies: US, NATO and UK Defence Relations* (eighth report of session, 2017–19), pp. 26–7, *https://publications.parliament.uk/pa/cm201719/cmselect/cmdfence/387/387.pdf*.

36 Hans Binnendijk, '5 Consequences of Life without NATO', *Defence News*, 19 March 2019, *https://www.defensenews.com/opinion/commentary/2019/03/19/5-consequences-of-a-life-without-nato/*.

37 Barry R. Posen, 'Trump Aside, What's the US Role in NATO?', *New York Times*, 10 March 2019, *https://www.nytimes.com/2019/03/10/opinion/trump-aside-whats-the-us-role-in-nato.html*.

38 John J. Mearsheimer and Stephen M. Walt, 'The Case for Offshore Balancing: A Superior American Strategy', *Foreign Affairs*, 95(4), 2016, p. 82.

39 Hal Brands, *The Limits of Offshore Balancing* (Carlisle Barracks, PA: United States Army War College Press, 2015), pp. 41–57.

40 A phrase derived from Michael G. Roskin, 'NATO: The Strange Alliance Getting Stranger', *Parameters*, 28(2), 1998, p. 38.

41 Joshua Shifrinson, 'Time to Consolidate NATO?', *Washington Quarterly*, 40(1), 2017, pp. 109–23.

42 Stuart Croft, Jolyon Howorth, Terry Terriff and Mark Webber, 'NATO's Triple Challenge', *International Affairs*, 76(3), 2000, pp. 495–518; Mats Berdal and David Ucko, 'NATO at 60', *Survival*, 51(2), 2009, pp. 55–76.

43 'Symposium. NATO at 70: Where Next?', *Politico*, 3 April 2019, *https://www.politico.eu/article/nato-at-70-where-next/*.

44 Thierry Tardy, 'Calibrating the Scope of NATO's Mandate', NATO Defence College, *Policy Brief*, No. 24, November 2019.

45 For this sort of problem, see Michael M. Atkinson, 'Lindblom's Lament: Incrementalism and the Persistent Pull of the Status Quo', *Policy and Society*, 30(1), 2011, pp. 9–18.

46 Andrew T. Wolff, 'The Structural and Political Crisis of NATO Transformation', *Journal of Transatlantic Studies*, 7(4), 2009, p. 489.

47 'The Future of NATO: NATO Flexes Its Muscle Memory', *The Economist*, 30 August 2014, *https://www.economist.com/international/2014/08/30/nato-flexes-its-muscle-memory*.

48 Luke Coffey and Daniel Kochis, 'At 70th Anniversary, NATO Must Return to Basics', The Heritage Foundation, *Issue Brief*, No. 4946, 1 April 2019, *https://www.heritage.org/defense/report/70th-anniversary-nato-must-return-basics.*
49 James Sperling and Mark Webber, 'NATO and the Ukraine Crisis: Collective Securitisation', *European Journal of International Security*, 2(1), 2017, pp. 19–46.
50 The basic idea here is inspired by (but goes some way beyond) a formulation used by John Bew in oral evidence to the House of Commons Defence Committee inquiry (28 March 2017) on 'The Indispensable Ally? US, NATO and UK Defence Relations', reply to Q107, *https://policyexchange.org.uk/wp-content/uploads/2017/04/49473.pdf.*
51 Patrick Porter, *The Global Village Myth: Distance, War, and the Limits of Power* (London: Hurst and Company, 2015), pp. 8–11, 18–50.
52 Alexander Mattelaer, 'Rediscovering Geography in NATO Defence Planning', *Defence Studies*, 18(3), 2018, p. 348.
53 Mattelaer, 'Rediscovering Geography', pp. 350–1.
54 Curtis M. Scaparrotti and Colleen B. Bell, *Moving Out: A Comprehensive Assessment of European Military Mobility* (Washington, DC: Atlantic Council, 2020), pp. 20–2.
55 Simon J. Smith, 'NATO and the EU: A Short History of an Uneasy Relationship', *The Conversation*, 2 December 2019, *https://theconversation.com/nato-and-the-eu-a-short-history-of-an-uneasy-relationship-126710.*
56 Alexander R. Vershbow and Lauren M. Speranza, *More in the Med: How NATO Can Refocus Its Efforts in the South and Italy Can Lead the Charge* (Washington, DC: Atlantic Council, December 2019), p. 11.
57 Lars Haugom, 'Turkish Foreign Policy under Erdoğan: A Change in International Orientation?', *Comparative Strategy*, 38(3), 2019, p. 209.
58 Recep Tayyip Erdoğan, 'How Turkey Sees the Crisis with the US', *New York Times*, 10 August 2018, *https://www.nytimes.com/2018/08/10/opinion/turkey-erdogan-trump-crisis-sanctions.html.*
59 Steven Erlanger, 'Turkish Aggression Is NATO's "Elephant in the Room"', *New York Times*, 3 August 2020, *https://www.nytimes.com/2020/08/03/world/europe/turkey-nato.html.*
60 Max Hoffmann, 'Responding to Turkey's Purchase of Russia's

S-400 Missile System', Centre for American Progress, 21 March 2019, *https://www.americanprogress.org/issues/security/reports/2019/03/21/467518/responding-turkeys-purchase-russias-s-400-missile-system/.*

61 Metin Gurcan, 'Can Ankara's Sudden Change of Heart on NATO Save the Day in Idlib?', *Al-Monitor*, 25 February 2020, *https://www.al-monitor.com/pulse/originals/2020/02/turkey-syria-united-states-ankara-change-of-heart-on-nato.html.*

62 Speculation that Turkey might request an Article 5 action has occurred on a number of occasions over the war in Syria, most recently in February 2020 following the deaths of thirty-three Turkish troops at the hands of Syrian government forces in Syria's Idlib province.

Chapter 6 American Leadership or European Autonomy?

1 John H. Aldrich et al., 'Foreign Policy and the Electoral Connection', *Annual Review of Political Science*, 9, 2006, pp. 477–502.

2 Constanz Stelzenmueller and Joshua Raiser, *Transatlantic Trends: Key Findings 2014* (The German Marshall Fund of the United States, September 2014), p. 44, *http://www.gmfus.org/publications/transatlantic-trends-2014.*

3 Stelzenmueller and Raiser, *Transatlantic Trends … 2014*, p. 45.

4 Michael Smith, 'Most NATO Members in Eastern Europe View It as Protection', Gallup, 10 February 2020, *https://news.gallup.com/poll/203819/nato-members-eastern-europe-protection.aspx.*

5 Guy Chazan and Michael Peel, 'Confidence in NATO in Sharp Decline', *Financial Times*, 20 February 2020, *https://www.ft.com/content/4cbd8196-4b29-11ea-95a0-43d18ec715f5.*

6 Moira Fagan and Jacob Poushter, 'NATO Seen Favourably across Member States' (Pew Research Center, 20 February 2020), p. 4, *https://www.pewresearch.org/global/wp-content/uploads/sites/2/2020/02/PG_2020.02.09_NATO_final.pdf.*

7 Dina Smeltz et al., *Rejecting Retreat: Americans Support US Engagement in Global Affairs* (Chicago: The Chicago Council on Global Affairs, 2019), p. 18, *https://www.thechicagocouncil.org/sites/default/files/report_ccs19_rejecting-retreat_20190909.pdf.*

8 Bertelsmann Foundation, the German Marshall Fund and Institut Montaigne, *Transatlantic Trends 2020: Transatlantic Opinion on Global Challenges before and after COVID-19*, p. 18, *https://www.gmfus.org/sites/default/files/TT20_Final.pdf.*
9 Fagan and Poushter, 'NATO Seen Favourably Across Member States', p. 3.
10 Stelzenmueller and Raiser, *Transatlantic Trends ... 2014*, p. 46.
11 Bertelsmann Foundation et al., *Transatlantic Trends 2020*, p. 19.
12 Mathew Smith, 'Support for NATO Falls in Key NATO Nations', YouGov, 3 April 2019, *https://yougov.co.uk/topics/international/articles-reports/2019/04/03/support-nato-falls-key-european-nations.*
13 Fagan and Poushter, 'NATO Seen Favourably Across Member States', pp. 11 and 13.
14 NATO Public Diplomacy Division, 'Defence Expenditure of NATO Countries (2013–2019)', COMMUNIQUE PR/CP(2019)123, 29 November 2019, *https://www.nato.int/nato_static_fl2014/assets/pdf/pdf_2019_11/20191129_pr-2019-123-en.pdf.*
15 V. Lance Tarrance, 'Americans Split on Outlook for US Power', Gallup, 20 February 2019, *https://news.gallup.com/opinion/polling-matters/246974/americans-split-outlook-power.aspx.*
16 Pew Research Center, 'Large Majorities in Both Parties Say NATO Is Good For the US', 2 April 2019, *https://www.people-press.org/2019/04/02/large-majorities-in-both-parties-say-nato-is-good-for-the-u-s/.*
17 Smeltz et al., *Rejecting Retreat*, pp. 10–12.
18 Pew Research Center, 'Large Majorities in Both Parties.'
19 See Julian Borger, 'World's Confidence in US Leadership under Trump at New Low, Poll Finds', *The Guardian*, 18 January 2018, *https://www.theguardian.com/us-news/2018/jan/18/us-leadership-world-confidence-poll.*
20 Gallup, *Rating World Leaders: 2019. The US vs Germany, China and Russia*, pp. 10–12, *https://www.gallup.com/analytics/247040/rating-world-leaders-2019.aspx.*
21 Richard Wike et al., 'Trump's International Ratings Remain Low, Especially Among Key Allies' (Pew Research Center, 1 October 2018), p.11, *https://www.pewresearch.org/global/2018/10/01/trumps-international-ratings-remain-low-especially-among-key-allies/.*
22 Susi Dennison, 'Give the People What they Want: Popular Demand for a Strong European Foreign Policy', *Policy Brief* (European Council on Foreign Relations, September 2019), p. 8,

https://www.ecfr.eu/page/-/popular_demand_for_strong_european_foreign_policy_what_people_want.pdf.

23 Noah Barkin, 'In the Post-Pandemic Cold War, America Is Losing Europe', *Foreign Policy*, 19 May 2020, *https://foreignpolicy.com/2020/05/19/coronavirus-pandemic-europe-opinion-polls-united-states-china-losing/.*

24 Thomas Colson and Adam Payne, 'European Diplomats Believe Joe Biden Will Repair the Damage Done by Trump to America's Broken Alliance with Europe', *Business Insider*, 4 July 2020, *https://www.businessinsider.com/europe-believes-biden-would-repair-trumps-damage-to-european-alliance-2020-7?r=US&IR=T.*

25 Fagan and Poushter, 'NATO Seen Favourably Across Member States', p.14.

26 Wike et al, 'Trump's International Ratings Remain Low', p. 12.

27 Körber-Stiftung, 'German Worldviews in Times of COVID-19', *https://www.koerber-stiftung.de/fileadmin/user_upload/koerber-stiftung/redaktion/the-berlin-pulse/pdf/2020/Koerber_TheBerlinPulse_Sonderausgabe_Grafikteilenglisch.pdf.*

28 The $6.5 billion enacted in 2019 was more than the national defence budgets of seventeen of NATO's twenty-nine allies for that year.

29 David B. Larter, '5 Takeaways: Top US Navy Officer Releases Updated Strategy Document', *Defense News*, 17 December 2018, *https://www.defensenews.com/naval/2018/12/17/top-us-navy-officer-releases-updated-strategy-document-five-takeaways/*; US Army, *2019 Army Modernization Strategy: Investing in the Future, https://www.army.mil/e2/c/downloads/567902.pdf.*

30 *National Security Strategy of the United States of America* (December 2017), p. 48, *https://www.whitehouse.gov/wp-content/uploads/2017/12/NSS-Final-12-18-2017-0905.pdf*; *Summary of the National Defence Strategy of the United States of America: Sharpening the American Military's Competitive Edge* (US Department of Defence, January 2018), p. 9, *https://dod.defense.gov/Portals/1/Documents/pubs/2018-National-Defense-Strategy-Summary.pdf*; 'Pre-decisional draft of the Nuclear Posture Review' (US Department of Defence, January 2018), extracted in HuffPost, 12 January 2018, *http://www.huffingtonpost.co.uk/entry/trump-nuclear-posture-review-2018_us_5a4d4773e4b06d1621bce4c5.*

31 'About DEFENDER – Europe 20', *https://shape.nato.int/defender-europe.*

32 David M. Herszenhorn, 'James Mattis Calls NATO My "Second Home"', *Politico*, 15 February 2017, *https://www.politico.eu/article/james-mattis-calls-nato-my-second-home/*.
33 Esper press conference at the NATO Defence Ministerial, 13 February 2020, *https://www.defense.gov/Newsroom/Transcripts/Transcript/Article/2084771/secretary-of-defense-dr-mark-t-esper-press-conference-at-nato-defense-ministeri/*.
34 Gardiner Harris, 'Tillerson Delivers NATO Allies a Familiar Message: Pay Up', *New York Times*, 31 March 2017, *https://www.nytimes.com/2017/03/31/world/europe/rex-tillerson-nato.html*; Pompeo remarks at the reception to mark NATO's seventieth anniversary, Washington, DC, 3 April 2019, *https://www.nato.int/cps/en/natohq/opinions_165208.htm*.
35 'Remarks by President Trump and NATO Secretary General Jens Stoltenberg before Bilateral Meeting', 2 April 2019, *https://www.whitehouse.gov/briefings-statements/remarks-president-trump-nato-secretary-general-jens-stoltenberg-bilateral-meeting/*; 'Press Point by NATO Secretary General Jens Stoltenberg and US President Donald Trump', 3 December 2019, *https://www.nato.int/cps/en/natohq/opinions_171542.htm*.
36 Paul Belkin, 'Assessing NATO's Value', *CRS Report* (Congressional Research Service, 28 March 2019), p. 13, *https://crsreports.congress.gov/product/pdf/R/R45652*.
37 Statement to the Senate Committee on Armed Services, 20 February 2020, p. 18, *https://www.armed-services.senate.gov/imo/media/doc/Wolters_02-25-20.pdf*.
38 Belkin, 'Assessing NATO's Value', p. 13.
39 Vincent Pouliot, *International Pecking Orders: The Politics and Practice of Multilateral Diplomacy* (Cambridge etc.: Cambridge University Press, 2016), pp. 59–66.
40 James Sperling and Mark Webber, 'Trump's Foreign Policy and NATO: Exit and Voice', *Review of International Studies*, 45(3), 2019, pp. 511–26.
41 On 'nodal defence', see Luis Simón, Alexander Lanoszka and Hugo Meijer, 'Nodal Defence: The Changing Structure of US Alliance Systems in Europe and East Asia', *Journal of Strategic Studies* (early view) 2019, *https://doi.org/10.1080/01402390.2019.1636372*.
42 Jolyon Howorth and John T.S. Keeler, 'The EU, NATO and the Quest for European Autonomy', in Howorth and Keeler (eds),

Defending Europe: The EU, NATO and the Quest for European Autonomy (New York: Palgrave Macmillan, 2003), pp. 5–6.

43 These were the so-called '3 Ds'. See Madeleine Albright, 'The Right Balance Will Secure NATO's Future', *Financial Times*, 7 December 1998, *https://www.jstor.org/stable/pdf/resrep06989.8.pdf.*

44 Cited in Jacopo Barigazzi and Joshua Posaner, 'EU to US: Don't Worry About Our Military Plans', *Politico*, 16 June 2019, *https://www.politico.eu/article/european-military-defense-army-nato/.*

45 Jennifer Rankin, 'Merkel Joins Macron in Calling for a "Real True European Army"', *The Guardian*, 13 November 2018, *https://www.theguardian.com/world/2018/nov/13/merkel-joins-macron-in-calling-for-a-real-true-european-army.*

46 Erik Brattberg and Tomáš Valášek, *EU Defence Cooperation: Progress Amid Transatlantic Concerns* (Carnegie Endowment for International Peace, November 2019), p. 12, *https://carnegieendowment.org/files/WP_Brattberg_Valasek_EU_Def_Coop_v3.pdf.*

47 *Official Journal of the European Union*, 115, 9 May 2008, pp. 0038–9.

48 'Notification on Permanent Structured Cooperation (PESCO) to the Council and the High Representative of the Union for Foreign Affairs and Security Policy', 13 November 2017, p. 3, *https://www.consilium.europa.eu/media/31511/171113-pesco-notification.pdf.*

49 Council of the European Union, 'Council Conclusions on Security and Defence in the Context of the EU Global Strategy – Council Conclusions', 13978/18, 19 November 2018, para. 5.

50 European External Action Service, 'The Military Planning and Conduct Capability (MPCC)', *Fact Sheet*, *https://eeas.europa.eu/headquarters/headquarters-homepage/54031/factsheet-military-planning-and-conduct-capability_en.*

51 Brattberg and Valášek, *EU Defence Cooperation*, p. 26, n. 25.

52 Thierry Tardy, 'European Defence: What Impact for NATO?', NATO Defence College, *Policy Brief*, No. 5, December 2018, p. 3.

53 Written comments to Nomination Hearings for position of Commander, US European Command and Supreme Allied Commander, Europe, Senate Armed Services Committee, 2 April 2019, p.24, *https://www.armed-services.senate.gov/imo/media/doc/Wolters_APQs_04-02-19.pdf.*

54 *2018 CDP Revision: The EU Capability Development Priorities* (Brussels: European Defence Agency, 2018), p. 4, *https://www.eda.europa.eu/docs/default-source/eda-publications/eda-brochure-cdp.*
55 'Fourth Progress Report on the Implementation of the Common set of Proposals Endorsed by NATO and EU Councils on 6 December 2016 and 5 December 2017', 17 June 2019, *https://www.nato.int/nato_static_fl2014/assets/pdf/pdf_2019_06/190617-4th-Joint-progress-report-EU-NATO-eng.pdf.*
56 Thierry Tardy and Gustav Lindstrom, 'The Scope of NATO–EU Cooperation', in Gustav Lindstrom and Thierry Tardy (eds), *NATO and the EU: The Essential Partners*, NATO Defence College, *Research Paper*, No. 5, September 2019, pp. 9–13.
57 Jeffrey A. Stacey, 'How to Take EU–NATO Relations from Words to Action', *Defence News*, 3 December 2019, *https://www.defensenews.com/opinion/commentary/2019/12/03/how-to-take-eu-nato-relations-from-words-to-action/*; Friends of Europe, 'EU–NATO Cooperation: A Secure Vision for Europe', June 2019, p. 11, *https://www.friendsofeurope.org/insights/eu-nato-cooperation-a-secure-vision-for-europe/.*
58 Marianne Riddervold and Akasemi Newsome, 'Transatlantic Relations in Times of Uncertainty: Crises and EU–US Relations', *Journal of European Integration*, 40(5), 2019, p. 505.
59 Alicia Von Voss and Florence Schimmel, 'NATO's Future Role in the Multilateral Rules-Based Order', in Tomáš Valášek (ed.), *New Perspectives on Shared Security: NATO's Next 70 Years* (Carnegie Europe, November 2019), *https://carnegieeurope.eu/2019/11/28/nato-s-future-role-in-multilateral-rules-based-order-pub-80412.*
60 Mark Rhinard and Gunnar Sjöstedt, 'The EU as a Global Actor: A New Conceptualisation Four Decades after "Actorness"', Swedish Institute of International Affairs, *UI Paper*, No. 6, 2019, *https://www.ui.se/globalassets/ui.se-eng/publications/ui-publications/2019/ui-paper-no.-6-2019.pdf.*
61 Sven Biscop, 'EU–US Consensus and NATO–EU Cooperation', in Valášek (ed.), *New Perspectives on Shared Security.*
62 Taesuh Cha, 'The Return of Jacksonianism: The International Implications of the Trump Phenomenon', *Washington Quarterly*, 39(4), 2016, p. 84.
63 Trump cited in Cha, 'The Return of Jacksonianism', p. 89.
64 Walter Russell Mead, 'The Jacksonian Revolt: American

Populism and the Liberal Order', *Foreign Affairs*, 96(2), 2017, pp. 5–6.

65 John Glaser, Christopher A. Preble and A. Trevor Thrall, *Fuel to the Fire: How Trump Made America's Broken Foreign Policy Even Worse (and How We Can Recover)* (Washington, DC: The Cato Institute, 2019), pp. 97, 136.

66 Glaser et al., *Fuel to the Fire*, p. 77.

67 Joseph R. Biden, Jr, 'Why America Must Lead Again: Rescuing US Foreign Policy after Trump', *Foreign Affairs*, 99(2), 2020, *https://www.foreignaffairs.com/articles/united-states/2020-01-23/why-america-must-lead-again*.

68 Elbridge A Colby and A. Wess Mitchell, 'The Age of Great-Power Competition: How the Trump Administration Refashioned American Strategy', *Foreign Affairs*, 99(1), 2020, *https://www.foreignaffairs.com/articles/2019-12-10/age-great-power-competition*.

69 Mira Rapp-Hooper and Rebecca Friedman Lissner, 'The Open World: What America Can Achieve after Trump', *Foreign Affairs*, 98(3), 2019, *https://www.foreignaffairs.com/articles/2019-04-16/open-world*.

70 Walter Russell Mead, *Special Providence: American Foreign Policy and How It Changed the World* (New York: Alfred A. Knopf, 2001), p. 130.

71 Mead, *Special Providence*, p. 100.

72 Mark Safranski, 'A New Nixon Doctrine: Strategy for a Polycentric World', *War on the Rocks*, 8 July 2014, *https://warontherocks.com/2014/07/a-new-nixon-doctrine-strategy-for-a-polycentric-world/*.

73 As paraphrased in Chad Pillai, 'The Return of Great Power Politics: Re-examining the Nixon Doctrine', *War on the Rocks*, 27 March 2014, *https://warontherocks.com/2014/03/the-return-of-great-power-politics-re-examining-the-nixon-doctrine/*.

74 Mead, *Special Providence*, p. 95.

75 Mead, who is the source of these categories, also outlines a Jeffersonian tradition that is antipathetic to the use of force, sceptical of overseas commitments and mindful that the principles of the American constitution guide how foreign policy is conducted.

76 The principle, which dates back at least to the French Revolution, was popularized by its association with the comic book character Spider-Man, the secret identity of Peter Parker, hence the name.

For an academic treatment, see Chris Brown, 'Do Great Powers Have Great Responsibilities? Great Powers and Moral Agency', *Global Society*, 18(1), 2004, pp. 5–19.

77 Winston Churchill, 'South African Native Races', House of Commons Debate, *Hansard* 152 (28 February 1906): 1239, *https://api.parliament.uk/historic-hansard/commons/1906/feb/28/south-african-native-races#S4V0152P0_19060228_HOC_307*.

Chapter 7 Cash, Capabilities and NATO Effectiveness

1 'Remarks by President Trump to the People of Poland', Warsaw, 6 July 2017, *https://www.whitehouse.gov/briefings-statements/remarks-president-trump-people-poland/*.

2 Richard Cornes and Todd Sandler, 'Easy Riders, Joint Production, and Public Goods', *The Economic Journal*, 94(375), 1984, pp. 580–98.

3 Timo Noetzel and Benjamin Schreer, 'Does a Multi-Tier NATO Matter? The Atlantic Alliance and the Process of Strategic Change', *International Affairs*, 85(2), 2009, pp. 211–26.

4 Peter Corterier, 'Introduction', in Keith Dunn and Stephen Flanagan (eds), *NATO in the 5th Decade* (Washington, DC: National Defence University Press, 1990), p. xxi.

5 Wallace Thies, *Friendly Rivals: Bargaining and Burden-Shifting in NATO* (Armonk, NY, and London: M.E. Sharpe, 2003), pp. 190–1.

6 Joshua Foust, '"Smart Defence": Should Europe's Militaries Specialize?', *The Atlantic*, 17 May 2012, *https://www.theatlantic.com/international/archive/2012/05/smart-defense-should-europes-militaries-specialize/257328/*.

7 NATO, 'Prague Summit Declaration', 21 November 2002, para. 4c, *https://www.nato.int/cps/en/natohq/official_texts_19552.htm?*.

8 Anders Fogh Rasmussen, keynote speech at the Munich Security Conference, 4 February 2011, *https://www.nato.int/cps/en/natolive/opinions_70400.htm*.

9 *NATO 2014 Wales Summit Guide*, p. 49, *https://www.nato.int/nato_static_fl2014/assets/pdf/pdf_publications/20141008_140108-SummitGuideWales2014-eng.pdf*.

10 Jennifer D.P. Moroney, 'A Framework for Developing Niche Capabilities', in Kristina Spohr Readman (ed.), *Building Sustainable and Effective Military Capabilities: A Systemic Comparison of Professional and Conscript Forces* (Amsterdam etc.: OIS Press, 2003), pp. 152–5.
11 Rihards Bambals, 'Threats to Euro-Atlantic Security and the Value of NATO', in Arnold H. Kammel and Benjamin Zyla (eds), *Peacebuilding at Home: NATO and Its 'New' Members after Crimea* (Baden-Baden: Nomos, 2018), p. 68.
12 Interviewed in *NATO Review*, Winter 2002, *https://www.nato.int/docu/review/2002/issue4/english/interview.html.*
13 Ojars Eriks Kalnins (special rapporteur), 'Burden Sharing Revisited', report of the NATO Parliamentary Assembly Political Committee, 8 October 2017, p. 10, *https://www.nato-pa.int/document/2017-burden-sharing-revisited-kalnins-report-210-pc-17-e-bis.*
14 Jerry Z. Muller, *The Tyranny of Metrics* (Princeton and Oxford: Princeton University Press, 2018), pp. 23, 45.
15 Kathleen H. Hicks et al., *Counting Dollars or Measuring Value: Assessing NATO and Partner Burden Sharing* (Washington, DC: Center for Strategic and International Studies), July 2018, p. 5, *https://www.csis.org/analysis/counting-dollars-or-measuring-value.*
16 Ian Davis, 'Mind the Gap: Has UK Military Spending Fallen Below the NATO Guideline and German Military Spending?', NATO Watch, *Briefing Paper*, No. 74, 28 April 2020, *https://natowatch.org/default/2020/mind-gap-has-uk-military-spending-fallen-below-nato-guideline-and-german-military.*
17 Lucie Béraud-Sudreau and Nick Childs, 'The US and Its NATO Allies: Costs and Value', *The Military Balance Blog*, 9 July 2018, *https://www.iiss.org/blogs/military-balance/2018/07/us-and-nato-allies-costs-and-value.*
18 Gary Schaub Jr and André Ken Jakobsson, 'Denmark in NATO: Paying for Protection, Bleeding for Prestige', *War on the Rocks*, 17 July 2018, *https://warontherocks.com/2018/07/denmark-in-nato-paying-for-protection-bleeding-for-prestige/.*
19 Richard Sokolsky and Gordon Adams, 'Penny Wise, Pound Foolish: Trump's Misguided Views of European Defence Spending', *War on the Rocks*, 7 March 2017, *https://warontherocks.com/2017/03/penny-wise-pound-foolish-trumps-misguided-views-of-european-defense-spending/.*

20 Wukki Kim and Todd Sandler, 'NATO at 70: Pledges, Free Riding, and Benefit–Burden Concordance', *Defence and Peace Economics*, 31(4), 2020, pp. 400–13.
21 Cited in *Newsweek*, 17 March 2017, *https://www.newsweek.com/military-costs-country-shouldnt-matter-nato-or-us-germany-insists-569607*.
22 See Hicks et al., *Counting Dollars or Measuring Value*.
23 Garrett Martin and Balazs Martonffy, 'Abandon the 2 Percent Obsession: A New Rating for Pulling Your Weight in NATO', *War on the Rocks*, 19 May 2017, *https://warontherocks.com/2017/05/abandon-the-2-percent-obsession-a-new-rating-for-pulling-your-weight-in-nato/*.
24 Patricia A. Weitsman, *Dangerous Alliances: Proponents of Peace, Weapons of War* (Stanford: Stanford University Press, 2004), p. 3.
25 Oral evidence to the House of Commons Defence Committee, hearing on 'The Indispensable Ally? The US, NATO and UK Defence Relations', 31 October 2017, *http://data.parliament.uk/writtenevidence/committeeevidence.svc/evidencedocument/defence-committee/the-indispensable-ally-us-nato-and-uk-defence-relations/oral/72419.html*.
26 *NATO Handbook* (Brussels: NATO Office of Information and Press, 2001), pp. 157–9.
27 See the NATO sources cited in David Yost, *NATO's Balancing Act* (Washington, DC: United States Institute of Peace Press, 2014), p. 78.
28 Wayne A. Schroeder, *NATO at Seventy: Filling NATO's Critical Defence-Capability Gaps* (Washington, DC: Atlantic Council, 2019), p. 10.
29 Press conference ahead of the meeting of NATO Defence Ministers, 25 June 2019, *https://www.nato.int/cps/en/natohq/opinions_167065.htm?selectedLocale=en*.
30 Press conference after a meeting of NATO Defence Ministers, 14 February 2018, *https://www.nato.int/cps/en/natohq/opinions_151504.htm*.
31 Yost, *NATO's Balancing Act*, p. 78.
32 McKinsey & Company, *The Future of European Defence: Tackling the Productivity Challenge* (London, 2012), pp. 14, 18; Jean-Marie Bockel (rapporteur), 'The State of Europe's Defence Industrial Base', NATO Parliamentary Assembly, Economics and Security Committee, 7 October 2017, p. 9, *https://www.nato-pa.int/*

document/2017-europe-industrial-defense-base-bockel-report-166-esc-17-e-bis.

33 *The Secretary General's Annual Report 2019* (Brussels: NATO Public Diplomacy Division, 2020), p. 50, *https://www.nato.int/nato_static_fl2014/assets/pdf/2020/3/pdf_publications/sgar19-en.pdf.*

34 Richard D. Hooker (project director), *Over the Horizon: NATO Joint Intelligence, Surveillance, and Reconnaissance in the Baltic Sea Region* (Washington, DC: Atlantic Council, 2019), pp. 5–8 and Appendix, *https://www.atlanticcouncil.org/in-depth-research-reports/report/over-the-horizon-nato-joint-intelligence-surveillance-and-reconnaissance-in-the-baltic-sea-region/.*

35 Monthly Press Briefing, 5 March 2012, *https://www.nato.int/cps/fr/SID-44D71EB3-2A164C8F/natolive/opinions_84865.htm.*

36 Alexander Mattelaer, 'Progress on Capability Development', in Gustav Lindstrom and Thierry Tardy (eds), *The EU and NATO: The Essential Partners* (Paris: European Union Institute for Security Studies, 2019), p. 37.

37 Schroeder, *NATO at Seventy*, p. 11.

38 Mattelaer, 'Progress on Capability Development', p. 37.

39 Attila Mesterhazy (rapporteur), 'NATO–EU Cooperation after Warsaw', NATO Parliamentary Assembly, Defence and Security Committee, 7 October 2017, p. 7, *https://www.nato-pa.int/document/2017-eu-and-nato-cooperation-mesterhazy-report-163-dsctc-17-e-rev1-fin.*

40 We owe this term to Margriet Drent, Dick Zandee and Lo Casteleijn, 'Defence Cooperation in Clusters: Identifying the Next Steps', *Clingendael Report*, October 2014, pp. 14–15, *https://www.clingendael.org/sites/default/files/pdfs/Defence%20Cooperation%20in%20Clusters_web.pdf.*

41 Air Marshal Sir Chris Harper, 'Foreword' to Schroeder, *NATO at Seventy*, p. 2.

42 See Jan Joel Andersson et al., 'Envisioning European Defence: Five Futures', *Chaillot Papers*, 137, March 2016, pp. 13–17, *https://www.iss.europa.eu/sites/default/files/EUISSFiles/Chaillot_Paper_137.pdf*

43 Marcin Zaborowski et al., 'Towards a New Level of European Defence Competence', GLOBSEC Policy Institute, February 2020, *https://www.globsec.org/wp-content/uploads/2020/02/GLOBSEC-European-Security-Initiative_Enhancing-European-Defence-Competence-Feb2020_web.pdf.*

44 *https://otan.delegfrance.org/Capabilities-NATO-a-facilitator-of-capability-development.*
45 Eva Hagström Frisell and Emma Sjökvist, *Military Cooperation around Framework Nations: A European Solution to the Problem of Limited Defence Capabilities* (Stockholm: Total Defence Research Institute, February 2019), p. 9.
46 NATO, 'Wales Summit Declaration', 5 September 2014, para. 67, *https://www.nato.int/cps/en/natohq/official_texts_112964.htm?mode=pressrelease.*
47 Diego A. Ruiz Palmer, 'The Framework Nations' Concept and NATO: Game-Changer for a New Strategic Era or Missed Opportunity?', NATO Defence College, *Research Paper*, No. 132, July 2016, p. 4, *https://www.jstor.org/stable/pdf/resrep10253.pdf?refreqid=excelsior%3A6d06586d67e3b500380c4b365bdacafe.*
48 Dick Zandee, 'Core Groups: The Way to Real European Defence', Egmont Institute, *Security Policy Brief*, No. 81, February 2017, pp. 2–3, *https://www.egmontinstitute.be/content/uploads/2017/02/SPB81.pdf?type=pdf.*
49 Rainer L. Glatz and Martin Zapfe, 'NATO's Framework Nations Concept', *CSS Analyses in Security Policy*, No. 218, December 2017, p. 3, *https://css.ethz.ch/content/dam/ethz/special-interest/gess/cis/center-for-securities-studies/pdfs/CSSAnalyse218-EN.pdf.*
50 Glatz and Zapfe, 'NATO's Framework Nations Concept', p. 3.
51 Robin Allers, 'The Framework Nation: Can Germany Lead on Security?', *International Affairs*, 92(5), 2016, p. 1186.
52 Hagström Frisell and Sjökvist, *Military Cooperation around Framework Nations*, pp. 16–21.
53 Glatz and Zapfe, 'NATO's Framework Nations Concept', pp. 3–4.
54 Reform of the German armed forces is discussed in Tom Dyson, 'The Challenge of Creating an Adaptive Bundeswehr', *German Politics* (early view) 2019, *https://doi.org/10.1080/09644008.2019.1612369.*
55 Drent et al., 'Defence Cooperation in Clusters', pp. 14–15.

Chapter 8 Mending NATO–Russia Relations

1 Stephen Walt, 'My Top 5 Foreign-Policy Unicorns – and Why I Want to Kill Them', *Foreign Policy*, 8 September 2016,

http://foreignpolicy.com/2016/09/08/my-top-5-foreign-policy-unicorns-and-why-i-want-to-kill-them/.

2 Marc Trachtenberg, *A Constructed Peace: The Making of the European Settlement 1945–1963* (Princeton: Princeton University Press, 1999), p. 129.

3 William H. Hill, *No Place for Russia: European Security Institutions since 1989* (New York: Columbia University Press, 2018), pp. 287–96.

4 *Kommersant*, 29 July 2008, in *CDPSP*, LX(30), 2008, p. 14.

5 Stuart Croft et al., *The Enlargement of Europe* (Manchester and New York: Manchester University Press, 1999), p. 131.

6 William H. Hill, 'The OSCE and the Moldova–Transdniestria Conflict: Lessons in Mediation and Conflict Management', *Security and Human Rights*, 24(3–4), 2013, p. 296.

7 Andrew Wilson, 'Ukraine's Orange Revolution, NGOs and the Role of the West', *Cambridge Review of International Affairs*, 19(1), 2006, pp. 25–6.

8 Wolfgang Zellner, 'Russia and the OSCE: From High Hopes to Disillusionment', *Cambridge Review of International Affairs*, 18(3), 2005, p. 390.

9 Hannah Claire Alberts, 'Russia's OSCE Policy and the Ukraine Crisis: Renewed Interest, Enduring Approach', Master's Dissertation, University of Texas at Austin, May 2016, *https://repositories.lib.utexas.edu/bitstream/handle/2152/41643/ALBERTS-MASTERSREPORT-2016.pdf?sequence=1.*

10 Olivier Schmitt, 'How to Challenge an International Order: Russian Diplomatic Practices in Multilateral Security Organisations', *European Journal of International Relations*, 26(3), 2020, pp. 922–46.

11 Samuel Charap and Mikhail Troitskiy, 'Russia, the West and the Integration Dilemma', *Survival*, 55(6), 2013–14, p. 50.

12 Strobe Talbott, *The Russia Hand: A Memoir of Presidential Diplomacy* (New York: Random House, 2002), pp. 131–2.

13 Nadia Arbatova, 'Russia and the West: Facing a New Bipolarity', European Leadership Network, 24 June 2014, *https://www.europeanleadershipnetwork.org/commentary/russia-and-the-west-facing-a-new-bipolarity/.*

14 Sergei Karaganov, 'Europe and Russia: Preventing a New Cold War', *Russia in Global Affairs*, 7 June 2014, *http://eng.globalaffairs.ru/number/Europe-and-Russia-Preventing-a-New-Cold-War-16701.*

15 James A. Baker III, 'Russia in NATO?', *The Washington Quarterly*, 25(1), 2002, pp. 102–3.
16 Martin A. Smith, *Russia and NATO since 1991: From Cold War through Cold Peace to Partnership?* (Abingdon: Routledge, 2006), pp. 51–2 and 92–3.
17 Konstantin Kosachev, 'Three Birds with One Stone? Russia's Failed Attempt to Join NATO', *Russia in Global Affairs*, 9(1), 2011, pp. 92–104.
18 Vincent Pouliot, *International Security in Practice: The Politics of NATO–Russia Diplomacy* (Cambridge: Cambridge University Press, 2010), pp. 158, 171, 218–19.
19 'Press Point by NATO Secretary General, Lord Robertson and Vladimir Putin, President of the Russian Federation', 11 November 2002, *http://www.nato.int/docu/speech/2002/s021111a.htm*.
20 *Izvestia*, 23 December 1991, in *CDPSP*, XLIII(51), 1991, p. 22.
21 Cited in Pouliot, *International Security in Practice*, p. 171.
22 Victor Kovalev, 'The Cost Russia Will Pay for NATO Rapprochement', *Strategic Culture*, 6 November 2010, *http://www.strategic-culture.org/news/2010/11/16/the-cost-russia-will-pay-for-nato-rapprochement.html*; Michael Bohm, '5 Reasons Why Russia Will Never Join NATO', *The Moscow Times*, 19 November 2010, *https://themoscowtimes.com/articles/5-reasons-why-russia-will-never-join-nato-3105*.
23 Michael Rühle, 'NATO Enlargement and Russia: Die-Hard Myths and Real Dilemmas', *NDC Research Report*, 15 May 2014, *http://www.ndc.nato.int/news/news.php?icode=676*.
24 'The Interview: Henry Kissinger', *The National Interest*, September–October 2015, *http://nationalinterest.org/feature/the-interview-henry-kissinger-13615*.
25 Andrew T. Wolf, 'The Future of NATO Enlargement After the Ukraine Crisis', *International Affairs*, 91(5), 2015, pp. 1104, 1118; Dmitri Trenin, *European Security: From Managing Adversity to a New Equilibrium* (Moscow: Carnegie Moscow Center, 2018), p. 19.
26 Michael O'Hanlon, *Beyond NATO: A New Security Architecture for Eastern Europe* (Washington, DC: Brookings Institution Press, 2017), p. 73.
27 Matthew Parris, 'It's Time We Washed Our Hands of Ukraine', *The Times*, 28 February 2015, *https://www.thetimes.co.uk/article/its-time-we-washed-our-hands-of-ukraine-tfd9mmd9pqs*.

28 John Mearsheimer, 'Why the Ukraine Crisis Is the West's Fault', *Foreign Affairs*, 93(5), 2014, pp. 77–89.
29 Vladimir Socor, 'Russia Trashes US–Russian–British Memorandum on Ukraine', *Eurasia Daily Monitor*, 11(45), 2014, *https://jamestown.org/program/russia-trashes-us-russian-british-memorandum-on-ukraine/#*.
30 For the text, see 'Charter on a Distinctive Partnership between the North Atlantic Treaty Organization and Ukraine', 9 July 1997, *http://www.nato.int/cps/en/natohq/official_texts_25457.htm*.
31 NATO, 'Wales Summit Declaration', 5 September 2014, para. 16, *https://www.nato.int/cps/en/natohq/official_texts_112964.htm*.
32 Uri Friedman, 'America Hasn't Always Supported Ukraine Like This', *The Atlantic*, 21 November 2019, *https://www.theatlantic.com/politics/archive/2019/11/how-vital-us-military-aid-ukraine/602407/*.
33 Obama cited in Jeffrey Goldberg, 'The Obama Doctrine', *The Atlantic*, April 2016, *https://www.theatlantic.com/magazine/archive/2016/04/the-obama-doctrine/471525/#3*.
34 Friedman, 'America Hasn't Always Supported Ukraine Like This'.
35 NATO, 'Warsaw Summit Communiqué', 9 July 2016, para. 12, *http://www.nato.int/cps/en/natohq/official_texts_133169.htm*.
36 NATO, 'London Declaration', 4 December 2019, para. 4, *https://www.nato.int/cps/en/natohq/official_texts_171584.htm*.
37 'Foreign Minister Sergey Lavrov's Address and Annual News Conference on Russia's Diplomatic Performance in 2014, Moscow, 21 January 2015', *http://www.rusemb.org.uk/foreignpolicy/2915*.
38 Jens Ringsmose and Sten Rynning, 'Now for the Hard Part: NATO's Strategic Adaptation to Russia', *Survival*, 59(3), 2017, p. 140.
39 'Latest NATO–Russia Council Meeting Fails to Bridge Key Differences', NATO Watch *News Briefs*, 27 October 2017, *https://natowatch.org/newsbriefs/2017/latest-nato-russia-council-meeting-fails-bridge-key-differences*; 'NATO–Russia Council Fails to Bridge Divide over INF Treaty', NATO Watch *News Briefs*, 7 July 2019, *https://natowatch.org/newsbriefs/2019/nato-russia-council-fails-bridge-divide-over-inf-treaty*.
40 Jamie Doward, 'Russia Offered Bounty to Kill UK Soldiers', *The Guardian*, 27 June 2020, *https://www.theguardian.com/world/2020/jun/27/russia-offered-bounty-to-kill-uk-soldiers*.

41 Richard Sakwa, *Frontline Ukraine: Crisis in the Borderlands* (London: I.B. Tauris, 2016), p. 55.
42 Smith, *Russia and NATO since 1991*, p. 70.
43 Quoted in 'Inside the Bear: A Special Report on Russia', *The Economist*, 22 October 2016, *https://www.economist.com/special-report/2016/10/20/inside-the-bear*.
44 Sergei Ivanov, 'As NATO Grows, So Do Russia's Worries', *New York Times*, 7 April 2004, *https://www.nytimes.com/2004/04/07/opinion/as-nato-grows-so-do-russia-s-worries.html*.
45 They declared that 'NATO's ongoing enlargement process has been a historic success in advancing the vision of a Europe that is whole and free, united in peace, democracy and common values. At our Summit next year, we aim to welcome Albania and Croatia as new members of the Alliance. [. . .] In a manner consistent with the principles of the United Nations Charter, NATO's door remains open to all European democracies willing and able to assume the responsibilities and obligations of membership.' See 'Final Communiqué, Meeting of the North Atlantic Council at the Level of Foreign Ministers', 3 December 2008, *http://www.nato.int/cps/en/natohq/official_texts_46247.htm?mode=pressrelease*.
46 In May 2019, two Russian military intelligence officers were found guilty *in absentia* for their involvement in a 2016 coup plot against the government in Montenegro. The charges, however, may well have reflected the murky politics of Montenegro, a country deeply divided on the merits of NATO membership. See Shaun Walker, 'Alleged Russian Spies Sentenced to Jail over Montenegro "Coup Plot"', *The Guardian*, 9 May 2019, *https://www.theguardian.com/world/2019/may/09/montenegro-convicts-pro-russia-politicians-of-coup-plot*.
47 Cited in Mark Webber, *The International Politics of Russia and the Successor States* (Manchester and New York: Manchester University Press, 1996), p. 100.
48 Cited in Andrew E. Kramer, 'Russia Claims Its Sphere of Influence in the World', *New York Times*, 31 August 2008, *https://www.nytimes.com/2008/09/01/world/europe/01russia.html*.
49 For discussion, see Andris Banka, 'The Breakaways: A Retrospective on the Baltic Road to NATO', *War on the Rocks*, 4 October 2019, *https://warontherocks.com/2019/10/the-breakaways-a-retrospective-on-the-baltic-road-to-nato/*.
50 Kimberley Martin, 'Reducing Tensions between Russia and

NATO' (Washington, DC: Council on Foreign Relations, 2017), *Council Special Report*, No. 79, p. 11.

51 Charles Dick, 'Russian Ground Forces Posture towards the West' (London: Chatham House, 2019), Russia and Eurasia Programme, *Research Paper*, *https://www.chathamhouse.org/publication/russian-ground-forces-posture-towards-west*.

52 Lt. Gen. (Ret.) Ben Hodges et al., 'NATO Needs a Coherent Approach to Defending Its Eastern Flanks', *War on the Rocks*, 12 June 2020, *https://warontherocks.com/2020/06/nato-needs-a-coherent-approach-to-defending-its-eastern-flank/*.

53 Aaron Mehta, 'Ukraine Sees Two Paths for Joining NATO. Will Either Work?, *Defence News*, 13 January 2020, https://www.defensenews.com/smr/nato-2020-defined/2020/01/13/ukraine-sees-two-paths-for-joining-nato-will-either-work/.

54 Timothy Garton Ash, 'There'll be No Peace While Putin is Squatting in Ukraine's Living Room', *The Guardian*, 17 February 2015, *https://www.theguardian.com/commentisfree/2015/feb/16/peace-putin-ukraine-moscow-kiev*.

55 Commitments contained in the CSCE's 'Charter of Paris for a New Europe', November 1990, *https://www.oscepa.org/documents/all-documents/documents-1/historical-documents-1/673-1990-charter-of-paris-for-a-new-europe/file*.

56 Igor Sutyagin, 'Zapad-2017: Moscow Rules', RUSI, *Commentary*, 14 September 2017, *https://rusi.org/commentary/zapad-2017-moscow%E2%80%99s-rules*.

57 Thomas Frear, Lukasz Kulesa and Denitsa Raynova, *Russia and NATO: How to Overcome Deterrence Instability?* (London: European Leadership Network, 2018), *https://www.europeanleadershipnetwork.org/report/russia-and-nato-how-to-overcome-deterrence-instability/*.

58 Asaf Siniver and Scott Lucas, 'Understanding Tacit Security Regimes', *Journal of Global Security Studies*, 4(4), 2019, pp. 510–25.

59 Siniver and Lucas, 'Understanding Tacit Security Regimes', pp. 511, 520.

Conclusion: Improvement, Repair and NATO's Future

1 Mark Webber, James Sperling and Martin A. Smith, *NATO's Post-Cold War Trajectory: Decline or Regeneration?* (New York: Palgrave Macmillan, 2012).
2 Horst W.J. Rittel and Melvin M. Webber, 'Dilemmas in a General Theory of Planning', *Policy Sciences*, 4(2), 1973, pp. 155–69.
3 'Germany's Merkel, Maas, Defend NATO after Macron's Rebuke', *Deutsche Welle*, 10 November 2019, *https://www.dw.com/en/germanys-merkel-maas-defend-nato-after-macrons-rebuke/a-51191565*.
4 Cited in James Sperling and Mark Webber, 'NATO and the Ukraine Crisis: Collective Securitisation', *European Journal of International Security*, 2(1), 2017, p. 34.
5 'Text of Newly Approved Military Doctrine', 5 February 2010, para. 8a, *https://carnegieendowment.org/files/2010russia_military_doctrine.pdf*.
6 John Mearsheimer, 'Why the Ukrainian Crisis Is the West's Fault: The Liberal Delusion that Provoked Putin', *Foreign Affairs*, 97(5), 2014, p. 7.
7 F. Stephen Larrabee et al., *Russia and the West after the Ukrainian Crisis: European Vulnerabilities to Russian Pressure* (Santa Monica, CA: Rand Corporation, 2017), p. ix.
8 Robert Levgold, *Return to Cold War* (Cambridge: Polity, 2016), p. 8.
9 Andrew Monaghan, *The New Politics of Russia: Interpreting Change* (Manchester: Manchester University Press, 2016), pp. 60–86.
10 Levgold, *Return to Cold War*, p. 2.
11 Michael Clarke and Helen Ramsar, *Tipping Point: Britain, Brexit and Security in the 2020s* (London etc.: I.B. Tauris, 2020), p. 1.
12 A scenario discussed in Richard G. Whitman, 'The UK's European Diplomatic Strategy for Brexit and Beyond', *International Affairs*, 95(2), 2019, pp. 383–404.
13 Hans Vollaard, 'One Down, Many to Go? European Disintegration after Brexit', 23 March 2020, *https://blogs.lse.ac.uk/brexit/2020/03/23/one-down-many-to-go-european-disintegration-after-brexit/*.
14 James Blitz, 'Boris Johnson's First Speech as Prime Minister

– Decoded', *Financial Times*, 24 July 2019, *https://ig.ft.com/boris-johnson-prime-minister-speech/*.

15 European Council, 'A New Strategic Agenda: 2019–2024', 20 June 2019, *https://www.consilium.europa.eu/media/39914/a-new-strategic-agenda-2019-2024-en.pdf*.

16 European Parliament, Directorate-General for External Policies, *CSDP after Brexit: the Way Forward*, EP/EXPO/B/SEDE/FWC/2013-2018/Lot6/20 (Brussels: European Union, 2018), p. 34.

17 Olivier de France, 'Strategic Autonomy and European Security after Brexit', *Analyses* (Paris: IFRI, 2020), at: *https://www.iris-france.org/135189-strategic-autonomy-and-european-security-after-brexit/*.

18 Nicholas Drummond, 'A Guide to the 2020 Integrated Review', *UK Land Power*, 6 July 2020, *https://uklandpower.com/2020/07/06/a-guide-to-the-2020-integrated-review/*. See also Lucy Fisher, 'Defence Chiefs Face Battle over Plan to Scrap Tanks', *The Times*, 5 August 2020, *https://www.thetimes.co.uk/article/defence-chiefs-face-battleover-plan-to-scrap-tanks-ws87tdgbg*.

19 'London Declaration', 4 December 2019, para. 6, *https://www.nato.int/cps/en/natohq/official_texts_171584.htm*.

20 Jens Ringsmose and Sten Rynning, 'China Brought NATO Closer Together', *War on the Rocks*, 5 February 2020, *https://warontherocks.com/2020/02/china-brought-nato-closer-together/*.

21 'Speech by Federal Foreign Minister Heiko Maas on the Occasion of the 70th Anniversary of the Founding of NATO', 3 April 2019, *https://www.auswaertiges-amt.de/en/newsroom/news/maas-70-years-of-nato/2207096*.

22 Stoltenberg probably had in mind here the DF-41 intercontinental ballistic missile, flight-tested by China since 2013. Stoltenberg, 'Remarks at the European Parliament Committee on Foreign Affairs (AFET) and Sub-Committee on Security and Defence (SEDE)', 21 January 2020, *https://www.nato.int/cps/en/natohq/opinions_172822.htm*.

23 Jonathan Holslag, 'China, NATO and the Pitfall of Empty Engagement', *The Washington Quarterly*, 42(3), 2019, p. 139.

24 Erik Brattberg, 'Time for NATO to Talk about China', Carnegie Europe, 26 March 2019, *https://carnegieeurope.eu/strategiceurope/78684*.

25 Andre Tartar, Mira Rojanasakul and Jeremy Scott Diamond, 'How China is Buying Its Way into Europe', Bloomberg, 23 April

2018, *https://www.bloomberg.com/graphics/2018-china-business-in-europe/.*

26 Stoltenberg, 'Remarks at the European Parliament'.

27 James Sperling, 'NATO and the Global Commons: A Perspective on Emerging Challenges', in NATO Supreme Allied Command Transformation, *Managing Change: NATO's Partnerships and Deterrence in a Globalised World* (Norfolk, VA: ACT, 2011), pp. III/3– III/16, *https://www.act.nato.int/images/stories/events/2011/managing_change_hr.pdf.*

28 Kadri Kaska, Henrik Beckvard and Tomáš Minárik, *Huawei, 5G and China as a Security Threat* (Tallinn: NATO Cooperative Cyber Defence Centre of Excellence, 2019), p. 4, *https://ccdcoe.org/uploads/2019/03/CCDCOE-Huawei-2019-03-28-FINAL.pdf.*

29 Jay Greene and Shara Tibken, 'Lawmakers to US Companies: Don't Buy Huawei, ZTE', CNET, 8 October 2012, *https://www.cnet.com/news/lawmakers-to-u-s-companies-dont-buy-huawei-zte/.*

30 Ringsmose and Sten Rynning, 'China Brought NATO Closer Together'.

31 Stoltenberg, 'Remarks at the European Parliament'.

32 See Mark Webber, 'The Perils of a NATO Rebalance to Asia-Pacific', in Alexander Moens and Brooke A. Smith-Windsor (eds), *NATO and Asia-Pacific* (Rome: NATO Defence College, 2016), pp. 83–100.

33 Julian Lindley-French (lead writer), *One Alliance: The Future Tasks of the Adapted Alliance* (GLOBSEC, NATO Adaptation Initiative, 2017), pp. 7, 18, *https://www.globsec.org/wp-content/uploads/2017/11/GNAI-Final-Report-Nov-2017.pdf.*

34 Figures from Johns Hopkins University, Coronavirus Resource Centre, as of 7 October 2020, *https://coronavirus.jhu.edu/map.html.*

35 António Guterres, 'A Time to Heal the Sick, and the Planet', *New York Times*, 28 April 2020, *https://www.nytimes.com/2020/04/28/opinion/coronavirus-climate-antonio-guterres.html.*

36 Colin Kahl and Arian Berengaut, 'Aftershocks: The Coronavirus Pandemic and the New World Disorder', *War on the Rocks*, 10 April 2020, *https://warontherocks.com/2020/04/aftershocks-the-coronavirus-pandemic-and-the-new-world-disorder/.*

37 Lawrence Freedman, 'Strategy for a Pandemic: The UK and COVID-19', *Survival*, 62(3), 2020, p. 25.

38 Richard Horton, *The COVID-19 Catastrophe: What's Gone Wrong*

and How to Stop It Happening Again (Cambridge: Polity, 2020), p. 127.

39 McKinsey and Company, 'When Will the COVID-19 Pandemic End?', 21 September 2020, *https://www.mckinsey.com/industries/healthcare-systems-and-services/our-insights/when-will-the-covid-19-pandemic-end*.

40 Ruchir Sharma, 'The Pandemic Isn't Changing Everything: It Is Just Speeding Up Trends that Were Already Underway', *New York Times*, 3 May 2020, *https://www.nytimes.com/2020/05/03/opinion/coronavirus-economy-nationalism.html*.

41 Stefanie Babst, 'The Coronavirus Pandemic Hits NATO: Five Potential Implications', European Leadership Network, *Commentary*, 14 April 2020, *https://www.europeanleadershipnetwork.org/commentary/the-coronavirus-pandemic-hits-nato-five-potential-implications/*.

42 Aaron Mehta, 'As Defender 2020 Drill Winds Down, US Army Plans for 2021 Edition', *Defence News*, 10 July 2020, *https://www.defensenews.com/news/your-army/2020/07/10/as-defender-2020-winds-down-army-planning-for-2021-underway/#:~:text=As%20we%20speak%2C%20we're,experiences%20between%20March%20and%20June*.

43 McKinsey and Company, 'COVID-19: Briefing Materials', 6 July 2020, *https://www.mckinsey.com/~/media/mckinsey/business%20functions/risk/our%20insights/covid%2019%20implications%20for%20business/covid%2019%20july%209/covid-19-facts-and-insights-july-6.pdf*.

44 Harry Lye, 'Crisis Response and Budget Cuts: Will Covid-19 Affect Future Military Funding?', *Army Technology*, 30 June 2020, *https://www.army-technology.com/features/crisis-response-and-budget-cuts-will-covid-19-affect-future-military-funding/*.

45 Carmen Reinhart and Vincent Reinhart, 'The Pandemic Depression: The Global Economy Will Never be the Same', *Foreign Affairs*, 99(5), 2020, *https://www.foreignaffairs.com/articles/united-states/2020-08-06/coronavirus-depression-global-economy*.

46 Thierry Tardy, 'COVID-19: Shaping Future Threats and Security Policies', in Thierry Tardy (ed.), *COVID-19: NATO in the Age of Pandemics*, NATO Defence College, *Research Paper*, No. 9, p. 19.

47 Tardy, 'COVID-19: Shaping Future Threats', p. 20.

48 Jamie Shea, 'Missing in Action: US Leadership Is the Biggest

Casualty of the Coronavirus Crisis', *Europe's World*, 22 April 2020, *https://www.friendsofeurope.org/insights/missing-in-action-us-leadership-is-the-biggest-casualty-of-the-coronavirus-crisis/*.

49 Joseph S. Nye Jr, 'Can We Recover Our Soft Power?', *The Hill*, 9 June 2020, *https://thehill.com/opinion/international/501812-can-we-recover-our-soft-power*.

50 Jonathan D. Moyer and Oliver Kaplan, 'Will Coronavirus Fuel Conflict?', *Foreign Policy*, 6 July 2020, *https://foreignpolicy.com/2020/07/06/coronavirus-pandemic-fuel-conflict-fragile-states-economy-food-prices/*.

51 Tardy, 'Introduction' in Tardy (ed.), *COVID-19: NATO in the Age of Pandemics*, p. 6.

52 'Remarks by NATO Secretary General Jens Stoltenberg at the Heritage Foundation in Washington, DC', 14 September 2018, *https://www.nato.int/cps/en/natohq/opinions_158078.htm*.

Index

Note: Page numbers with italic *t* and *b* denote Tables and Boxes, respectively